Dash before Dusk

A slave descendant's journey in freedom

Joe Khamisi

Kenway Publications

Published by
Kenway Publications
an imprint of
East African Educational Publishers Ltd.
Brick Court, Mpaka Road/Woodvale Grove
Westlands, P.O. Box 45314 – 00100
Nairobi,
KENYA.

email: eaep@eastafricanpublishers.com
website: www.eastafricanpublishers.com

East African Educational Publishers Ltd.
C/O Gustro Ltd.
P.O. BOX 9997
Kampala,
UGANDA.

Ujuzi Books Ltd.
P.O. Box 38260
Dar es Salaam,
TANZANIA.

East African Publishers Rwanda Ltd.
Tabs Plaza, Kimironko Road,
Opposite Kigali Institute of Education
P.O. Box 5151,
Kigali,
RWANDA.

© Joe Khamisi 2014

First published 2014

All rights reserved.

ISBN 978-9966-25-989-9

Printed in Kenya by
Printwell Industries Ltd.
P.O. Box 5216-0506
Nairobi, Kenya

To
Doretha, Maria and Sydney, Josephine and
Chiza, Bryan, Pauline, Noa, Luka

In memory of
Charles, Lydia and Faida

Kenway Biographical Works

1. *A Fly in Amber*, Susan Wood
2. *A Love Affair with the Sun*, Michael Blundell
3. *Facing Mount Kenya*, Jomo Kenyatta
4. *From Simple to Complex: The Journey of a Herdsboy*, Prof Joseph Maina Mungai
5. *Illusion of Power*, GG Kariuki
6. *The Mediator: General Sumbeiywo and the Sudan Peace Process*, Waithaka Waihenya
7. *Madatally Manji: Memoirs of a Biscuit Baron*, Madatally Manji
8. *My Journey Through African Heritage*, Allan Donovan
9. *Nothing but the Truth*, Yusuf K Dawood
10. *Tales from Africa*, Douglas Collins
11. *Theatre Near the Equator*, Annabel Maule
12. *The Southern Sudan: Struggle for Liberty*, Elijah Malok
13. *Wings of the Wind*, Valerie Cuthbert
14. *Tom Mboya: The Man Kenya Wanted to Forget*, David Goldsworthy
15. *Not Yet Uhuru*, Jaramogi Oginga Odinga
16. *Freedom and After*, Tom Mboya
17. *Dreams in a Time of War*, Ngũgĩ wa Thiong'o
18. *Beyond Expectations: From Charcoal to Gold*, Njenga Karume with Mutu wa Gethoi
19. *A Profile of Kenyan Entreprenuers*, Wanjiru Waithaka and Evans Majeni
20. *Running for Black Gold: Fifty Years of African Athletics*, Kevin Lillis
21. *Kiraitu Murungi: An Odyssey in Kenyan Politics*, Peter Kagwanja with Humphrey Ringera
22. *In the House of the Interpreter*, Ngũgĩ wa Thiong'o
23. *Kenyan Student Airlifts to America, 1959-1961: An Educational Odyssey*, Robert F Stephens
24. *A Daunting Journey*, Jeremiah Gitau Kiereini
25. *Dash before Dusk: A slave descendant's journey in freedom*, Joe Khamisi

Contents

Dedication .... *iii*
Preface .... *vi*
Acknowledgements .... *viii*
Abbreviations .... *ix*
Chronology of events .... *xi*
Chapter 1: How it all began 1
Chapter 2: My Parents Separate 11
Chapter 3: Rituals and Superstition 22
Chapter 4: My Father and Politics 29
Chapter 5: Father Re-Marries 38
Chapter 6: Struggle for *Uhuru* 45
Chapter 7: Tough Times at Home 53
Chapter 8: Nocturnal Tunes 67
Chapter 9: My First Trip Overseas 78
Chapter 10: Kenyatta, Odinga, VoK 86
Chapter 11: The Love of My Life 97
Chapter 12: Corruption Exposed 113
Chapter 13: The Poaching Menace 124
Chapter 14: Business Attempt 140
Chapter 15: Namibia Surprise 151
Chapter 16: Kanu Membership by Force 160
Chapter 17: Protocol 169
Chapter 18: I Thrive on Africa's Chaos 177
Chapter 19: Journey Across the Border 186
Chapter 20: A Lucky Entry into KBC 195
Chapter 21: A Political Journey Begins 206
Chapter 22: Things to Remember in Parliament 216
Chapter 23: The Pain of Losing 227
Chapter 24: Money, Money, Money 237
Chapter 25: Bombay Africans 243
Chapter 26: The Last Word 251
Glossary of Non-English Words *256*
Index *260*

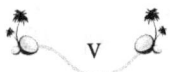

Preface

Dash before Dusk; A slave descendant's journey in freedom represents my life history of more than sixty-five years, spent abundantly in five foreign countries, three of them while in the service of the Kenya government. It is a story of my humble beginnings in a slum town in Mombasa at the end of World War II and my journey as a journalist, diplomat and politician.

In this autobiography you will read about my multiple ethnicity in a background anchored on the abominable slave trade, and about my agonising early upbringing in a single parent home. As a descendant of slavery, I have included a narration – at the back of the book – of the significant role my people played and continue to play, in the development of our adopted country, and the pain and struggle for recognition we continue to endure.

This is my second book. The first one, *The Politics of Betrayal: Diary of a Kenyan Legislator*, was a political memoir that narrated the intrigues and political corruption in the regimes of Jomo Kenyatta and Daniel arap Moi, as well as the backroom tricks played out by Mwai Kibaki in his first tenure in office. Conversely, *Dash before Dusk* is my own story, told by me and based on my own life experiences.

Usually, an autobiography presents a special challenge to the writer: one of trying to balance between telling the whole truth, half-truth and concealing the truth altogether. I had a unique leeway therefore to decide what to include and what to exclude, what to emphasise and what to de-emphasise. As I compiled this book, I found myself with the challenge of recalling and extracting information that had remained docile in my mind for decades, sifting through it and presenting it in an interesting and readable format. The more I thought, the more I found myself recollecting even the very minute details of things that took place in my life many years ago. What you are about to read, therefore, represents a significant part of my life history.

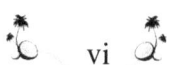

I decided to include in this book only those memories that stand out as the most pivotal events in my life. I hope my readers will not feel too offended if I have, here and there, gone too far in my narration of events. This is because certain events are not generally easy to condense without distorting or altering content. If there is anything I did not cover, it is because it failed the scrutiny test.

I have tried to be as truthful, as frank and as complete as possible. Where it became necessary to include names I have done so. In a few cases I have deliberately avoided mentioning names, either for legal reasons or because such an endeavour would not add any value to the text. I have also avoided mentioning occurrences that were included in my first book. *Dash before Dusk* therefore contains fresh information only known to me and, perhaps, only to a few in my family.

I have borrowed some of the information, especially pertaining to my family tree, from notes prepared by my father, Francis Joseph Khamisi, before he died in 2000. I have also included information from an interview with my mother, Maria Faida, at Rabai in 2010, and my recollections of people and events told to me by my grandparents.

I hope you will enjoy this rare opportunity of getting a glimpse into my personal life.

Joe Khamisi
Indianapolis, Indiana, USA
June 2014

Acknowledgements

I want to thank God for giving me a life and the many abundant opportunities I have enjoyed throughout my life. I have lived a blessed life full of spiritual richness, personal satisfaction and familial gratification. I am not rich and I have never aspired to be. But I have enjoyed the best that life can give in my own very blessed way. All this would not have been possible without the grace of God.

I also want to thank my father, Francis, and my mother, Maria, for bringing me to this world. Childhood challenges were many because life in a divided family was not fun. I loved both of them, though in starkly different ways.

In my beloved wife Doretha I have everything to be grateful for. She offered me comfort and love, and persevered through difficult times. She gave me two wonderful children, Maria and Pili, who now have their own families. It was therefore proper that Doretha, Maria and Pili should be the ones to read the first draft of this book. I thank them for their useful suggestions which I incorporated in my final draft.

To all my relatives and the many friends, I say thank you for your fellowship. They are many and I cannot list them all here.

To the offspring alive now, and to those who would come later, I hope this book will make them proud of their ancestry and allow them to appreciate, in a very real sense, the life I shared with others in this world.

Abbreviations

AEMO	–	African Elected Members' Organisation
AfriCog	–	Africa Centre for Open Governance
ANC	–	African National Congress
ASP	–	Afro Shiraz Party
AWOL	–	Absent without official leave
BBC	–	British Broadcasting Corporation
BH	–	Broadcasting House
BVR	–	Biometric Voter Registration
CBD	–	Central Business District
CCM	–	Chama Cha Mapinduzi
CCTV	–	Central China Television
CDF	–	Constituency Development Fund
CEE	–	Common Entrance Examination
CIA	–	Central Intelligence Agency
CLF	–	Coast Leaders' Forum
CMC	–	Cooper Motors Corporation
CMS	–	Church Missionary Society
CPF	–	Coast People's Forum
CPG	–	Coast Parliamentary Group
DRC	–	Democratic Republic of Congo
EAPLC	–	East African Power and Lighting Company
ECK	–	Electoral Commission of Kenya
EPLF	–	Eritrea People's Liberation Front
FLs	–	Frontline states
GMT	–	Greenwich Mean Time
GNA	–	Ghana News Agency
GoK	–	Government of Kenya
HIV/Aids	–	Acquired Immune Deficiency Syndrome
ICC	–	International Criminal Court
ICDC	–	Industrial and Commercial Development Corporation
IEBC	–	Independent Electoral and Boundaries Commission
IPK	–	Islamic Party of Kenya
IQ	–	Intelligence Quotient
KADU	–	Kenya African Democratic Union
KANU	–	Kenya African National Union
KAPE	–	Kenya African Primary Examination
KAPU	–	Kilifi African People's Union
KASU	–	Kenya African Study Union
KAU	–	Kenya African Union
KBC	–	Kenya Broadcasting Corporation
KFL	–	Kenya Federation of Labour

Abbreviations

KFL	–	Kenya Federation of Labour
KICC	–	Kenyatta International Conference Centre
KIM	–	Kenya Independence Movement
KNA	–	Kenya News agency
KNP	–	Kenya National Party
KPU	–	Kenya People's Union
KTN	–	Kenya Television Network
KWADU	–	Kwale African Democratic Union
LDP	–	Liberal Democratic Party
LegCo	–	Legislative Assembly
MADU	–	Mombasa African Democratic Union
MIT	–	Massachusetts Institute of Technology
NAC	–	Nyasaland African Congress
NAK	–	National Alliance of Kenya
NARC	–	National Rainbow Coalition
NASA	–	National Aeronautical and Space Administration
NDP	–	National Development Party
NFD	–	Northern Frontier District
OAU	–	Organisation of African Unity
ODM–K	–	Orange Democratic Movement–Kenya
OPC	–	Ovambo People's Congress
PAFMECA	–	Pan-African Freedom Movement of East and Central Africa
Pan Am	–	Pan American World Airways
PFLP	–	Popular Front for the Liberation of Palestine
PGA	–	Parliamentarians for Global Action
PSC	–	Public Service Commission
SABC	–	South African Broadcasting Corporation
SADF	–	South African Defence Force
SDP	–	Social Democratic Party
SPK	–	Shirikisho Party of Kenya
SRC	–	Salaries and Remuneration Commission
SWAPO	–	South-West Africa People's Organisation
TANU	–	Tanganyika African National Union
TJRC	–	Truth Justice and Reconciliation Commission
UNICEF	–	United Nations Children's Fund
UNTAG	–	UN Transition Assistance Group
UPI	–	United Press International
USA	–	United States of America
USAID	–	United States Agency for International Development
USD	–	US Dollar
VIPs	–	Very Important Person (s)
VoA	–	Voice of America
VoK	–	Voice of Kenya
ZNP	–	Zanzibar Nationalist Party

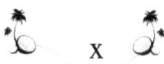

Chronology of events

1941	–	Parents wed; Francis Joseph Khamisi and Maria Faida
1942	–	Brother, Charles, is born
1944	–	Born at the Native Civil Hospital, Mombasa; birthday celebrated as 31 December. Father resigns from *Baraza* to form the Kenya African Study Union (KASU)
1946	–	Parents separate; father nominated to the Nairobi Municipal Council
1950	–	Enrolls in Standard One at Makupa School, Mombasa
1952	–	Father re-marries
1957	–	Father appointed a Member of the East African Central Legislative Assembly
1958	–	Sits for KAPE and fails; transfers to Buxton School. Father vies and captures the Mombasa seat to become a Member of the Legislative Council (LegCo)
1959	–	Visits Jaramogi Oginga Odinga in Kisumu
1961	–	Employed as a clerk at the New Zealand Insurance Company
1962	–	Leaves leaves the insurance company and joins *The East African Standard* in Nairobi as a copy holder
1964	–	Leaves *The East African Standard* and joins the Nation Newspapers
1965	–	Moves to Voice of Kenya (VoK); Travels to Bombay for a nine-month attachment at the *Times of India*; Nyanya Emilia dies
1969	–	Travels to Washington DC to begin work with Voice of America (VoA)
1972	–	Weds Doretha Savage on 28 October
1973	–	Relocates to Nairobi, Kenya. Takes up employment with the Department of Information, Ministry of Information and Broadcasting
1973	–	Maria is born on 15 September at Jamaa Maternity Hospital
1974	–	Appointed press attaché in the Kenya mission in Addis Ababa, Ethiopia; military coup in Ethiopia
1975	–	Moves to the Ministry of Tourism and Wildlife as a public relations officer; disappearance and murder of politician J. M. Kariuki
1976	–	Josephine Pili is born on 10 June at Nairobi Hospital
1977	–	Starts tour of duty in Paris, France.

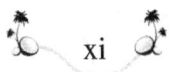

1979	–	End of tour of duty in Paris, France; returns to Nairobi and sets up a tour company, Jetset Africa Tours and Safaris
1982	–	Attempted military coup, disrupts the tourism industry; Jetset Africa Tours and Safaris collapses
1983	–	Returns to the United States and takes up appointment with VoA in Washington DC
1988	–	Pays a visit to Kenya and rural home in April; My brother Charles passes on shortly after the visit
1989	–	Joins the Foreign Service as Senior Assistant Secretary in the Ministry of Foreign Affairs, Asia Division
1990	–	Namibia gains independence; (mid-year) returns to Kenya after setting up a diplomatic mission in Windhoek
1991	–	Resigns from the Ministry of Foreign Affairs; joins Safari Park Hotel as Public Relations Manager
1992	–	Resigns from Safari Park Hotel; registers private enterprise, Copy Deadline Ltd
1993	–	Maria is married on 11 February in the USA
1998	–	Copy Deadline closes; relocates to Dar es Salaam as Chief Editor of *The Express* owned by Media Holdings Ltd
1999	–	Moves from Media Holdings' *The Express* to Business Times Ltd's the *Business Times* as chief editor
2000	–	Appointed Managing Director, Kenya Broadcasting Corporation (KBC)
2002	–	Resigns from KBC and enters active politics; joins LDP and wins the Bahari parliamentary seat on a NARC ticket in December
2003	–	Pili weds Chiza
2007	–	Defends the Bahari parliamentary seat on an ODM-K ticket but loses
2008	–	Travels to the USA and begins writing *The Politics of Betrayal: Diary of a Kenyan Legislator*
2013	–	Tries to recapture seat in newly established Kilifi North constituency but loses. Returns to the US and starts writing *Dash before Dusk*
2014	–	Full author in the USA, now writing a scholarly book on the slave trade along the East African coast

Chapter 1

How it all Began

As African nationalists prepared to transform the Kenya African Study Union (KASU) into the Kenya African Union (KAU) in readiness for Kenya's struggle for independence, a peasant woman in the rustic surroundings of Rabai in the Kenyan coastal region was counting her days to delivery. It was around that time too that German bombs were raining on Allied Forces in the Battle of the Bulge in Belgium, one of the bloodiest of the World War II encounters.[1]

Maria Faida was expecting her second child. The first one, Charles Juma, had been born two years earlier. At the start of her contractions she was assisted to walk three kilometres to Mazeras on the Mombasa/Nairobi highway from where she got a vehicle to transport her to Mombasa. From the bus stage at Mwembe Tayari she walked the half kilometre stretch to the Native Civil Hospital. On the night of 31 December 1943 and 1 January 1944, after hours of exhaustive labour, I popped out of my mother's womb ending a nine-month journey. I was conceived in Nairobi, carried to full pregnancy at Rabai, and delivered in a segregated ward in a paradise holiday town along the Indian Ocean coast. When I was born, my father was in Nairobi working as a full-time Secretary General of KASU. He missed my first shrill of life.

What I don't know is the day and hour of my birth. My mother insisted I was born on the last day of the year. My father on the other hand thought I was delivered on New Year's Day. That confusion may have been caused by a misinterpretation of the Greenwich Mean Time (GMT). I really don't know; and I really don't care. I don't care either where, under what tree, in what village, in what country, my placenta was buried. It could have been incinerated at the hospital, or it could have been flushed down the drains and then found its way into the Indian Ocean where it still sits in the belly of a shark. The most important thing

---

1   According to History Learning Site, the Americans lost 81,000 men while the Germans lost 100,000 – killed, wounded and captured.

is that I celebrate 31 December as my birthday. I chose it only because it gives me an illusion of heavenly superiority – of being able to close the gate on the last day of the year to all those sinners and do-gooders just like St Peter has done for more than two thousand years as per the Christian belief.

My forefathers believed the burial place of one's placenta defined one's origin and outlined the beacon of one's territory. The umbilical cord, they believed, had to be buried in the ground immediately after birth in a ceremony witnessed by elders. That ceremony is a confirmation, a testimony, of one's affinity to the clan. So, whenever a person's true origin is in dispute, the question of where their placenta was buried becomes a fundamental subject of discussion. For me, that was not an issue.

Other than the two nurses – one white and one black – and my mother, no one else was present in the grey delivery room of the hospital. There were no elders and no ceremony. The umbilical cord was cut with a pair of silver-coloured scissors fished from a jar containing a bluish solution. That was the last time my mother saw that cord. What is important is that I am here – more than six decades later – with abundant memories of the past and a story to tell.

One may wonder why I was born in a "native" hospital. In those days, all Africans were natives in the eyes of the British colonialists. We were natives because we were not considered intelligent. We were foolish and could not think rationally. Colonialists used the word *toto*, a child, to describe grown-up Africans old enough to be their grandparents. According to them Africans were inherently retarded and were comparable only to baboons. The description of Africans as natives was just one of those derogatory expressions of racial iniquity that were so common in British colonies everywhere in the former Commonwealth club of nations.

So we had the Native Civil Hospital built by the British colonialists in 1908 for use by Africans. Europeans had the Mombasa Hospital established in 1891 as the English Hospital and Asians the Aga Khan Hospital opened in 1944. The Native hospital was situated where the General Post Office building is in Mombasa, next to Makadara recreational grounds. Even though the hospital was moved in 1957 to the Tononoka area, overlooking the Nyali Creek, the name Makadara in reference to the hospital has stuck like super glue. Sometime in the 1950s, I went back to the Native Hospital when my father was admitted there for a vermiform appendix operation. It hadn't changed a bit. It was overcrowded, floors and walls were chipped and the workers looked unmotivated. There were cots lined up along the corridors the same way it is in some of our public hospitals today.

At birth I was given only one name: Joseph. Coincidentally, this was also the second name of my father. Common sense tells me that if that was my sole name then my full name would have been Joseph Francis Joseph Khamisi. That didn't sound clever. In the community of slave descendants, European names were commonly used, as you will see later in this book.

It was, and still is, almost culturally mandatory for people at the Coast to carry a second name. Because my parents forgot to give me one, I created one for myself. I adopted the name Matano, which belonged to my favourite uncle, Leones. So, when I applied for my birth certificate I registered as Joseph Matano Khamisi and used that identity on all official documents until I officially changed it to Joe Khamisi in September 2009, through a Gazette Notice No. 10920.

The reason for changing my name was simple. Other than my childhood friends, no one knew me as Joseph. Everyone called me Joe and that's the name I have used in my career in journalism and in politics. I also thought Joe, like Bill and Jack, was trendy and rather sexy in a positive way.

* * *

I come from a slave ancestry. My village of up-bringing at Rabai, Simakeni, which roughly means "don't be shocked", is about twenty-five kilometres north-west of Mombasa. From its hilly perch, one could look down during the dry season when trees were bare and see the shadows of the first Church Missionary Society (CMS) mission in Kenya. The mission was started in 1844 by two German missionaries, Rev. Johann Ludwig Krapf and Johannes Rebmann, and became the resting place for thousands of rescued slaves. This was where my maternal grandmother, Pauline, was matched to Stephen Sepetu, a person who was to be her life-long husband.

In the late 1880 when the Sultan of Zanzibar issued letters of freedom, former slaves were asked to choose their future husbands or wives from a multitude of people at the station. After selecting partners, they would then be joined in matrimony in a Christian ceremony before being settled on small plots of farms surrounding the mission. Some reports indicate that by the year 1889, two-thousand slaves were issued with freedom papers by the Sultan. Under that arrangement, Babu Stephen and Nyanya Pauline were settled at Kinyakani on a three-acre plot overlooking the main Mombasa/Kaloleni road. My paternal great grandmother, Kalekwa, was settled at Simakeni, not far away from Kinyakani. She was married to Khamisi Sadala who had retired from the British Army. Both Kalekwa and Sadala were from Nyasaland.

The Sultan of Zanzibar ruled over one-thousand miles of offshore territory, stretching from Mozambique to Somalia. The ten miles from the Mombasa shores of the Indian Ocean into the interior, for example, belonged to him. He was the one who controlled all trade, including selling and buying of slaves, spices and ivory. No one knows exactly when Mombasa was founded, but some believe it was around 900 AD. Situated at the mouth of the Indian Ocean, Mombasa has since those early days continued to play an important role in trade between East Africa and the world.

Until Independence, Mombasa was ruled by different powers. It was originally administered by Arabs until 1505 when the Portuguese invaded the East African coast and destroyed the town triggering a war with the Arabs that lasted for 200 years. It was during that time that the Portuguese built Fort Jesus, a magnificent edifice overlooking the sea entrance for defence purposes. "Mvita", the local name for Mombasa literally means the place of war. By 1698 the Portuguese had been defeated and they left the region for good. In 1887, the Arabs relinquished the town to the British who handed it over to the new Kenya government at independence in 1963.

In the early days, Arabs occupied third place in the race tier. They had their own educational institutions called Arab schools. Rich Arabs however shared medical facilities with whites. The poor ones, the dark type referred to as *Washihiri,* mostly from the Southern Yemen coastal town of Hadhramaut, were ranked lower than the "white" Arabs and often ended in native hospitals. So, it was first the Europeans, the Asians and then the Arabs. Africans occupied the very bottom position in all aspects of life. They did the dreariest of jobs, earned much less than anyone else, and lived in designated slum areas.

I don't remember Babu Stephen, my maternal grandfather, at all. He must have died before I was born or, perhaps I was too young to remember him. However, I do remember Nyanya Pauline. She was a small (she wasn't more than four-and-half feet in height), wide-nosed, and sunken-cheeked woman who emphasised syllables – all of them – with a deep, heavy Zaramo accent. She did not shake off that Tanganyika accent despite years of stay among the native Arahai. Nyanya Pauline was captured while still in pre-teens as she returned home from fetching water somewhere in the Tanganyika interior. This is how she narrated her experience in the hands of her captors:

> There were three of them, one an Arab and others African. The Africans grabbed my hands and carried me in the air as I kicked my legs and screamed for help. They walked me to a place where I found a group of perhaps twenty other captured people, young and old. They were chained. They tied my hands and those of the other children with a long rope before we started a long walk. They did not give us food or water to drink. We just walked until we came to some houses where there were many other Africans. Later we were transported by dhow to Unguja. Some of the people were sold off in Unguja but most of us were packed in a ship. I just cried most of the time because I didn't know where my parents were and there was no way I could find out.

While she was being shipped away from Zanzibar, the dhow was intercepted. According to her, a British ship approached the vessel, which was packed to the brim with frightened slaves and, closing in, asked them to declare whether they were slaves or free human beings *"Nyinyi ni watumwa au ni wangwana* (Are you slaves or free)?" is how she explained. They had been taught to say they were free people when approached by others. But on seeing the British cruiser, the people shouted in unison: "We are slaves!" At that point, the Arab captors dived into the sea and the human cargo with legs and arms shackled was rescued and taken ashore.

The treatment of slaves after capture and the suffering and humiliation they went through were callous according to numerous accounts recorded by historians. A British naval officer who participated in one rescue operation between Zanzibar and Mombasa gave a heart-rending account of what he saw of a slave ship:

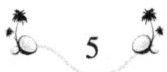

> She was just a huge open boat filled practically to the last chink of space with black humanity; men, women, some children and infants in arms, but no old people. Old slaves like horses are not marketable. The sun cooked the closely packed mass of people and the smell was awful. We had tried once or twice to give the poor creatures some relief from burning thirst and hunger, particularly the women with small infants, but the attempt caused such a fierce fighting scramble in which everything was spilt or scattered and nobody profited that we gave up.[2]

This description of the deplorable state of life in a slave ship matched closely what Nyanya Pauline had told me. She had talked of stuffed dhows, hunger, disease and neglect. Could she have been in that particular vessel or was she in another similar one? I have asked myself that question all my life.

After their melodramatic rescue, Nyanya Pauline and others were released to the Rabai mission. She lived there through puberty before Stephen Sepetu took her hand in marriage.

Nyanya Pauline's community, the Zaramo, inhabit an area around Dar es Salaam, the chief seaport of Tanzania, and within the vicinity of Bagamoyo, once an important trading centre and capital of German East Africa. It was from Bagamoyo that caravans left into the interior to hunt for slaves. The captors would march the people back to Bagamoyo – sometimes a distance of hundreds of miles – for processing and shipment to Zanzibar and beyond where they would be sold. I suspect Nyanya Pauline and, most possibly, Babu Stephen, came from somewhere along those nebulous routes; and that what she explained as a few houses was probably the Bagamoyo receiving centre. The name Bagamoyo itself means a place where you "drop your heart" – a place of temporary relief before the next phase of adventure begins.

When I tried to probe further, Nyanya Pauline could not pinpoint exactly where she came from in Tanganyika. The only thing she remembered was that many people in her village were fishermen who spent days at sea before returning home, bringing with them fish and other food items. They inhabited a cluster of huts abutting a forested area where certain types of animals wondered desultorily. Through the forest was an opening that led to a ridge and a river. It is along that route that Nyanya Pauline was seized by strangers.

---

2 Marshall Macphee, *Kenya* (New York: Frederick A. Praeger, 1968): 32.

Slave trade across the Indian Ocean started early in the 8th century AD when Arab traders sent slaves from the East African ports to the markets all over Arabia and India. At that time, Zanzibar on the island and Kilwa on the mainland were the two largest African shipping points for captured slaves. The British declared slavery illegal in 1807 although it continued in Zanzibar for years.

Thus, my maternal grandparents were Babu Sepetu and Nyanya Pauline. Together they had five children – three boys and two daughters: Francis, reticent and dour; Livingstone, a born-again Christian who didn't marry until he was fifty-five years old and worked together with Francis as mosquito catchers[3] at the Municipal Council of Mombasa; Leones, the uncle I took my name from and who was a ticket examiner in passenger trains plying the vast, winding East African Railway routes; Regina, a pleasant woman married to Athanas Matano, a bumptious Mnyaturu from Singida region in north-central Tanganyika; and, Maria, my mother, who was married to my father, Francis.

On the paternal side, my grandmother was Emilia Salama, a tall, former nursery school teacher in Mombasa who loved to tell frighteningly ghostly stories that scared my brother Charles to death. She was the child of Sadala and Kalekwa, a woman my father described as "a diminutive, gentle lady". Sadala and Kalekwa bore Nyanya Emilia and Juma Sadala at Rabai.

In notes he wrote before he died, my father remembers his grandmother Kalekwa singing songs in Chinyanja, one of Nyasaland's main tribes. The story of how she was captured is not very different from that of Nyanya Pauline. In her case, she was bought by missionaries from Arab traders because, according to my father, "... she was not considered good for the overseas market" due to her young age. What is not clear is where in Nyasaland Sadala and Kalekwa came from.

Nyanya Emilia was not married when she became pregnant by a man who came to Rabai from Sagalla in the Taita hinterlands. My father did not know his father. Later in life he found out that he had a half-brother called Walter Kivure Elijah. Both Walter and my father were sired by

---

3   This term is no longer in use but in those days, mosquito catchers were public officers tasked with fighting mosquitoes in their breeding grounds. Their daily routine was therefore to scout stagnant waters, the most likely place to find mosquitoes, and spraying them with insecticides carried in tanks on their backs.

the same person, Frederick Elijah Mwang'ombe. Walter's mother was Lydia Kadzo. Like Nyanya Emilia, Kadzo was a slave descendant from the Yao tribe on the shores of Lake Malawi and part of the large group of rescued slaves at the Rabai mission. My father's half-brother married Margaret Nadzua from Tsunza in the south coast, and they had four children: Frederick who became a banker and worked for some time in London; Lydia who was the first woman graduate in Rabai; and Arthur and Florence. The last three are now deceased.

My father was born at Simakeni on a date his mother could not remember. The only thing Nyanya Emilia remembered was that he was born either at the beginning or at the end of the "big war". She couldn't explain which war it was, but we understood it to mean World War I. My father nevertheless adopted 4 August 1913 – the day of his patron Saint, Francis of Assisi – as his official birthday.

Later, when Father was still young, Nyanya Emilia was married at the Holy Ghost Cathedral, Mombasa, to Augustine Louis Mpanda, a self-taught painter residing in Mombasa. The two did not have any children which meant Khamisi was the only child of Nyanya Emilia. After losing her job as a teacher upon becoming pregnant, Nyanya Emilia spent some years working as a domestic worker, care-taking children in a European household of British descent.

British colonialists loved cucumber and egg sandwiches especially for their morning and afternoon teas, and liked their bread trimmed on the edges without the crusty sides. Nyanya Emilia told us how she carried home those hard crumbs and enjoyed them with her *siturungi* (black) tea. I didn't know she was that cheeky, but her stories of spoon-feeding *mzungu* (white) babies under her care with hard liquor to put them to sleep were horrendous, but side-splitting. It was from Nyanya Emilia that I learnt my only two Chinyanja phrases: *muli bwanji* (how are you) and *ndili bwino* (I am fine).

Nyanya Emilia's elder brother, Juma Sadala, a burly, adventurous former soldier and train driver, was a hunter and loved to hunt wild game with his long, double-barrel gun. During World War I, he was deployed to Tanganyika to fight alongside the British in the East African Campaign. On his return, he got married to a kindly nurse called Mary and the two bore two children before they separated; Jimmy, the elder one, had bloodshot eyes and walked with a gangster's swagger, while his sister Salama, was a tall, good-looking girl who was married to a man – I forget his name – whose job was to shuttle wagons at the railway station in Mombasa.

My uncle Jimmy was a renegade, a bandit of some sort who stayed away from home for months on end. He would show up without notice and suddenly leave as mysteriously as he came, lifting from home whatever he could get his hands on. He was insipid and as sly as a cat. The last time anyone heard of him before he died hundreds of kilometres away from home was when he was masquerading as a witchdoctor, fleecing unsuspecting villagers with useless roots he claimed could cure chronic diseases. Jimmy, for lack of a better description, was the devil in the family.

After the collapse of his marriage, Juma Sadala – his children Jimmy and Salama now fully grown – moved in with his sister, Nyanya Emilia, who was then a small-scale farmer at Simakeni. To me Sadala was a great man. He talked slowly with a hoarse voice and appeared to be limping slightly, perhaps from a wound from the war years. He loved hunting and treasured the bush life. Every time he came home from his hunting expeditions, he would bring with him carcasses of different types of wild game – all nicely cured and dried. We always looked forward to his return because we knew that our menu of *ugali* (maize meal) and *mchicha* (wild greens) would instantly be replaced by chunky pieces of impala, dik dik, deer or guinea fowl meat. Of all the meats, dik dik was my favourite. It was tender and very tasty.

But nothing enthralled me more about Babu Sadala than watching him clean his gun. He was meticulous. His eyes would glow with delight each time he took a clean piece of cloth, drew the gun from its wooden box ready to clean and polish. He would fold the cloth twice, and with a lot of care, apply a solution that smelt like burnt gum to the barrel and then to the handle. He would tenderly caress the weapon in the same way a mother does to a baby. When it was all clean and shiny he would spray it with spit before finally giving it a final glow. He was closely attached to his gun. The bullets were big and pointed – the size of an adult index finger. He stored them in a special pocket made from gazelle skin. Once in a while he would take them out, count them like coins, give them a shine and thereafter slide them into their pocket slowly one at a time. When his bullet supply dwindled he travelled to some office in Mombasa to replenish them.

In 1952 after the colonial government announced a state of emergency in the wake of the Mau Mau liberation war and recalled all guns from civilian hands, poor Sadala wept incessantly and refused to talk to anyone for a whole week. The mourning ended only after the gun was returned to him a few years later. In the meantime, he assumed a languid demeanour and began sniffing *tumbaku,* a powdery substance made from tobacco leaves plucked from a garden behind the house. He would either draw the *tumbaku* in through his hairy nostrils or put a small chuck of the substance under his tongue to let it take effect slowly. Spit residues from chewed *tumbaku* looked like soft brown mud and smelt like chicken entrails.

There was a lot of sibling love between Babu Sadala and Nyanya Emilia. They never publicly demonstrated it, but I could see they totally depended on each other by the way they talked and worked together.

Chapter 2

My Parents Separate

Two years after I was born my parents separated. Both Charles and I were too young to comprehend what had taken place. I had this weird, innocent feeling that something was wrong when Nyanya Emilia came to take us away from Kinyakani where my mother was with us then. She exchanged some harsh words with Mother, then stood up and just said *twendeni* (let's go). As we were leaving, Mother was crying, "Please, don't take them away! Please, don't take them away!" Nyanya Emilia just gathered a few of our clothes from atop a dresser, stuffed them in a *kikapu* (basket) made of fibre, and we left. She tied me on her back with a *leso* and held Charles's hand as we took the small path past the fat baobab trees into an opening on our way to Simakeni.

All of a sudden we found ourselves with neither a father nor a mother close by. We felt abandoned. At that tender age we yearned for the undivided attention of our parents. We needed the motherly affection of gentle cuddles and warm kisses that many children take for granted. Since we were boys, we also needed fatherly presence and mentoring. We had none of that.

We loved our Nyanya and she loved us too, but she was our grandmother and not our mother. That was not all. Father had left instructions that we were not to be taken back to visit mother. I don't think Nyanya Emilia fully agreed with that because once in a while she would take us to Kinyakani for brief periods of time. For a few hours we would talk and laugh and thoroughly enjoy the company of our biological mother. Mother was still in her early twenties. Exhaustively stressed out she took to heavy drinking of *mnazi* (palm wine), lost weight, and her face became pale for lack of nutrients. Her drinking habits deteriorated and got to a point where Nyanya Emilia didn't want us to see her in that state of hopelessness. She therefore stopped taking us to Kinyakani. It was several years before we got to meet her again.

Nyanya Pauline, my maternal grandmother, was still alive. During our visits to Kinyakani, she would gather us at her favourite spot under a neem tree beside the house and tell us many stories about her childhood. When she laughed, her raised cheeks would dance to what I thought were Zaramo ancestral tunes and her body would quaver. Sometimes she would sing for us, occasionally interspersing the melodies with heavy belching. Her stories revolved around her experiences at the Rabai mission; the night singing, the weddings and deaths. But she would smile subtly whenever she remembered her suitor, Stephen, "the young man with good manners and handsome looks", how they fell in love at first sight and how they were joined as husband and wife and sent off to Kinyakani. Her early experiences as a slave girl appeared far off, but once in a while she would talk of her tribulations on the difficult journey from Tanganyika to the Kenyan coast. We would listen intently and laugh hilariously when she described her Arab captors as "smelling like spice".

I was too young to ask questions as to why Father and Mother were not living together. Not that the two had lived together for any long periods of time. She was in Nairobi with Father for only a short time after marriage. When she got pregnant with Charles she was sent back to Nyanya Emilia at Rabai. Sporadically, she would travel to Nairobi for short stays, but she spent most of her time either with her mother, Nyanya Pauline, at Kinyakani or mother-in-law, Nyanya Emilia, at Simakeni.

Many years later I saw a black and white picture dated 1941, which clearly indicated that the union may have been doomed from the start. It showed the two of them seated in a photo studio, way apart, neither of them smiling; my father in a light suit and an English hat, and my mother in a sparkly and a beautiful head-gear. The picture, my mother told me, was their wedding photo. Maybe the stony expressions on their faces signalled the pain in their relationship.

When I grew older I learnt that my father did not really want to marry mother after all. He didn't want to marry anyone. His goal was to become a priest. He dreamt of going to the Gregorian Seminary in Rome for theological studies and thereafter work as a parish priest. Before his marriage to my mother, he had rejected another girl who had also been imposed on him by his mother. When he rebuffed her, Nyanya Emilia was angered. Unable to deal with the pressure from his family, he ran away from home and stayed with relatives and friends until he got a scholarship to go to Kabaa High School where he joined the seminary after completing high school. He was away from his parents for seven tormenting years. During holidays, he would stay behind to do various jobs at the school to earn pocket money. My father was determined to become a parish priest, but perhaps God did not will it.

There are two versions of how he eventually left Kabaa School. According to his own notes, he, along with seven other African candidates for priesthood, left one by one after they saw the person who had inducted them into the seminary, Rev. Father Alfons Loogman, being humiliated by his white colleagues. Father Loogman was the Founder and Principal of Kabaa School, but his stewardship did not sit well with other priests. After his students – Joseph Ngugi and his brother Stephen Kimani, Alois Obunga, Rocki Kaberere, Josephat Mbaria and Khamisi – left following that discord, Father Loogman too departed for Kilungu Mission, in Ukambani, before returning home to Holland (Netherlands). Paul Njoroge was the only one who remained. He proceeded to Rome where he died as a priest and his remains were interned at the Vatican.

The second version is more interesting and this was given to us by Nyanya Emilia herself. She told us that after failing to convince her son to marry, and after receiving reports that her fugitive son was at the seminary, she travelled all the way to Kabaa. Holding a big knife, she demanded his release. She threatened to kill herself if she was not allowed to leave with her son. Pleas from priests to persuade her to return home only increased her determination to take her mission to fulfilment. Finally they agreed to let him go and on that day, 15 December 1937, Khamisi reluctantly abandoned his journey to priesthood. Nyanya Emilia's version, if true, represented a dramatic show of resolve by a peasant woman against a revered missionary order. May God forever keep Nyanya Emilia in eternal peace because had it not been for her, and Khamisi had become a Catholic priest, I would not have been born and you would not be reading this autobiography.

At Rabai, Nyanya Emilia had a bride ready for him. She had already paid a dowry of three hundred shillings to Mzee Stephen. Not wanting to disappoint his mother for the second time, my father unenthusiastically entered into a marriage arrangement he knew he wouldn't honour. He considered himself too educated to be married to a peasant primary school drop-out whose furthest point of travel was the mission school. The fact that he had travelled many miles away to foreign lands made him wiser and modern, he thought. That was the reason, I was told, why he walked away from the marriage so soon.

After their church wedding, my father left for Nairobi where he found a job as an assistant personal secretary at the Meteorological Department. He was moved to Station 710 of Cable and Wireless Ltd to become the first African broadcaster. He worked there until he was appointed the first African editor of *Baraza*, a Kiswahili newspaper, in 1937.

The separation of my parents was bitter and the two did not talk again for the rest of their lives. My father willed that his soul would be unsettled if Maria attended his funeral. When that time came, she didn't. To Charles and me the separation was the beginning of a very difficult period of our lives. We loved both of them, but we were sometimes compelled to make a choice between the two, an abstruse situation that bothered us for many years.

Within the compound of the CMS mission in Rabai is the Isaac Nyondo Primary School, the country's oldest formal school. It was at this school – in a classroom built of mud and mangrove poles – that I first read my ABCs as a nursery school pupil in 1948. I was only four years old. Isaac Nyondo was the name of the second African to be baptised at the mission by the missionaries after his father, Jana Abegunga. The school and the church are located on high ground, but my class was situated on low ground across from small farms and country homes. During break we would play either by chasing each other or, my friend Josiah and I, would be throwing stones and sticks at ripe mango fruits. If lucky, we would get a mango or two to snack on, otherwise our stomachs would growl in hunger until we got home late in the afternoon.

I must admit I wasn't good at arithmetic right from the start, the only subject that was taught in the class other than English. I couldn't understand why zero times two was zero and why after ninety-nine we didn't go to ninety-ten instead of one hundred. English was easier because all examples the teacher gave us were based on our daily existence. It was not difficult, for example, to remember things like mango, egg, cow, chicken and so on. We could write them and draw their pictures on our slates because we had a physical connection with them. Our teacher was a cheerful petite girl with a chin that stuck out like a chisel and thick black hair that shone from applying layers of coconut oil. She carried a small stick but I don't remember her using it on us. If she thought a child was unruly, she would just raise it and slam it down as if trying to hit him or her. Bai Joyce was a comely lady.

I loved Rabai. The name, some say, came from a Kiswahili word "*raha hii*" (a place of pleasure). Rabai was a laid-back, rural community with a century old market selling dry fish and hot peppers. The fishes, mostly *papa* (shark) and *nguru* (king fish) or simply salt fish, were usually buried deep in a pit for seasoning purposes. By the time of harvest they would be dripping worms and other creeping creatures and smelling worse than skunk. *Papa* cooked in coconut is delicious and *nguru* fried in oil is irresistible. The salty taste of *nguru* comes very close to that of anchovies. In fact, it could easily replace anchovies in certain dishes such as pizza. *Nguru* has now been scarce in Kenya for years and Coastarians (communities living along the coast) blame the violence in Somalia and the disruption of fishing activities there as the main reason for its scarcity. Most of the king fish consumed in Mombasa came from the Somali coast.

Rabai, also known as Rabai Mpya, is framed by palm and mango trees stretching as far as one's eyes can see. From Simakeni, where my father was born, one had to walk downhill on a single-file path, cross the Mombasa/Kaloleni road to get to the mission area. In essence, there were two Rabais, one inhabited by indigenous Arahai and the other by former slaves and their descendants.

When I was growing up, Rabai had many farms of juicy oranges, fat, fluffy tangerines and pink guavas. Mangos came in many varieties: *ngoe, dodo, shikio la punda* and many others. Every day traders, mostly women in *handos* (traditional pleated skirts) packed the fruits in baskets made of coconut straws and transported them to Mombasa markets for sale. They would also take with them cassava, coconuts and sweet potatoes.

Rabai was agriculturally very fertile. The coconut tree was, and still is, an important cash crop for Coastarians. It yields products that range from roofing materials and broom sticks, hair and cooking oil, to refreshing soft and alcoholic brews. *Mnazi* is the primary drink of intoxication.

Because there are thousands of toddy-producing coconut trees, there are equally hundreds of people working as tappers. Wine tapping is generally a risky career requiring good motor skills and sobriety. An average tree is about fifteen metres high, but some go even higher. Without a safety belt, and with the wind swaying the tree from one side to the other, a climber must be able to maintain composure and balance. At Simakeni one man named Washe was a celebrity tapper who worked on up to twenty trees every day. Seeing him dash from one tree to another was operatic: confident, whistling or singing away a popular tune, his oversized shorts folded at the waist, and his sharp pointed knife tucked on his side. One rainy day, he slipped and fell from atop a tree. The sharp knife pierced his stomach and severed the lungs. He didn't survive.

Every tree marked for tapping must have *pandizo* (steps) chipped off the stump by either a *panga* (machete) or a *jembe* (hoe) to aid the climber in safe navigation as he goes up and down the slippery tree. To catch the sap, a gourd (nowadays a plastic jug) is fastened to the cut flower that grows at the centre of the branches. It is from the tip of that branch that the sap drips out. The flower tip is cut afresh every harvest time which is twice every twelve hours or so to facilitate easy flow of the sap. A tapper must, therefore, climb the tree holding a knife and carry an additional container into which the sap is poured.

The fresh sap is very sweet, like sugar cane juice. When mixed with flour dough it works the same way as yeast. Left overnight it ferments and raises the dough which becomes ready for baking *chapati* (an unleavened flatbread) or *mahamri* (form of deep-fried doughnuts) the following day. At the Coast, the sweet sap is also used for making vinegar. Left to ferment for a few days, the liquid becomes sour and people can, at that time, use it to manufacture a strong form of gin popularly known as *pyuwa* or *chang'aa*.

Palm wine plays a very important part in the customs of the Coast people. When slaves arrived at Rabai from as far away as Mozambique, northern and southern Rhodesia as well as Tanganyika, they brought with them different customs and rituals applied in special occasions in their own countries of origin. Over time though, the traditions of the newcomers fused with those of the Arahai and a sort of common approach to birth, circumcision, marriage and burial rituals emerged. Up to date, for example, slave descendants still follow the Mijikenda custom of *kuhaswa*, a special blessing given to prospective marriage partners. My daughter Josephine Pili, for example, underwent that ceremony as you will see later. In such a ceremony, like in others, the palm wine forms a central part of the rituals. The Mijikenda tradition mandates that before one takes the first sip from *mboko* (a slim gourd container) they must pour a little of the wine on the ground to appease the spirits. Sometimes that brief ritual is accompanied by a quiet prayer with eyes gazing upwards.

Mnazi, the alcoholic drink, is just as addictive as any alcohol. Careless drinkers end up ruining their health and becoming social misfits. Since it is readily available and affordable, it is a common recreational drink for many young people. But more importantly, *mnazi* the tree plays a vital role in local customs. It features in poetry and songs such as the one below, which we sang while waiting for the evening meal.

> *Ukuti, ukuti*
> *Wa mnazi, wa mnazi,*
> *Ukipata upepo,*
> *Watete, watete, watetemeka.*

> The straw, the straw
> Of a coconut tree, of a coconut tree,
> When the wind blows,
> It rattles, and rattles, and rattles.

Ukuti can refer either to a coconut tree branch or a single straw. When singing this dirge, children hold hands and go round in a circle. When it gets to "When the wind blows" they circle faster and faster and by the time they get to the last line, they suddenly drop to the ground in a sitting position. They repeat the song many times until they get tired and turn to some other form of dance.

At Rabai trading centre, all the shops – about four or five – were owned by Arabs. They controlled the retail business and were so rich that some of them ran commuter bus services between Mombasa and Rabai and beyond. The Rabai Arabs, like most traders in the hinterland, were generally kind and generous and allowed trusted locals to buy on credit. Nyanya Emilia had an account at Abdalla's shop where we took provisions on credit and paid at the end of the month when Father sent subsistence money. The store sold almost everything; sisal rope for building, household utensils, *lesos*, wrap-ups and food. For us, our purchases were restricted mainly to *unga* (maize meal), beans and bread. I liked the dry round buns called scones which were my favourite replacement for unsliced bread. The buns were crunchy, and because the baking process sucked away all the liquid in them, their shelf life was long. I would immerse one in *siturungi* (black tea) to make it soggy and soft and then munch it slowly to savour its goodness.

In my childhood, we ate a lot of *ugali* and cassava. The latter, which looks like a long thick root, is uprooted from the ground complete with the plant. After separation from the stump, the root is peeled and eaten raw, boiled or roasted on a wood fire. During the dry season when maize crops failed, cassava, as an all-weather crop, was our source of survival. In those times, my grandmother would sun-dry it, pound it into pulp using a *kinu* (wooden mortar) and a *mchi* (wooden pestle) and then grind it in a *kijaa* (grinding stone) to produce flour for *ugali*. Cassava *ugali* is dark, sour and sticky. I didn't like it as much as I liked ordinary *ugali* made from maize meal, but during difficult times I had no choice. For vegetables we had *mchicha* or *mvuna* which thrived during the wet seasons. If these were unavailable, Nyanya Emilia would go into the bushes to look for *mtsunga*, a bitter tasting leafy vegetable that was our last resort. Its extremely harsh taste is said to be good for treating malaria.

The traditional architecture at Rabai involved the use of *fitos* (thin long sticks) fitted together to make circular walls which would then be plastered with muddy soil. For roofing, thick layers of wild grass would be packed together to prevent any leakages of water into the structure. When slave descendants began to settle in the area, they made significant modifications in the way houses were built. They built theirs in a square form or rectangular shape. Inside the structures were rows of rooms and a roofless courtyard at the centre where people would sit to watch stars and to tell and listen to fairy tales. Our house was not different. We spent several evening hours at the courtyard of our home where Nyanya Emilia often sat us around a crackling fire on a *jiko* (three-stone wood stove) and told us stories.

After sunset, once we moved to the rooms, a stubborn family of bats hiding between planks up in the ceiling would begin its nightly rounds.

That happened only at night. Early every morning, the bats would fly out through a small opening on the wall and spend daylight hours ravaging through guava and mango trees, weakening the fruits at their stumps and forcing them to fall. On our daily rounds in the bush we would find half-eaten fruits strewn all over the place. Once dusk set in, the animals would sneak back through the same hole and patch themselves upside down like black, menacing kites, clinging tightly to the palm fronds. But they would only be feigning sleep. Soon one or two would zip through blindly, knocking out the small kerosene-powered tin lamp and leaving the house in darkness.

When I was a child I equated bats with evil. My nursery school teacher had taught us that light symbolised good while darkness symbolised evil. Why would bats descend on the house, turning off lights and making us blind, if they weren't evil? Moreover, no animal I knew slept upside down, eyes directed at the humans below. During those moments of blackouts, I would bury my small body under the sheet, cover myself from head to toe and breathe silently like a fly lest the bat smelt my breath and zoomed in on me. Those scary childhood experiences stayed with me for the rest of my life and darkness became anathema.

Also etched in memory is the day when my grandmother found a snake under my pillow. As a matter of practice, we never really made our beds after waking up in the morning. So the beddings would go undisturbed for days. One morning as we played outside, I heard a loud shout of "*Nyoka, nyoka*" and sounds of a coconut straw broom hitting something. Charles and I rushed to the door only to see Nyanya Emilia hysterically banging the floor, her eyes bulging out in fear, and a slim, dark-coloured serpent lying dead. She believed it was poisonous. With a stick she lifted its limb body and threw it in a pit where a fire consumed it. We believed a dead snake must be burnt otherwise its relatives would descend on the household and cause deaths. Snakes love to inhabit frond thatched roofs because that is where they find their prey: lizards and rats.

The snake-under-the pillow incident was my second encounter with the slithering type. My mother told me that when I was a baby, a snake came to me as I slept under a cassava tree shade. Remembering an old belief that snakes never harm babies, she did not panic but went out looking for a specific root, and when she found it she threw it close to where I was. The snake uneventfully slithered away leaving me safe. Since then, though, I have developed a morbid fear of snakes.

Rabai was a lot of fun, but there were also some painful moments. One day on our way to school, for example, we came across a partly fallen coconut tree lying on an angle that children used as a swing. We climbed on it and swung up and down. As it was coming down, I slipped under, and the full weight of the tree pressed on my back. I cried in pain all the way home. Nyanya Emilia quickly gave me a hot water massage and applied warm coconut oil, but my back was permanently injured. Even today that pain traumatises me. Despite Nyanya's warning that I stay away from the tree, I returned to that swing over and over again. I learnt to firmly grip the trunk, and as a result avoided another mishap.

We played many different games at the village other than football, which every boy played. We had marble contests, the winner being the one who could toss as many marbles as possible into a hole. Once in a while we would also join girls on hop-skip-and-jump, more as a cynical way of mocking them in the way their skirts took to the air, than a genuine desire to participate. We would jump a few times and then laugh off the game and leave. We would also play cards and use soda tops as award trophies.

During the fruit season, we would invade farms and eat as many tangerines, oranges and mangoes as our stomachs could take. We did this until some farmers complained and threatened us with witchcraft.

A lot of imagination went into the building of toy cars using sticks, cardboards and soda tops as wheels. Some of the toy vans were as big as bread boxes and looked real. We would then use charcoal chalks to decorate them and write slogans on them just like real vehicles: *Matunda Express*, *Simakeni Bus*, *Rabai Delimeli*, and so on. *Delimeli* was a Swahili distortion of "Daily Mail", the bus that brought mail to Rabai from the main Post Office in Mombasa. At Rabai, people would buy stamps and leave their letters with a local shop to be collected by the bus conductor for dispatch to Mombasa. The arrangement worked well in the absence of a permanent facility.

In those days there was a cigarette brand called *Clipper*. For some reason, we liked that name. Just for mischief, my friends Josiah, his brother Kuwaka and a neighbourhood friend Keni would gather at a spot. We would roll up some soft coconut reefers in a piece of paper to resemble a cigarette and smoke. We called it *Clipper*. The result of our escapade would be an incessant cough all around. That was the closest I came to smoking. I have been a non-smoker all my life.

Chapter 3

Rituals and Superstition

Decades have gone by, but many of the rich memories of my childhood are still vivid. They are as clear and defined as this morning's day break. I can still feel the soft winds whistling through the air propelled by swaying coconut trees and swishing pregnant mango plantations. I can still remember the unshakable calm and the simplicity of village life and the ubiquitous games of hide and seek. I can still see the unpredictable bare knuckle fights over the dimple-cheeked girl in the village and the unending reprimands from my grandmother over all manner of minor infractions. All these memories are etched in my mind like a footprint on concrete.

And, how could I forget the man who arrived at our home in Simakeni at the crack of dawn as the moonlight faded into the horizon? I was not even ten years of age, but I can still smell his breath spewing out a mixture of crude tobacco snuff, stale booze, and yesterday's meal. I can still see the musty rags on his body, his brow farrowed with foul sweat and eyes bloodshot. I had not seen this man before, but I knew something was wrong when I saw a pair of knives on his belt.

That man with a high wattage grin was a circumciser brought in to conduct a ritual that was mandatory for all boys in Rabai. With him were two other men: one, brown-toothed with a breathy voice; the other, gaunt and tardy. The two suddenly – without notice at all – got hold of my legs and splayed them. I was filled with fear and revulsion and cried madly. My grandmother, who was only a few feet away, did nothing to rescue me from the strangers. She stood there, her face twitching, her expression sorrowful.

The main man grabbed my tiny penis and a sharp pain ran through my body. I let out a piercing sound that must have been heard many villages away. My body jerked and my stomach lurched. In that nanosecond, the job was done. I felt a warm stream of blood jet out and I momentarily collapsed on the palm frond-carpeted ground. As my mind and body floated in stratosphere, I felt and smelt a putrid concoction of liquid dripping through my private parts, and then my grandmother carrying me back into the house. In my pain I cried to sleep in her arms.

Until that day, I had been awakened at dawn only once. That was when Nyanya Emilia got Charles and I out of bed for a foot journey in darkness. I remember we walked for a long time. As we fought off straws of tall grass blocking our imperceptible path, and the morning dew splashing droplets of water on our faces, we could hear cocks crow from behind tall trees in some hidden villages. At one time we even heard the laughs of a hyena in the distance.

As we came out of a clearing, we saw in front of us a faint silhouette of structures made of mud and grass-thatched roofs. Nyanya slowly led us towards them and with a *hodi* (knock) a plump man with a goatee emerged, bending his weighty body to clear himself through the short wooden frame. We discovered soon enough that he was the medicine man waiting to cut off our troublesome tonsils. When we left home, grandmother did not tell us where we were going. Local legend surmises that it is taboo to do so lest the targeted tonsils disappear, not to be seen by the medicine man. It was therefore a mystery journey that culminated in a surprise crude operation that permanently and surprisingly ended our frequent bouts of coughing.

Rabai has always been known for its obsession with superstition. Stories of *jinni* and ghosts invading houses and tormenting villagers were common then and are still common. Nyanya Emilia had a mortal fear for phantasm and always kept a dry bone of a pig dangling on the main door of her house to scare away the *jinni*. It was widely believed that a *jinni* would not enter a house that had traces of pig remains. But as much as Nyanya Emilia was afraid of the evil, she was not afraid of narrating ghostly tales as we sat around a fire in the evening, fresh maize (corn) roasting on the gentle three-stone stove.

Her favourite story was about the spirits of her ancestors who, she claimed, emerged from their burial grounds on the same day and at the same time every Christmas eve. They would land atop her hut in the middle of the night and in unison whisper to her: we have come. Are you coming with us? She would reply: not yet. The same scenario would repeat itself year after year. One Christmas eve, she told us, the spirits once again descended over her hut and again they blurted out quietly: we have come. Are you coming with us? This time around she responded, yes, I am coming. Immediately, she was hurtled through the star-filled sky and landed at a burial site in what seemed to be a far, far away place from her house. There she danced with the spirits until the first cock crowed at three-thirty in the morning. Accompanying the crow was a loud thundering sound. Suddenly, the spirits vanished into their macabre burial grounds, and she found herself alone in her house.

As she told the horrifying story, her face would streak with fear and her voice would thrum with emotions. She would look to the heavens as if in supplication while holding tightly to the beads of her rosary which she permanently wore on her neck. Charles and I would be left sputtering in nightmarish fright with our mouths unable to open. On a night such as this, we would turn and toss on our matted bed until morning.

Life in Rabai during those days was dictated by two things: good and evil. When it was good it was too good and when it was evil it was just horrible. The coming of Europeans to Rabai was perhaps the best thing that ever happened there. The introduction of Christianity and the conversion of people from atheism to religiousness opened up many avenues for enlightenment, though it didn't vanquish local rituals and traditions. People continued to believe in the power of witchcraft, but at least they had an option in the teachings of Christ. They would, for example, believe that drought was human-controlled, and that famine only occurred when rainmakers, in their mischief, withheld rain. I remember one rainmaker, an innocuous old man who travelled with all his paraphernalia – animal skin, gourds, bones and a wooden stool – and who was always blamed in times of drought for withholding rain. For rain to fall he had to shed tears. People would capture him and give him a merciless beating until he cried. The flowing of his tears would then trigger a thunderstorm and the rains would fall. That belief was so strong among the Arahai that after that ritual there would actually be a downpour. How much of that belief was responsible for the precipitation was hard to say.

In our home there was a special way of discarding body portions such as nails and hair, lest they be found and used by the evil spirits to bring disaster to the family. We had to mix cut nails with seven small sticks. The sticks and the nails would then be thrown into the trash pit. That way, we believed, the evil spirits would not see the nails but only the sticks. Why seven sticks? I have no idea. The hair had to be covered in white paper and buried on the ground. Nails, hair and even spit were believed to be tools of witches. Once a witch got hold of any of those items, life could be in danger. One could die or they could be turned into zombies. That is why anyone seen walking in a daze and dressed in rags at Rabai was thought to be a victim of superstition. The other common belief involved the presence of an owl in the village. We believed that whenever an owl perched itself on a tree, someone in a nearby household would die.

There was only one house at Rabai that was roofed with galvanised sheets and there was an explanation for that. Galvanised roofing materials were invariably associated with jinni, and whoever had such a house was suspected to be harbouring evil spirits. Only palm fronds were used for roofing. As children, we feared passing anywhere near the big white-washed house near the market roofed with corrugated iron sheets. We would rather take a circuitous route than risk being dragged into that house by dark forces. The owner, an old woman, was rarely seen in public. The story was that she sequestered herself with the wicked creatures in a room that was always shut, venturing out only in the dark for her night runs.

And talking about night runners, I can say for sure that I saw one with my own eyes. We were going home in the middle of the night from a wedding dance. Suddenly we heard the thumping sound of a solo drum coming from a footpath just ahead of us. I was in a group of about seven young boys and girls. As the sound drew nearer, I saw a naked lady dancing to the beat of the drum and chanting some mumbo jumbo. We immediately recognised the woman as the same one who sold *mahamri* (Swahili doughnut) outside a house in that village. Panicking, we made a sudden about-turn and ran back as fast as we could. Shaken and very afraid, we took another route home. After that bizarre and frightful incident, I avoided passing anywhere near that house and never again bought *mahamri* from her.

Not too far from our Simakeni village is a river called Mwakuchi where my friends and I always went for a swim. That river was not too deep and was much calmer and safer compared to the fast-flowing Kombeni River not too far away. As days in Rabai were constantly hot, we liked to go swimming at the dormant pool of water on the side of the river. From an elevated position on the banks, I would dive into the dam with much funfare, my small legs bent and my hands raised as I made some spunky shouts. On landing, sheets of bubbled water would swirl helter-skelter and the robins atop the nearby neem tree would scatter feverishly. I would repeat the dive many times over until my skin went pale perhaps due to floating cow and goat urine. The river was not the cleanest in the world but it offered a much appreciated cooling effect on a hot day. Humans shared that water for drinking with cows, goats and sheep. In introspection, I now recognise the high health risks we were taking by swimming in that river.

After the swim, on our way home, we would catch grasshoppers of different types and shapes. We would chase them through the shrubs, dive at them and cup them with our palms. My favourite was the big, fat one with colourful wings in the shape of a locust, but many times I would end up catching the smaller one with an over-sized head and round, protruding eyes. We would then stake the little winged creatures and, at home, roast them on fire. The flesh of a grasshopper tasted a little like mud fish, but the wings were crunchy like the tails of fried shrimp. Those flying insects were our appetiser before the big meal.

There were other delicious creatures we longed for that made delectable appetisers. During the rainy season, winged ants would crawl from underground holes and fly out in droves. Generally known as *kumbikumbi* in Kiswahili, the ants would land in our small containers and later in frying pans. They provided us with a rich source of protein.

One of the arsenals we carried everywhere we went as children was a *panda,* a form of catapult made of a v-shaped stick, two rubber strips tied at the end of the stick and a leather piece at the top. We made and used either dry clay marbles we called *sokota* or used stones to shoot at birds. On lucky days we would shoot down one or two small birds which we would then take home and roast.

* * *

I was baptised at the Holy Ghost Cathedral, Mombasa, soon after birth, but it was at the Sunday School at Rabai CMS Church, officially known as St Paul's Church, that I was introduced to the teachings of the Bible. In those days, Catholics were not allowed to read the Bible, at least that is what we were told. There were just too many mysteries, too many questions the Vatican did not want the faithful to ask. Perhaps, it was thought, Africans lacked the capacity to understand the Word, to rationalise the many parables and miracles before and during the lifetime of Jesus. That was not so with the Anglicans.

Nyanya Emilia was a Catholic, but since there was no Catholic Church at Rabai, we had to go to the CMS Church. It was not until many years later that Catholics were able to infiltrate the heavily Anglicised area and build their own Church at Jimba, several miles into the interior. Today, there are several Catholic Churches in the area.

At the Sunday School in Rabai, I would sit, my ears sticking up like a fox to ensure I did not miss anything of the teachings of Christ. I was particularly awed by the miracles performed by Jesus: First of all, His own Resurrection and Ascension, then the multiplication of bread and fish, making the blind see, walking on water and others, left me wondering what kind of a an Jesus was. But it was the story of Lazarus, more than many others that reaffirmed my faith in the omnipotence of Christ. The Bible says, Jesus cried out: "Lazarus, come out! The dead man came out, his hands bound with bandages and his face wrapped with a cloth. Jesus said to them (those present), "Unbind him and let him go."

At that point my imagination would go to the image of Jesus, then to the crowd present at the graveside and over to Lazarus. What was Jesus wearing? Why did He have to cry out? Was Lazarus happy when he emerged from that tomb or was he angry that He had awakened him from slumber? And what was the reaction of those present? "Lazarus, come out." That phrase, delivered in a loud shrieking voice by our teacher, rang in my ears throughout a Sunday school day until I went to sleep.

I thoroughly enjoyed the singing during service at the Anglican Church. The slave influence was clearly present in some of the songs. Remembering them now I see great similarities in melody with the Negro spiritual songs during the slave era in the United States.

When I visited the Church recently fond memories came rushing into my mind. The historical edifice hadn't changed a bit since I was a child. The organ was exactly where it had been more than fifty years ago. The pulpit was raised high and the pews as vintage as ever. I could hear the echo bouncing back and forth as Reverend Samuel Kuri delivered his sermon and the choir belching out godly tunes. The galvanised roof was a little rusty but the huge bell atop the structure was still in place.

The Church is now part of the Rabai Museum which also includes the Rebmann's cottage now used as a school, Krapf's house, the Mission Market and an exhibition hall. Opened on 18 June 1998, the Museum represents what the official pamphlet calls "a mixture of the history of Christianity, slavery and the Mijikenda culture …"

Chapter 4

My Father and Politics

The year I was born, my father resigned from *Baraza* and joined Eliud W. Mathu and others to form the Kenya African Study Union (KASU), a quasi-political group aimed at sensitising Africans on their freedom rights. The first meeting to draw the KASU constitution was held in my father's rented quarters at Ziwani. Among those who were present at that meeting were Jimmy Jeremiah, Edward Binns (a slave descendant), Samuel Josiah, James Njoroge, Frederick Ng'ang'a, James Gichuru and J. D. Otiende. It was about that time too that Mathu was nominated into the colonial legislature as the first African member of the Legislative Council (LegCo). Since he could not find a decent hotel in Nairobi because of the colour-bar, he slept at my father's house until he bought a second-hand car that got him to and from his village.

It wasn't long before African leaders discovered that KASU was too benign and was not the right vehicle to take Africans to self-independence. What was needed was a political party to articulate the aspirations of Kenyans more vigorously, especially on the issue of land. So at a meeting at Pumwani Social Hall in October 1944, the Kenya African Union (KAU) was formed to take the place of KASU. My father remained the General Secretary with James Gichuru as President and Albert Owino as Treasurer.

On 12 June 1946, my father was nominated, together with Muchohi Gikonyo, to the Nairobi Municipal Council as a Councillor, through Gazette Notice No. 554 signed by C. E. Mortimer, a member of the Health and Local Government.[4] While all that was happening, Jomo Kenyatta, who was recognised as the leader of the nationalist movement in Kenya, was in London agitating for the country's freedom. When he finally returned home that year to take charge of KAU, all office holders were asked to resign to give him a chance to pick his own preferred officials.

---

4   *The Official Gazette of the Colony and Protectorate of Kenya*, Vol. XLVIII, No. 28 (18 June 1946): 308

Before the expiry of his one-year term at the Nairobi Municipal Council, my father was invited to travel to India as a guest of the Kenya National Indian Congress. He was to translate into Kiswahili the biography of Mahatma Gandhi, the iconic Indian non-violent crusader. When he heard about the journey, Kenyatta objected to Khamisi's selection and instead recommended that James Beauttah, a fellow Kikuyu, proceed to India. However, when Kenyatta made the announcement, my father was already aboard a ship on his way to Bombay. On arrival, and upon receiving the order from Kenyatta, he abandoned the assignment but remained in Bombay for a while to await the next ship to take him home. In the meantime, he survived by writing articles for an Indian newspaper called *Blitz*.

Before his travel, my father was editing a newspaper in Nairobi called *Mwalimu* (meaning Teacher), and had left it in the hands of his assistant, Mureithi Wambugu. Along with Oginga Odinga's *Ramogi* and Henry Muoria's *Mumenyereri* (the Guardian), *Mwalimu* was among the pioneer African publications in the 1940s intended to champion African interests.

After his mission aborted, my father returned to Kenya and came to Rabai to visit us. It was a joyous but short reunion. He spent only one week with us before rushing to Nairobi to take over the running of the paper. In Nairobi, he met a hostile reception from some Kikuyu leaders who denounced *Mwalimu* for supporting peaceful ways of achieving independence; they wanted a more radical approach or an armed rebellion. He was personally threatened and told to go "where you came from". He decided time had come for him to relocate to the Coast.

Soon after arriving in Mombasa, my father was invited to become an Honorary Secretary of the Mombasa African Advisory Council. He was then appointed chairman of the Housing Committee and, that same year in 1948, he inaugurated the Tudor Estate overlooking the gateway into the island and the Changamwe Estate, popularly known even today as the Khamisi Estate. The two were the first decent African housing projects in Mombasa.

My father's return to Mombasa meant we now had at least one parent in the household. Nyanya Emilia remained in Rabai while Charles and I moved to Majengo King'orani and enrolled at a kindergarten in Makupa in 1949. Our teacher was Nora, a short, bow-legged Luo lady who came to Mombasa when she was young and stayed on to become a respected nursery school teacher. Bai (a respectful term associated with child care providers) Nora improved our reading and writing skills, showed us how to draw images on a slate using crayons, and taught us how to pray, the Catholic way. That is when I learnt how to make the sign of the cross. Easy as it may look, the sign of the cross provided a challenge during the initial period. I was often confused as to which shoulder to start with, left or right.

I enjoyed my kindergarten days. We drank fresh milk brought to school every day by a big truck full of shiny, silver containers. We had a few hours' nap every afternoon and played a lot. Bai Nora was a joyful mother-type who led us in songs and dance and told us tales. We would all join in and shake our small bodies, just like puppets do, and do so vigorously until the bell rang for us to go home. One of the rhymes went like this:

> *Tumbili kala kunazi*
> *Usiku kucha halali*
> *Nikimfata hataki*
> *Ni vipi hajali?*

> The monkey ate the berries
> All night it doesn't sleep
> When I try to catch it, it runs
> How come it cares not?

While singing we would raise our hands to mimic the greedy monkey, put our palms on a slanted head to show sleep, pretend to be running after the monkey, and then show surprise that the animal doesn't care. It was all great fun. After we had done all that, we would wipe out our slates, put them on the teacher's desk and rowdily walk out of the classroom.

To take care of us at Majengo was my aunt Salama, renegade Jimmy's sister and Juma Sadala's only daughter. She was at the time engaged to her future husband who lived only a few houses from our own. As we grew a little older the aunt taught us how to cook simple meals on a *jiko*, a three-legged cooking stove made of pieces of iron sheets. We would fill charcoal bricks through the opening at the top and pour kerosene to light it, or we would stuff papers into the door on the side. Placing it in the direction of the wind the charcoal would turn red within minutes. On days when the air was still, we would take a hard board and fan it until the charcoal got agitated and threw sparks everywhere. Later on, primus stoves came to town and we were among the first in the neighbourhood to own one. The primus worked on air pressure, and just as one would fan a *jiko,* one would need to pump air into the belly of the primus to fan the flames. The new stove was more efficient and less messy.

There was a time when we thought father had found a wife in a tall Kamba lady called Mary who worked as a nurse at the municipal clinic next to the chief's camp opposite Majengo market. The colonial chief's name was Kitonga, a big man with a menacing voice. When dressed in khaki uniforms with a bowler hat, Kitonga exuded authority. He is the person who signed my first *kipande* (identification card) after I turned 18. I came to learn later that he was the father of Nzamba Kitonga, the celebrated lawyer who years later chaired the Committee of Experts that reviewed the Kenya Constitution and produced the draft that was subjected to the referendum in 2010.

At the beginning, Mary would only visit for a few hours. Later, she and her two equally tall boys, Douglas and Silas, moved in with us. The two were rude and out of control and talked back at my father whenever he tried to discipline them. I didn't particularly like the lady, but whenever we got sick we would go to her clinic for treatment and she would reward us with candy from a big jar sitting in her office. It made going to the clinic a pleasant experience. That, I liked a lot.

The Kamba, who inhabit the savannahs of eastern Kenya, have this traditional dish made of dry maize and beans called *isyo*. Mary used to cook a lot of *isyo,* which we called *puree,* while they stayed with us. Although I tolerated it at the beginning, it made me sick after a while. That is why to this day, I am not particularly attracted to beans.

My father's relationship with Mary the nurse lasted for less than a year. One day, Charles and I came from playing football and found her and her children packing their personal items to leave. I have no idea why their friendship ended. Mary however continued to work at the Majengo clinic, but we changed clinics to avoid any possible nasty incidents.

Majengo was a near middle-class location inhabited by politicians, small African traders, and Christian and Muslim religious leaders. It was relatively clean; it didn't have entertainment joints that played music all night long, and it didn't have lodging houses for one-night stands. There were several *majengos* (the name simply means makeshift structures). Ours was called Majengo King'orani, so named after the siren (*king'ora*) from a nearby aluminium factory that served as a timer for employees to enter and leave work. There was also Majengo Mapya, Majengo ya Msaji, Majengo Sokoni and others. They all combined to make one humongous African location.

During my childhood, the Asians – Indians and Goans – resided mainly in Ganjoni, south of the island, and the whites in Nyali in the north. The Arabs, who were the subjects of the Sultan of Zanzibar, preferred the areas now known as the Old Town, conveniently located near Fort Jesus, the hub of the slave trade. That living arrangement underlined the segregationist policies of the British colonial regime. I remember many times when we were chased by dogs in white and Asian neighbourhoods while searching for *kunazi* (wild berries). Other than house servants, Africans were not allowed anywhere near those areas.

Then, the Muslim *muazin* was announced not by loudspeakers – as it is today – but by Islamic criers who walked the estate calling people to prayers in the crack of dawn. "*Swalaa! Swalaa!* (Prayers! Prayers!)" the criers would call out loudly from dark alleys. Adherents would scamper out of bed, wash their faces, put their *kanzus* and leave for the mosque. The ritual was as sacred as it was predictable, serving as a wake-up call even for us non-Muslims.

Mombasa was a safe, tranquil place with no serious security problems and the criers would move unworried from one estate to another. People left their doors open and slept on open verandas to enjoy the cool ocean breeze without any fear of attacks by thugs. However, as it became more cosmopolitan, crime went up, and the criers were withdrawn for security reasons in favour of the electronic version of *muazin*, beamed directly from the mosques.

The land in the whole of Majengo was owned by one family, the Swalee Ngurus. Before that, it belonged to the Sultan of Zanzibar. The family rented out plots at a monthly rate of fifteen shillings and people built houses according to their means. Every end of the month, my father would give me the money and the rent book. I would go to the land agent, pay the money and get a receipt. Even now, few house owners in Majengo own their own land.

The houses were built using sand, mangrove poles and palm fronds and were decently plastered and painted to look modern and presentable. Those who could afford used cement blocks. They were built in long rows with just enough space for people and handcarts to pass in between them. A veranda built on the front side of the house was the most popular rendezvous for family and friends after dusk. There, gossip would be exchanged and stories would be told until people retired to their rooms, way past midnight. Each house had an internal pit latrine and a bathroom. Although that may sound convenient, the latrines were a reservoir of huge cockroaches which left their murky crevices at night to venture into bedrooms and crawl on sleeping bodies. In their wake, they would leave tiny ants that always seemed to be in their company.

The sewerage system at Majengo was horrendous. During the rainy season houses and streets would flood and unmask raw human waste. To address that issue, the Municipal Council of Mombasa had dug a big trench through Majengo to take waste and rain water into the sea at Tudor Creek. I remember that trench well because to cross it one had to balance over pieces of wood stretched across it. It was a harrowing experience, especially when flood waters were raging below. The trench was not replaced until after independence when a more efficient waste disposal system was put in place.

Illegal drugs were present in Mombasa even then and the most potent drug was *bhang*, a form of marijuana. Heroin and cocaine did not exist. Traditional brews were available and were sold legally in government social halls in Majengo, Tudor and Tononoka. In the evenings, the halls would be full of noisy drunks. Once in a while fights would erupt and the police would be called to pick up the culprits. Since drinking of local brews was allowed only in the halls, people caught brewing their own home versions of *matingasi* or *buzaa* – both products of fermented grain – or drinking in public, were arrested and prosecuted. Once in a while a van called *Black Maria* (children called it *haraka*, meaning fast) filled with plain-clothes policemen would swoop in, dig out tins of booze buried underneath the ground, arrest screaming and kicking men and women, and haul them to jail.

If there was anything the colonialists enjoyed doing was arresting Africans for the flimsiest of reasons. One day, my friend and I were coming home to Majengo from a dance in Freretown. I was cycling and my friend was a passenger seated on the frame. A police car stopped us and took us, along with the bike, to Makupa Police Station. Luckily, a detective at the station called Kazungu knew my father and ordered that we be kept at the reporting office instead of being detained in the cells. At about seven in the morning a *haraka* (police van) came and collected us and the other suspects in the cell for the journey to the law courts which were then situated next to Fort Jesus. I was charged for carrying a passenger on the bike frame and my friend, Donald Gandani, was charged for being a passenger. We were both fined 10 shillings each. It was Kazungu who paid the fine for us. However, he kept the bike as collateral until we paid him back the money which I did a few days later.

Almost throughout the year, there were many social activities in Majengo including street theatres called *sarakasi*, commercial mobile cinemas and *gwarides*, brass bands that passed through the neighbourhood especially during Muslim holidays. Brass band musicians wore Scottish skirts and played bag pipes apart from drums and horns. Weddings were social events and anyone was invited to attend. At the coast, we had the advantage of attending both Muslim and Christian weddings and both featured different types of foods.

Makupa School where I enrolled in Standard One in 1950 when I was six years old was also located at Majengo. The school was run by the Catholic Archdiocese of Mombasa and was a walking distance from our home. The principal was a short, grim-looking Irish priest called Father Boniface (we just called him Father Bonny) who had spent years as a missionary in Kenya. He was very strict, especially when it came to attending mass.

I was chubby-faced and plump, so children at school called me Kimbo, the brand name of a popular cooking fat. So, it was, "Kimbo kick the ball here; Kimbo, let's go play." I didn't feel insulted at all because the cooking fat was promoted as an energy-building product. On the can was a picture of a muscular, healthy-looking individual. What my playmates were insinuating was that I was as strong as the man with the thick biceps on the can. That was more flattering than annoying. Between the two of us, Charles was much quieter and more conformist than I. He was the interventionist while I was the initiator when it came to small scuffles in school.

We no longer used slates and chalks when we went to primary school, but books and pencils. Father made arrangements with an Indian shop nearby for us to collect all our writing supplies, exercise books and pencils, and be billed at the end of the month. So we were not short of books. Also, while we were not required to wear uniforms at kindergarten, in primary school we wore khaki shorts and khaki shirts called *marekani* and this uniform was mandatory. However, instead of the light fabric which was more popular, our father bought us blue khaki uniforms, and that earned us the nickname "fire brigade" because those were the colours worn by fire fighters. My school mates now had a second name to call me other than Kimbo. The only good thing about the blue khakis was that they hid dirt and did not require to be washed every day.

Despite being a Catholic institution where one would expect discipline to reign, Makupa School harboured quite a few bullies, *bhang* smokers and misfits. Many pupils dropped out and ended up in juvenile detention centres. The one I remember most was a rugged boy called Onyango Mazera. Although that was not his real name, his six missing bottom teeth gave him up as a Luo from Nyanza (it was customary for the Luo along Lake Victoria to pluck out the bottom six teeth). Mazera had bulbous biceps and a jerky walk and was a menacing miscreant. He was also bellicose and anti-social. He started as a petty thief in Majengo and smoked *bhang* while in primary school. He never finished school as he routinely missed classes and often assaulted teachers who tried to punish him.

We had several local teachers but there were two who were seconded to Makupa by the Moshi Catholic Diocese. Daudi and Michael were strict and exacting, but they found their match in Onyango Mazera. He would curse them and walk out of class to smoke *bhang*. Even Father Bonny could not handle him. Because of his unruly behaviour, Onyango was arrested, taken to court and sentenced to three years at the Kabete juvenile detention facility (near Nairobi). Upon his release, he had graduated to a master burglar. One day, a police dog was brought in to flash out suspected burglars from business premises and Onyango Mazera was arrested among others. He was jailed for seven years at the Fort Jesus Prison, currently a museum. In an attempt to escape, Onyango jumped from the top of the fort to the Indian Ocean below. Other than breaking a few bones, he was good enough for a re-arrest and re-imprisonment. He died sometime in the nineties, poor and sick.

Chapter 5

Father Re-Marries

After years of bachelorhood, my father finally re-married in 1952. He found a young woman called Tabu, a petite country girl introduced to him by a friend and a fellow Mnyasa called Chirwa who was then a metre reader with the East African Power and Lighting Company. My father did not directly court Tabu. Chirwa did the initial contacts because his own wife was Tabu's elder sister. For my father, it must have been love at first sight. When she first arrived at our home, she had only a few belongings and was dressed simply. Father took her shopping and ensured she dressed well. Soon thereafter, she was baptised as a Catholic and christened Mary. We thought it was a coincidence that all his women were named after Jesus's mother. My mother was Maria, the Kamba lady was Mary, and now his new wife was also Mary. Years later when he opened a retail store at his Kanamai farm he called it Mary's Store, and the church he built in his compound, St Mary's Catholic Church.

We had suspected that something was afoot in the weeks preceding Tabu's arrival. There was a lot of activity at home which was not of a political nature. Strange old men and women that I hadn't seen before came in and were joined by some familiar faces. The two groups would spend hours behind closed doors in a room discussing what appeared to be serious matters. Charles and I were only allowed into the room to serve tea. While in there, they would stop talking and everything would be quiet only for the exchanges to resume upon our stepping out of the door.

As much as we wanted a mother figure in our life, we had difficulty accepting the step-mother in our household. My brother, Charles, and I resented the marriage and did everything to make life difficult for her. In return, she made the point of reporting us to Father every time we did something wrong, however minute. We still did not want to let go the memories of our biological mother. To us, the new wife was a stranger in our household who had come not just to replace the one person we loved most but to take away the love and attention Father had for us.

Because Father spent a lot of time away from home, the step-mother would tell on everything while he was away. Without waiting to hear our side of the story, Father would take out a whip of some animal tail we called *mkia wa taa* and slash our bare buttocks until they turned red. This whole scenario created a vicious circle of animosity in the house; we would disobey the step-mother, Father would punish us, we would hate both of them, and defiance would continue. The circle would repeat itself over and over.

* * *

There was one event during my childhood that I would never forget: that is the Coronation Day in 1953 when Queen Elizabeth II assumed the throne. All along, we had been praising King George VI in our songs, and all of a sudden, at the morning assembly in school, Father Bonny announced that the King had died and that his daughter, Princess Elizabeth, who was at that time visiting Kenya, would become Queen. We didn't know what that meant other than that from that morning onwards we were not going to sing about King George VI any more.

On Coronation Day, which was a public holiday, thousands of miniature Union Jack flags were distributed to pupils in schools. The celebrations were all over Mombasa. If I recall correctly, some of the festivities were at Tononoka, so we had to walk all the way from Majengo to participate. The event was presided over by white men. We were made to line up along the street and wave our flags as the British representative and other government officials dressed in white cotton suits and dresses drove by. After the event, we were herded under a tree and given small Vimto sodas and biscuits. From that day, Coronation Day was observed every year.

In order to keep myself away from the wrong crowd, I enrolled as an altar boy at Makupa Catholic Church, which was in the same compound as the school. I also joined the church choir and spent a lot of time in rehearsals. I also helped around the church, dusting the altar and ironing vestments. During those days, Masses were conducted in Latin and, as a server, I had to memorise all the prayers in that foreign language.

I recited them beautifully without knowing exactly what I was saying. Priests serving mass faced the altar instead of facing the congregation so attendees were reduced to mere spectators instead of participants in the liturgy. However, there was a lot of singing and I liked to sing.

One thing I am proud of is that I was among those who were lucky enough to serve a young priest called Maurice Otunga who, many years later, became a Cardinal. Otunga was posted to Makupa as a young priest fresh from the seminary. Even in those early days of his priesthood, he was a humble, godly person, a good listener and a mentor. He had entered Kabaa High School just as my father was leaving and the two knew each other well.

Before a roster for altar boys was drawn, it was free for all, meaning whoever arrived first in church and put on the vestment was free to serve. That often triggered physical fights and caused bad blood among boys in the altar club. Charles and I devised a method to ensure that we served in as many masses as possible. We would wake up at the crack of dawn and walk to Makupa, arriving there well before 5 am. That way we were able to serve the six o'clock and seven o'clock masses. Eventually a roster was prepared and the fights ended. The most enjoyable part of serving was sipping wine drops from containers after mass. We really never got much, but I think it was the smell of it that made us feel happy afterwards.

In the Catholic religion, Confirmation is an important ritual in the journey to righteousness and during that event one is allowed to pick up a new name. At my confirmation, I selected the name Lawrence after Lawrence Kazungu, a friend and classmate of my father's at Kabaa High School. I have never used that name in any official or non-official transaction in my life, but it remains part of me. It reaffirms my commitment to my religion and to God. Kazungu was the first Town Clerk of Malindi, a tourist town north of Mombasa.

I was interested in music at an early age, so when my school bought musical instrument for a marching band I joined and learnt to play the drums. The band performed mainly at sports and social events. I was very proud to wear the band uniform, blue khaki shorts and shirts with maroon flaps on the shoulders. We played at many schools and social events and one of the songs we often played talked of beautiful flowers.

Our six-person flute section did a good job on this one, bringing out a melodious tune that always attracted public applauses.

> *Maua mazuri yapendeza*
> *Maua mazuri yapendeza*
> *Ukiyatazama yatakupendeza*
> *Hakuna moja usilolipenda*
> *Ukiyatazama yatakupendeza*
> *Hakuna moja usilolipenda.*

The flowers are beautiful
The flowers are beautiful
You look at them, they are beautiful
Not a single one you wouldn't like
You look at them, they are beautiful
Not a single one you wouldn't like.

My most memorable school event was a visit to Malindi. I was in a party of about thirty children, invited by one school to play games and demonstrate our marching band skills. Malindi has one of the most beautiful beaches on the East African coast, but unlike the beaches near Mombasa where the waves are gentler, waves in Malindi are humongous and scary. One must be a good swimmer to beat them.

On the day of our arrival we made an uneventful visit to the beach and returned to the host school safely. The following day when we returned to the beach, we found the waters choppy and the waves unwavering. Nevertheless, we took our clothes out and jumped in relying on our self-taught swimming skills. Not long thereafter, we found ourselves trapped by swirling salty waters that rose up in a rage and came down in a thrust. However much I tried, my small feet could not touch the bottom of the sea. A vigorous pedalling of my legs and arms only left me tired and helpless. I found myself drowning. I tried to shout but I couldn't. When I opened my mouth a gush of water rushed through my throat. I raised my hand to draw attention, but a wave pushed it down. The last thing I remember doing was to look at the blue, cloudless sky and say a silent prayer, before a mysterious pair of rescue hands reached me. One big boy had noticed my troubles. He reached at me, got hold of my limping body, and swam with me out of the dangerous waters.

Since that incident, there have been many questions in my mind I have been unable to answer. When is a person ready to die? And, why doesn't a person die when every sign shows that they must die? Also, if one doesn't die in situation as dire as the one in Malindi, are they supposed to thank the preserver of life? More importantly, did that small prayer said in the midst of an angry sea save me from impending death? I still don't have answers to those questions. In Christianity we are told death is inevitable and that everlasting life exists in the afterlife. As I sank down that morning, the only thing I could see in the near depth of the sea was a terrifying darkness, a blank frame of nothingness below.

Strewn along the shores were dozens of other children who had escaped death just like me. Our stomachs were bloated from ingesting gallons of dirty, salty water. The liquid was pumped out by using a technic of squeezing the lower part of the stomach. Together with the nasty liquid, came remnants of mashed green mangoes we had eaten that morning. That was the closest I had been to an accidental death.

* * *

Back in our neighbourhood, my brother and I started a soccer team called Majengo Stars. We took newspapers and other scrap paper and bound them together, fashioning them into a nice round ball. Later, someone gave us a tattered ball whose tube was so patched up it resembled a battered human torso dressed in bandages. The ragtag team did not go beyond neighbourhood competitions because of lack of resources and equipment. We had neither footballs nor uniforms. It was a makeshift team meant to keep children busy rather than winning competitions. We eventually disbanded it because no one was willing to pay the weekly contribution of ten cents. Because the balls were tattered they needed constant patch ups at the local cobbler, which cost money we couldn't raise without members' support.

* * *

Every end of the month when pockets were full, some of my relatives would get together for drinks and dance. Men wearing their finest, usually white flannel or cotton suits, beige pointed shoes and brim hats, and women in long white dresses trimmed with embroideries and bright headgears would converge at a house and jive for a better part of the night.

Charles and I would be the DJs. Since juke boxes had not yet arrived in Kenya, the cherished music machine was the wind-up gramophone with a picture of a dog and the inscriptions, On His Master's Voice. When I was little I thought it was the dog that was singing all those rumba songs. Later on, I came to know the fox terrier on the machine represented the brand of a big music company in England.

Our job on those musical nights was to crank the machine, change the pins whenever they began to wobble, and spin the 78 rpm double-sided records. The cranking had to be continuous, almost, otherwise the music would snore and come to a halt and then everyone on the floor would go, aaahhh!! They would curse us. So, we made sure the music was non-stop, interrupted only by instructions from the adults. "Put GV 15," one would shout drunkenly. "No, no, no. This time let's have GV 30," another would yell back. The most popular genre of music then was rhumba, which came on the GV label from as far away as Cuba, Puerto Rico and Brazil. The GVs were numbered and we could pick up the correct record just by its number. So, we had GV 20, for example, GV 48, etc. Many do not know that it was the Cuban music that influenced the contemporary Congolese/Lingala rhumba that is so popular throughout the continent today.

For me, Christmas time was the most fun period. That was the only time in the year when we would be outfitted with new clothes. Father would send us to an Asian tailor in the neighbourhood to choose the fabric of our choice for trousers. We were even allowed to select how we wanted the trousers to be tailored; ankle flaps or not, one or two back pockets, and so on. Our preferred fabric for trousers was cotton gabardine. We also had a choice of shirts. The most popular imported brand during those days was Arrow. We would pick the colours of the shirt to match the pair of trousers. Then we would go to the Bata shop near the Majengo market for shoes. I really liked the loafer type made of canvas material. They cost nineteen shillings ninety-nine cents. We just called them nineteen-ninety-nine. Finally, we would go to a bald-headed Kikuyu barber for a haircut under a huge mango tree across from our house. The barber was an old geezer who took hours to complete a head. He would scrape my scalp with a hard commercial brush as if flushing out stubborn lice before slowly attacking the hair, one at a time, with a sharp pair of scissors. Electric shavers had not been introduced then.

We looked dandy on Christmas Day and ready for our annual pilgrimage to relatives. This was the most valuable part of the holiday. We did not believe in Father Christmas or even in reindeers or chimneys. Our presents came from real people, mostly in the form of pennies, which we would later use to hire bikes for boisterous, noisy joy rides. Most bike hire shops were owned by *Washihiri* (Yemeni Arabs) the same people we blamed for the slave trade. A half-an-hour bike hire cost twenty cents. Because we usually collected cash presents amounting to up to two shillings, we were assured of plenty of rides for weeks.

After one Christmas, I decided to go to Mwembe Tayari market to buy myself a T-shirt that cost one shilling fifty cents. It was the only big market in town selling everything anybody needed. I held tightly to my money all the way from Majengo until I got to the market entrance and came face to face with three card tricksters. The fast-talking gamblers happily shuffled the cards as I carefully watched, and saw one or two bystanders actually winning. It looked so easy. What I didn't know was that the pretentious winners were actually part of the flimflam cartel.

I put my one shilling and fifty cents on the table and waited for a jackpot. Instead of winning I quickly learnt I had lost. I had thrown away all my savings in a blinker. I stood there shocked and unbelieving. The tricksters quickly disbanded the camp and dispersed in different directions, perhaps to re-group elsewhere and await another prey. A few good people who saw what had happened only shook their heads and walked away. For a moment, I felt like fainting as my tiny heart pounded like a clock. I had a sudden attack of migraine. My body was shaking. My legs were heavy and they could not move. I just stood there gazing at the market entrance. I saw no point for me to go in and despairingly walked back home crying, promising myself never to gamble again.

Chapter 6

Struggle for *Uhuru*

Sometime in 1951, I began hearing radio reports about oath-taking activities and secret meetings in forests upcountry. It was around that time too that I heard for the first time of a group called Mau Mau which was terrorising Europeans demanding land rights. Then in October 1952 came news of the killing in Nairobi of a prominent Kikuyu leader, Senior Chief Waruhiu. Most of us Coastarians knew very little about the tribal leaders of the Kikuyu people, leave alone the slain official. The news therefore made little sense to most people in Mombasa. Waruhiu, it was alleged, was an ally of the British colonialists and was therefore considered an enemy of the independence struggle.

While the Coast remained relatively quiet, tension was rising upcountry. Immediately after the murder of Waruhiu, the British colonialists flew into Kenya one thousand troops that were camped in the Suez Canal Zone to deal with the escalating Mau Mau rebellion.

Freedom fighters were raiding and killing Europeans, especially around Mt Kenya and the Aberdare Mountains, initially armed only with home-made guns, swords, bows and arrows, and spears. They mutilated settler-owned cows and hunted down their sympathisers. Reports were coming in of police stations being attacked and arms stolen.

I remember planes flying low over Mombasa on several occasions dropping leaflets warning people to report Mau Mau sympathisers to the police. The leaflets had pictures of dead and maimed European cattle and of burnt houses, as if to suggest that Mau Mau were criminal elements who should not be followed. There were swoops everywhere and thousands of suspected supporters of the liberation movement were being arrested and detained.

That October, the British colonialists declared a State of Emergency and issued a shoot-on-sight order. They also formed the Kikuyu Home Guard, a brigade of several thousand Africans who were tasked to spy and flush out Mau Mau freedom fighters. Consequently, thousands of Africans were rounded up and sent to detention camps where torture, disease and starvation were rampant. The following year in 1953, KAU was banned, accused of working in cahoots with Mau Mau. It was not until 1955 that the ban on political activities was lifted – everywhere in the country except in the Kikuyu-dominated Central Kenya – and Africans were allowed to form regional political parties.

That same year, my father formed the Mombasa African Democratic Union (MADU). Among the founder members were W. Mukeka, William Mbolu Malu, Shekue Ali, Mohamed Jahazi, Abdulla Mwidau and Msanifu Kombo, who at independence became the first African Mayor of Mombasa. Similar regional organisations were started elsewhere in the country; for example in Rift Valley there was the Kalenjin Political Alliance, in Western the Kenya African People's Party, in Nairobi the Nairobi District African Congress and the Nairobi People's Congress, and in Maasailand the Maasai United Front. There were also the Abaluhya People's Association, the Abagusii Association of South Nyanza District, the South Nyanza District African Political Association, the Nyanza North African Congress, the Taita African Democratic Union, the Nakuru District Congress and the Nakuru African Progressive Party. All these organisations were formed between 1955 and 1958.

In 1957 Dedan Kimathi, believed to be the leader of Mau Mau, was arrested and executed. The news reached us in class from teacher Daudi. Most of us had heard of Dedan Kimathi, but none had seen his picture so he had remained a myth in our minds. I was then in Standard Seven at Makupa Primary School. The day after he was executed, the news was published in the *Mombasa Times*, a British owned paper affiliated to the *East African Standard* in Nairobi. Every morning before going to school I would go to the newspaper vendor to get a copy of the broadsheet. The shop was owned by Mzee Okoth, father of Joseph Okoth Waudi, a businessman who later became a political point man of Raila Odinga in Mombasa. Waudi was also the owner of two popular night clubs, the Casablanca and Toyz. He succumbed to cancer in 2013.

Within a short period of time, MADU had amassed massive support from the people far beyond the island. Two satellite parties worked parallel with MADU: the Kilifi African People's Union (KAPU), north of the island, and the Kwale African Democratic Union (KWADU) in the south. It was at that time that I began to take interest in politics. I was thirteen years old, but even at that age I became an active youth member of the party. Whenever time allowed I joined other activists aboard an ageing Land Rover on a tour of town, singing and drumming freedom songs. Our leader was a trade unionist from the western region of Kenya, a heavy-drinking man called Menya, who sang with such passion and vigour that his voice disappeared sometimes for days. I still remember the lyrics of one of the songs:

Walisema tutachoka
La, hatuchoki, hatuchoki
Hatuchoki, mpaka uhuru upatikane
Wazungu wataenda,
Wataenda, wataenda
Na sisi Waafrika tutatawala Kenya.

They say we would tire (to fight for our rights)
No, we would not tire, we would not tire
We would not tire, until freedom is attained
The British will leave,
Will leave, will leave
And we Africans will rule Kenya.

During weekends I hawked the party newspaper, *Sauti ya Madu,* the Voice of MADU – a cyclostyled A4 paper-size – earning myself pocket money and getting to understand the art of selling. Usually business boomed during public meetings. Moving around quickly amongst people and shouting the headline of the day, I could sell several hundred copies of the six-page paper within a matter of hours.

The *Sauti ya MADU* printing machines were at my father's private office next to the elephant tusks showcase along Moi Avenue in Mombasa. Outside, hundreds of people would line up patiently waiting for a copy of the paper. My job at the office was to staple the pages, and at times feed the machine with ink. Thereafter, I would go around town selling the publication.

One of the editions that sold out carried the story of the Hola massacre in March 1959. Hola (now known as Galole) is situated in Tana River County, a part of the former Coast Province. At that time it was the site of a detention camp where thousands of Africans, mostly hard-core Mau Mau suspects, were held. Eleven detainees were killed during a fracas with prison warders after the former refused to go to work. The killings raised questions about the treatment of African detainees by British prison officers and the matter was discussed in the British House of Commons. Africans made a lot of noise too about that massacre, but nothing much came out of it. Arrests of suspected Mau Mau sympathisers continued throughout the country and the State of Emergency remained.

* * *

After the Common Entrance Examination (CEE) which was taken at Standard Four, the Kenya African Primary Examination (KAPE) was the most important examination at the Intermediate Educational level. Those who failed CEE could not go further and those who flunked KAPE had no chance of continuing to a government secondary school. I sat for my KAPE in 1958 and when the results came I had failed, so had Charles.

Charles drifted away to work as a mechanic apprentice, first at a bicycle shop owned by our father, and later at the Cooper Motors Corporation (CMC), dealers in Volkswagen and Land Rover brands. For me, continuing with my education was important. I wanted to do well in school, get a good job, move away from Majengo and drive a car. Therefore, my failure in the KAPE did not deter me from seeking other options in order to further my education, although it was certainly a setback.

I transferred to Buxton School the following year to repeat the examination. Unlike Makupa, Buxton (named after John Buxton, a leading British anti-slavery campaigner in the 1800s) was a more serious school with determined students whose collective goal was to go to Shimo la Tewa Secondary School, the only government-run institution for Africans in Mombasa at that time. My Principal at Buxton School was Hary Fanjo, a no-nonsense person who imitated Europeans by wearing knee-high stockings and khaki shorts. He would blurt out *"utapata shida"*, meaning you will be in trouble, every time a pupil made a mistake. I had no choice but to take my studies in earnest. I was not the brightest student in Class 8A, but I was quite competitive and looked forward to another stab at the examinations.

At Buxton, I found friends from Rabai and Freretown, people like Sylvanus Nasibu who in later years joined me in the journalism profession; Edgar Manasseh, later to become Commissioner of Income Tax, and Price Uledi and the Farrahs. But in getting ready for the examination something went wrong. I discovered my name had not been submitted to the examining authorities for registration. Without a serial number I could not sit for the tests. My father was infuriated and I was crushed. What shocked us was that the Principal was a family friend who came from a clan of scholars and church leaders. His home was only a short walking distance from my mother's house at Kinyakani. Why did he do that to me? It was not that my father had not paid the examination fees. He had. Fortunately in those days, there was an external equivalent examination administered by the government. I registered for it the following March and I passed; and the door was now open for me to get admission to a private school, the Kenya Indian High School.

As the name suggests, the school was owned and run by Indians. By that time, the colour bar had eased and Africans were allowed to attend such schools. The school's emphasis was on mathematics and sciences, subjects which I didn't particular like. My bias was on history, geography and English. The fees were fifty shillings a month and we had to purchase our own books and other requirements.

High school gave me a completely new perspective in education. I toned down my rebellious attitude, became more sanguine and worked hard in my studies.

***

Our house at Majengo was always a beehive of activity. MADU offices were only three houses away and party workers and leaders from outside Mombasa found it easy to locate us. Important visitors to our home at Majengo included Masinde Muliro, Martin Shikuku, Daniel arap Moi, John Keen, and Justus ole Tipis, all of whom later became national leaders in independent Kenya. They all came to address meetings in Mombasa at the invitation of MADU. Ronald Ngala visited regularly, at times accompanied by Kabwere, the celebrated witch-hunter, who would remain in the car outside for all the time Ngala would be conversing with my father. I always wondered why Kabwere, a well-known Giriama ghost buster, was relied upon not only by the locals, but also by British administrators to handle increased cases of witchcraft-related killings across the length and breadth of the Coast.

But it was the visit of Julius Kambarage Nyerere, the leader of Tanganyika African National Union (TANU), in 1957 that excited Mombasa. Like many people, I had heard of Mwalimu Nyerere who was leading his people towards independence. Nyerere was a guest of MADU and stayed with us at Majengo during his stay at the Coast. I had expected to see a giant of a man with wide shoulders, but I found Nyerere to be much thinner and smaller than what my mind had pictured him. He spoke gently and his smile, exaggerated by a well-trimmed moustache, was inviting. MADU had organised a meeting and people from all over the Coast were expected to come and listen to his captivating speech at the Tononoka Social Hall. He was known to be a witty but fiery speaker. Worried about the euphoria, the colonial government banned him a day before the meeting. The action angered many people, but there was nothing my father or MADU could do.

There was also one prominent Nyasaland leader who regularly visited us in Mombasa. He was Christopher Kanyama Chiume, one of the leading nationalists in Malawi and a close ally of Hastings Kamuzu Banda, the future President of Malawi. In fact, Chiume was staying at our house in Mombasa when a state of emergency was declared in Nyasaland in February 1959. Banda and his colleagues of the Nyasaland African Congress (NAC) were rounded up and detained. My father quickly booked a train ticket for Chiume to Nairobi from where he boarded a plane to London. By the time police came for him at our house he was already gone.

Makerere-educated, Chiume spent most of the pre-independence years in exile in Tanzania where he worked with several state-run newspapers alongside Benjamin Mkapa, later Tanzania's President. Chiume's friendship with my father was cemented in 1958 during a meeting of the Pan-African Freedom Movement of East and Central Africa (PAFMECA) in Mwanza, which was attended by representatives from Uganda, Tanganyika, Zanzibar and Nyasaland. PAFMECA had been established to coordinate political parties in the member countries.

At that inaugural meeting convened by Julius Nyerere, my father, who was elected chairman of the organisation, together with Chiume and Dr Julius Gikonyo Kiano of Kenya, were tasked to go to Zanzibar to mediate in the political crisis between the African-leaning Afro Shiraz Party (ASP) led by Sheikh Abeid Amani Karume and the Arab-leaning Zanzibar Nationalist Party (ZNP) led by Sheikh Ali Muhsin. The two groups were feuding over the control of the island's political landscape. The officials did not succeed in uniting ASP and ZNP. Since then, Chiume became a close friend of my father. To honour both Chiume and Banda, my father named two of his boys – Christopher and Gregory – after them.

Former slaves and ex-soldiers from Central Africa residing in Mombasa had a social association whose objective was to forge closer bonds and to give the people a platform to reminisce about their past. It was called the Nyasaland, Southern and Northern Rhodesia Association. People just called it the Nyasaland Club. It brought together natives from countries that are now known as Malawi, Zambia and Zimbabwe. There were quite a few of them in Mombasa. They bought a Swahili house at Majengo just a few metres away from our own and used it as a club house. Many of them had integrated into the local customs through marriage, but that did not stop them from making regular contributions to their countries' independence struggle. My father was the association's president. I remember going to Freretown and all over Mombasa many times to deliver letters to members.

In 1958, when Banda was on his way home after a prolonged stay in the United States where he had gone to study medicine, he stopped over in Mombasa and was warmly welcomed at the association club by Central Africans living there. I remember there was a big party with dances, speeches and a lot of food. So, when Nyasaland was approaching independence on 6 July 1964, President-elect Hastings Kamuzu Banda was kind enough to invite my father to attend the festivities in Blantyre. He went there as a representative of the Kenyan descendants of former slaves in a sentimental journey. Upon his return he informed us that Banda had offered him a piece of land if he ever decided to settle in

Malawi. That offer was not only to him, but also to all slave descendants in Rabai and Freretown. He politely declined preferring to live in his country of birth.

In 1957, my father battled Ngala for a seat in the LegCo to represent the Coast. I remember accompanying him to several public meetings in and outside the island. I would blush with excitement whenever he posed to introduce me as his son. I liked the ululations, the high-pitched calls for *uhuru* (freedom) and the violent punching of fists into the air by emotion-filled crowds. Through the megaphone he would shout; *uhuruuuu*...and the crowd would roar back *sasaaaa*, meaning freedom now. *Uhuruuuu*... the people would roar back Kenyattaaaa!

Political meetings resembled carnivals where people danced and threw themselves on the ground and sang freedom songs for hours. Unfortunately, my father lost to Ngala who was hugely supported by his kinspeople in the Kilifi African Peoples' Union (KAPU) and the Mijikenda Union. Ngala got 3,406 votes, Dawson Mwanyumba 2,439, Khamisi 2,267, Claudis Mwashumbe 712 and Jimmy Jeremiah 488 votes. Soon after that my father was appointed a Member of the East African Central Legislative Assembly.

The eight African Members elected during those country-wide polls were: Tom Mboya (Nairobi); Oginga Odinga (Nyanza); Lawrence Oguda (South Nyanza); Masinde Muliro (North Nyanza); Daniel arap Moi (Rift Valley); Ronald Ngala (Coast); Bernard Mate (Central); and James Miumi (Ukambani). They soon pressured the colonial authorities to increase the number of legislators by an additional six as a result of which another round of LegCo elections were held in 1958 and my father beat Edward Binns, also a native of Rabai, to capture the Mombasa seat. Also elected to LegCo were Taaita Towett, Jeremiah J. Nyagah, Justus ole Tipis, David Mumo and Julius Gikonyo Kiano. That brought to fourteen the number of representatives in the legislative body.

* * *

At Majengo, the Kikuyu community had a social club and every Sunday afternoon men and women dressed in their traditional clothes made of skin and beads would gather to dance to *mwomboko* traditional music. At the height of the uprising, the dances stopped.

Chapter 7

Tough Times at Home

To go with his status as a Member of LegCo, my father upgraded from a Raleigh bicycle to a second-hand black Humber Pullman, a British-made motorcar with an interior that smelt like baby powder. The seats were all genuine leather and the steering wheel was as big as a hula loop.

My father was among only a few Africans owning motor vehicles then. Vehicles seen on the streets of Mombasa belonged mainly to Europeans and rich Arabs like the Liwali, the Sultan's representative. My father never drove the Humber for his weekly travels to and from Nairobi preferring instead to go by train. In those days, the overnight train was the most convenient and reliable means of travel between Mombasa and the interior. As a legislator, he was allowed to travel in first class sleepers which ordinarily were reserved for whites.

While he was away, my brother Charles and I would fetch the car keys and take turns at the steering wheel of the Humber pretending to be driving. That annoyed our step-mother who would snatch the keys, hide them and, of course, report us. We would be punished with whiplashes. We detested the way our step-mother was treating us and she responded to our negative attitude towards her harshly. Whenever we came home from school at lunch time, we would have to fire the primus stove and cook our own *ugali* and then walk a mile away to the dairy to buy a cup of sour milk with which to eat the *ugali*. We didn't think our biological mother would have treated us that way. Everything that our step-mother did only aggravated our relationship and led to more punishment on our part. Whiplashes were not the only form of punishment my father used on us. There were two others. One we just called *kupiga magoti* (kneeling).

Before the Mombasa stadium was built, the only decent soccer field was Tononoka grounds. Charles and I always went there to watch matches between different local teams. One day, the last match ended late. Although we rushed to get home, by the time we arrived it was already dusk. Our father was there waiting, but this time round, not with his black tail. After the usual verbal reprimands, he ordered us to kneel down at a corner in the sitting room and chant: *taa ikiwaka lazima niingie ndani...taa ikiwaka lazima niingie ndani,* which basically meant that we had to be home before dusk every day. We got to our knees and chanted that monotonous line for hours until he got tired of it, then he let us go. From that day, and regardless of what we were doing, we had to drop everything and dash home before dusk. It was a regiment we followed until he left Mombasa for Nairobi in 1961.

The other form of punishment was less painful, though irritating. We called it *jaza kitabu* (fill a book). Father would send us to buy two 36-page exercise books. He would then order us to write one line over and over again until the book was full. If, for example, we forgot to wash dishes, then the line would be: *I must wash dishes after every meal...I must wash dishes after every meal.* That dreary exercise would keep us at the main table in the sitting room for hours. After completing the punishment, we would still wash the dishes. Compared to the others, this method of punishment was like a walk in the park, albeit time-consuming and boring.

The Humber vehicle my father bought was a bad second hand car that broke down often. He therefore sold it and bought a fairly good used VW Beetle. Instead of travelling by train he was now using his car to travel between Nairobi and Mombasa. One day while in Mombasa he was informed that Jaramogi Oginga Odinga, his colleague in the LegCo, was sick in Kisumu. He asked that I accompany him for the eight-hundred kilometre journey. I was very excited. I had not been anywhere further than Rabai and the very idea of crossing the causeway and venturing into the wild country gave me joyful shivers.

It was during the school holidays sometime in 1959 when we left Mombasa for Kisumu. The Mombasa-Nairobi road was all murram and very dusty. In some sections he had to slow down to a crawling speed in order to safely navigate the big pot-holes and boulders sticking up on the road. On the way up, I saw herds of elephants, zebras, impalas and giraffes – for the first time – grazing in the vast Tsavo terrain. Once, we came face to face with a colony of baboons that had pitched camp right in the middle of the road. They scattered away laughing as we passed by.

I was very fascinated by people of different tribes I met on the way. The Duruma I saw at Samburu reminded me of step-mother Tabu when she first came to us; simple in demeanour, but callous in determination. And since we had been told our renegade uncle Jimmy had been seen in Duruma country, I kept on looking at everyone on the roadside to see if I could spot him. I didn't.

We stopped at Voi and I found the Taita to be explicitly blustery and innocuous, while the Kambas I saw at Mtito Andei appeared quaint and old-fashioned with a taste for too many colours in their clothing. We arrived in Nairobi in the evening and went to my father's flat at Jericho for the night.

The following day we tackled the picturesque hills and valleys of the Great Rift Valley. Driving through part of what was once the White Highlands was breathtaking. I marvelled at the vast green landscapes, the tall pine trees and the livestock that grazed nonchalantly behind fenced farms with no herder on sight. I just could not compare the beautifully spotted Jerseys and the Ayrshires I saw in upcountry farms to the ill-bred local cows I was used to in Rabai.

The sight of Lake Elementaita and Lake Naivasha, which I had read about in my textbooks, was quite educative. We bypassed tea plantations that spread as far as the eyes could see. Finally, we left the huge farmlands behind and began to notice small scale plots with traditional round dwellings of the Luo people as we entered Kisumu. The blue waters of Lake Victoria were visible and fishermen's boats could be seen anchored on its banks. We went straight to Odinga's home where we found him recuperating from a bad bout of malaria. Odinga's aide, Dick Makasembo, towering and dark like most Luos of those days, was there. I did not see Odinga's wife and suspected she was away. At lunch time, Makasembo was ordered to take us to Kisumu Hotel for meals.

Kisumu Hotel was one of the few places in Kenya that had abandoned colour bar before we visited. I saw whites and Indians mingling in the big dining room. Apart from the waiters, we were the only Africans in the restaurant on that day. The setting was far from being comfortable for me. That was my first time in a big hotel and I had this overarching feeling that I was in the wrong place. But what scared me even more was the sight of the cutlery on the table. Three forks were carefully paraded on the left and three knives on the right of the plate. Over the plate were more forks and spoons. It was scary. How am I, I thought, going to deal with all these things? All my life I had used my bare fingers, now this!

My father ordered fried chicken and some chips for me. My stomach was churning with hunger, but when I tried to use the utensils, I couldn't. Every time I tried to hold the chicken leg with a folk it slipped spitting oil on my shirt. At one time the little bird almost jumped out of the plate. I looked at my father with the corner of my eyes to draw his attention, but he was engrossed in discussions about politics. When he finally noticed me he hinted that I could use my fingers. Frustrated, I decided I was not that hungry after all. I ended up eating the chips and leaving the entire chicken untouched. It must have been humiliating for the two adults, but they said nothing more to add to my troubles. We spent the night at a smaller hotel and returned to Mombasa the next day.

That trip to and from Kisumu gave me a welcoming opportunity to reconnect with my father. I don't remember any time before that when we had a one-to-one talk. It was too tense at home most of the time and he spent most of the time away engaged in other activities. During the trip, we talked and laughed as if no barriers existed between us. I temporarily forgot the incessant lashes and relaxed to enjoy the passing scenery outside. For the first time I discovered a deferential part of him. He was, after all, gentle and human. I was tempted on several occasions to bring up the issue of my mother, you know, the separation thing, but I thought that would spoil the mood in what was a moment of cordiality. So, we just talked about mundane things: politics, people and education. It was at that time that I raised the issue of wanting to go to a boarding school. My father did not warm up to that idea for reasons he did not explain. My view was that the stress of family feuds was hurting my school work and taking a toll on my self-esteem. My close friends, Sammy Makwida and Alex Obondo, were doing well in school. I wanted to follow their path. Noting his negativity, I abandoned that line of talk altogether.

* * *

Indeed, the instability at home was causing a lot of damage to my school work. It also thrust Father in the middle of an inevitable position of having to choose between believing us, his children, and siding with his wife. That was not an easy decision, even though most of the time he sided with the latter, leaving us with no defence. It was during such occasions that I hated everything. I hated my father; I hated my step-mother; I hated school; and even hated to be alive. At one time, I ran away to Uncle Morris, a few houses away from ours. Since the uncle was my step-mother's brother, I was promptly returned home.

Corporal punishment on children was not illegal during my time. I got so many beatings at home that I would not even dare to count. At first, I used to yell whenever the lash landed on my buttocks. As time went by, and as I became more infuriated at the treatment we were receiving, I only winced. I didn't allow a single drop of tears to show. That was my way of protesting, of showing all that whiplashing didn't matter to me anymore. It was a way of sending a message to Father that I could be defiant and brave at the same time.

Unlike now when there are laws against abuse on children, parents and teachers had no limits as to how to discipline children during my time. *Kikoto*, a lash made from a tropical frond called *miyaa* – the same material used to make African baskets – was the preferred tool of correction in *Madrassa*, Muslim religious classes. In secular schools anything went, from neem tree sticks to leather belts, to rulers, to tails of an animal like the one my father was using, or to slaps and kicks.

To escape from those punishments, I looked forward to the end of the term to go to Rabai and stay with Nyanya Emilia. There I would have no curfews; I would be free to climb trees for mangoes and wild berries; I would catch grasshoppers and indulge in all kinds of mischief without expecting any punishment. And because weddings were invariably held during school holidays, we would attend all wedding festivities and dance to music until the wee hours of the morning. During the rains when we were younger, we would shed all our clothes and run naked all over the village, splashing our ashy bodies in stagnant pools of water in joyful playfulness. Not once, but several times, we came down with bilharzia, a waterborne disease, and had to be taken to the dispensary for treatment.

My step-mother was an excellent cook, however. I don't know how she became such an expert in culinary delights. Her place of birth was Tsunza, a bucolic small fishing village in the south coast overlooking the harbour with no known reputation for turning out outstanding chefs. At Christmas she would make the sweetest *mahamri*, cook the most sumptuous *pilau* and the most delicious fish-on-coconut. During the Christmas season, our love for her was unflinching. It was the only time when we could indulge in a wide variety of tasteful foods without any restrictions. After returning from the midnight mass, we would go home and stuff ourselves with sweet munchies. We would then spend the day feasting on different types of Swahili foods and chasing them with copious amounts of Fanta. So, while we abhorred her, we had a soft spot when it came to her culinary skills.

It was during one of our visits to Rabai that Juma Sadala, the hunter and brother of Nyanya Emilia, died. I cannot remember what caused his death. We just discovered in the morning that he had passed on. Nyanya Emilia was profoundly saddened and wept quietly for many weeks. Sadala was her only brother and companion. They had grown, played and grieved together when their parents died. Sadala was buried at a cemetery in Rabai called *Mtakuja – You will come here*. That cemetery had been operating before I was born. It is a modest plot off the road to Kokotoni village, and although it filled up many years ago, the dead are still being buried there even today. Diggers have to push away old bones to bury new bodies.

It was after Sadala was buried that I began to wonder about his gun. From the cemetery I went to his room to look for it. It wasn't there. I suspected it had been taken to the village chief by a relative immediately after his death for, although ex-soldiers were allowed to keep arms at the Coast after the War, the weapon was always deemed to be government property.

* * *

In the intervening period, my father bought a farm at Kokotoni, about five kilometres from Simakeni. The piece of land was marshy and good for rice growing. Nyanya Emilia, with assistance from a worker called Obonyo, often reaped good harvests of *mpunga*. Obonyo, a fifty-plus year old farm hand from the shores of Lake Victoria, was a work-horse. After smoking a few joints of *bhang* (marijuana), he would work like a tractor; planting, clearing, weeding and harvesting. In the evening he would eat a whole *sufuria* of *ugali* with green vegetables and spend his evening drinking palm wine. When he first came to us, he admitted he had not visited his home village, just outside Kisumu, for over ten years.

Every morning during school holidays my cousins, Fred, Lydia and Arthur – children of my father's step-brother, Walter Kivure – would pass through our home to walk with us to the farm. Kivure had a farm next to ours. On the way, the cousins would crack the craziest of jokes. We would laugh hilariously which made the long journey appear shorter. We would work at the farm until late afternoon then begin the journey back home. Much later, my father built a small house for Nyanya Emilia at the farm and that was where she spent most of her remaining years in this world.

My father had invested in two businesses. The first dealt in bicycles; he was importing bicycles in kits from Eastern Europe, assembling and selling them on easy terms to Africans. In those days, bicycles were a status symbol and my father was among the first Africans in Mombasa to own one, a double-framed Raleigh, which was sturdier and more durable than any other brand. The ones he imported for sale were of a cheaper variety but good bikes nevertheless. He opened a sales and repair shop at the Saba-Saba building in Majengo, and that was where Charles apprenticed after flunking his examinations in 1958.

Out of belief that every African should at least own a bicycle, my father introduced a hire purchase scheme that allowed small monthly payments over a period of time. He had launched a campaign called *sisi kwa sisi* (literally meaning "us by us"), to rally Africans to boycott Asian and Arab shops and patronise only African-owned retail shops. It had been a huge success. By offering easy terms, he drew Africans away from Asian shops. The campaign also opened new opportunities for small African entrepreneurs and created jobs. But the hire purchase arrangement was a disaster. A year down the line, he discovered he could not sustain the business because people were not paying. Many accounts became delinquent forcing the business to close. He had to absorb a massive loss.

My father's other business was the Sisi kwa Sisi Bar opposite the Kikowani Muslim cemetery. He was one of only two Africans who operated bars in Mombasa at that time. On weekends, and sometimes during the school breaks, I would help at the bar counter; selling and ordering drinks from wholesalers – the management type of work. The business was good at the beginning, but as more African bars opened, sales suffered. He had to close down this business too.

The other bar owner was Mzee Mbogori, whose flagship was Maendeleo Bar at Ziwani. Mzee Mbogori, a Meru from Central Kenya, had made Mombasa his home. He was the sole distributor of beer throughout the island and surrounding areas. He had two sons, Edward and Peter, who went to school with me at Makupa. I remember times when the two, still very young to drive, commandeered a beer truck and drove it to school. They went around in circles with children clinging dangerously at the back and on the side of the truck. Because of their father's social status, no teacher dared to reprimand them.

* * *

By late 1959 the tension at home had somewhat eased. Charles and I felt that since we did not have an immediate Plan B, the only option was to call a truce and accept to live in peace with our step-mother. In any case, the frequent verbal brawls had become too stressful for everyone. There was no longer joy in the family. My father had metamorphosed too, before my own eyes, from a loving, forbearing patriarch who loved to burst out in paroxysms of melodious laughs, into a toned-down, obsequious father-figure who only listened and took commands from his wife. At most times, we felt neglected. We decided to put all that behind us.

But the ceasefire did not mean that corporal punishments had ceased. The lashes and other forms of punishment were still on the menu, though this time around they were only applied in extreme cases such as when one broke a valued utensil or when father discovered we had sneaked and gone to the beach. My father never swam in the sea in his entire life and barred us from swimming. Once in a while, however, we would lie we were going to visit relatives when in actual fact we were headed to the beach at Bamburi. To my father, going to the beach was a very serious violation of rules that attracted severe punishment. To remove any traces of salt residues behind our ears, we would first go to Railway housing quarters at Makande near Majengo where Auntie Salama lived, take a shower and then head home.

As we got a little older, my father got tired of expending his physical energy on us and just hoped God would be kind enough to save us from societal malfeasance. Suddenly, corporal punishment at home stopped.

As all this was going on, a double tragedy struck. Francis, my uncle, the mosquito catcher, died. Not too long after that my aunt, Regina, also passed on. Francis was sick on and off, but I didn't know exactly what he was suffering from. He was a hard-working individual who never missed work until his health began to fail. He would spend weeks at the Native Hospital, be discharged and then be re-admitted. What we didn't know was that he was slowly dying. One night he slept and never woke up. Later, I heard whispers within the family that he had died of syphilis which at that time was incurable. On her part, Regina, a woman with an ardently religious disposition, had endured a life of domestic abuse. Athanas, the gentleman from Singida who married her in a colourful ceremony, was a staunch Catholic; in fact, he was editor of a weekly Catholic publication and a respected church elder, but a heartless domestic abuser. Although the family knew of their marriage problems, no one dared to interfere. During the final months before her death, she looked frail and afraid, and finally she refused to eat and lost the will to live.

To Regina the option of divorcing her husband was never in the cards. She was a devoted Catholic and wanted to live through her marriage vows; "till death do us part". Ironically, it was death that finally separated them. She died peacefully at home. Her body was laid out in a casket outside their house at Majengo Mpya, and I remember kissing her powdered face just before the casket was closed for the final journey to Manyimbo cemetery. The two left behind only one child, Anthony Matano, a short, dark-skinned chummy fellow who went to school in Tanzania, and worked as a clerk at the Department of Trade along Moi Avenue in Mombasa. Before Anthony returned home from Tanzania, he married a beautiful, shy Mmnyaturu girl and the two were blessed with six children. After Regina's death, Athanas went back to Tanganyika and married another wife.

*　*　*

Meanwhile, the movement by Mombasa Arabs, backed by their counterparts in Zanzibar, to push for the secession of the ten-mile strip from the shores to the interior had picked up steam and was now dominating area politics. "The Arabs wanted the ten miles coastal strip to either be given autonomy or secede to join the Sultanate of Zanzibar instead of being incorporated in independent Kenya."[5]

Whenever my father got an opportunity, he spoke against *Mwambao* autonomy, insisting there was only one country called Kenya and the Queen was the head. He went further to urge the British government to cease paying any levies to the Sultan of Zanzibar who was controlling the ten-mile strip. He received overwhelming support from up-country leaders. The Arabs formed a political party, the Mwambao United Front and launched a newspaper, *Mwongozi*, as a propaganda tool for their cause, but the drive for a unified Kenya did not slack.

Back to the LegCo, the African Members formed the African Elected Members' Organisation (AEMO) to foster unity. Jaramogi Oginga Odinga was elected the first Chairman with Tom Mboya as Secretary and James Muimi as Treasurer. However, the organisation was marred by a leadership struggle and the movement eventually split into two groups. There was the Kenya National Party (KNP) which was formed in the absence of Oginga Odinga and was led by Daniel arap Moi as President and Ronald G. Ngala as Secretary General. When Oginga Odinga learnt about it he disowned it and was backed by Tom Mboya. The two registered their own party called the Kenya Independence Movement (KIM). KNP, which also had Asian elected Members, advocated a gradual process towards independence, while KIM demanded *independence now*. My father supported the former.

AEMO became quite a threat to the colonial authorities. Its clout was felt when its members walked out of Parliament en masse during a Communication from the Chair, which the Governor, Evelyn Baring as the Queen's representative, was delivering on 4 November 1958. In his address, Governor Baring made clear the position of the British government: that Africans were not ready for independence; the position had not changed. As a punishment for their protest, which was considered

---

5 John M. Mwaruvie, "The Ten Miles Coastal Strip: An Examination of the Intricate Nature of Land Question at the Kenya Coast", *International Journal of Humanities and Social Sciences*, Vol. 1, No. 20 (December 2011): 179.

an insult to the Queen, the Members were suspended from LegCo for three days, but they chose to boycott sessions for the whole week.

Even with their internal differences, the two groups in AEMO agreed to attend the Lancaster House independence conference in London in January 1960, as a united front. I remember that time well because my father had forgotten his favourite Stetson hat and a walking stick in Mombasa. I was therefore asked to travel by train to deliver the items in Nairobi. That was my first long travel alone.

I had been to Nairobi only once before, when we spent the night on our way to visit Jaramogi Oginga Odinga in Kisumu. This time around, I arrived in Nairobi in the morning upon which I had to ask for directions since I didn't know how to get to Jericho. And when I got there, I couldn't remember which house was my father's; all the flats looked the same. When I finally located it, my father was not at home and I had to sit on the stairs the whole day until he came home in the evening. He was more surprised that I had made it to Nairobi by myself rather than the fact that I was there. The next day I boarded the return train to Mombasa.

The first Lancaster conference in January 1960 was marred by a boycott by the Kenya African delegates who wanted the inclusion of Mbiyu Koinange, working in the African Affairs Bureau of the Goverment of Ghana in Accra, as their adviser. The Secretary of State for Colonies, Ian MacLeod had refused to admit him. The boycott lasted for five days. He was later admitted as an informal adviser but was not allowed to sit in the committee or plenary sessions. Recently, I stumbled on a picture held by the US-based Historic Images Store, an online photo company, which showed Khamisi, Ngala, Oginga and Moi, smartly dressed in winter coats and clutching briefcases and files, as they arrived at MacLeod's office on 19 January to try to jumpstart the talks.

Upon their return the AEMO members agreed to form a countrywide political organisation and, at a meeting in Kiambu in March 1960, the Kenya African National Union (KANU) was born. Ngala was away overseas and did not attend, but he was elected Treasurer with James Gichuru as President and Tom Mboya as Secretary General. On his return, Ngala refused to take up the position and instead joined Moi, Abaluhya and Maasai leaders to form the Kenya African Democratic Union (KADU) which advocated a federal system of government known as *majimbo*. My father followed Ngala into KADU and was later appointed the party's coast secretary with the task of registering members in the region where it got a lot of support.

There was one final election that my father took part in on 27 February in 1961, which was a contest between KANU and KADU. My father stood on a KADU ticket against KANU's Mwinga Chokwe, a former political detainee, for the Mombasa constituency seat. He lost. He was shattered. The polls left him with a huge debt with printers and transporters. He was also out of a job. Seeing him in that sorry situation affected me. Since he could no longer afford to pay my fees of fifty shillings a month, I dropped out of secondary school after only two years. That was in August 1961. It made me fretful and angry, not with my father, but with myself. I cried a lot during the first few days at home. I had to confront the reality that I was no longer in control of my future; that my dreams of getting away from Majengo were no longer tenable; that the possibility was high now that I would end up as a loader at the port like so many people I knew. Such feelings nearly drove me insane.

As much as father honourably accepted defeat, he was not happy that he had to exit politics in such an inglorious manner. Until his death in 2000, he believed his loss was caused by a tribal conspiracy engineered by elements in the Mijikenda community. After that defeat, he retired from politics altogether.

The Mijikenda people, of a Bantu extraction, originated from Shungwaya in Somalia many centuries ago. After a clash with the local Oromo tribesmen, they left and trekked southwards, hid in forests along the way which they called *kayas*, and developed a collective identity. While seven tribes settled north of Mombasa, two of the tribes, the Duruma and Digo, crossed the sea into the south Coast where they still live. The *kayas* became their sacred shrines and up to today Mijikenda elders retreat there for special prayers to *Mulungu* (God).

Until Ngala came along as the community leader, the Mijikenda prided on a petite woman called Mekatilili wa Menza who in 1913 rose against the British, resisting the recruitment of her tribesmen to fight in the World War I and opposing the control of the palm wine trade. Mekatilili was arrested and exiled in Mumias, western Kenya, for five years. Legend has it that she mysteriously escaped and returned to her village near Malindi. In recent years, the Mijikenda have been celebrating her anniversary every year with song, dance and story-telling.

A pipe-smoking middle-sized man of scholarly demeanour, Ngala went to Alliance High School and then to Makerere University in Uganda. For several years thereafter he taught at Buxton School until my father convinced him to enter politics in 1957. He was brilliant, placid but tough. In those days, people of Ngala's calibre were few in Coast politics. Many years later when I was a reporter with *The Standard*, I was captivated by his mastery of English. One day he emerged from Government House (now called State House) – obviously exasperated – after a meeting with officials. He told the press camped outside: "... there is going to be a flare-up in this country." With my Form Two English, I didn't know what the word flare-up meant. It surely sounded big to me. I had to look it up in the dictionary when I got back to the office.

* * *

Although my father was out of a job, we were not actually poor. He had built a house at Changamwe and was getting a little rent from his tenants. He also got rid of the Volkswagen Beetle. By that time, he had added several more children into the household and maintaining the family was becoming burdensome. But we never went hungry.

Waking up one morning, I decided I was no longer going to be a burden to the family. I did what any sensible person would do in such a situation: I went to look for a job. Instead of writing endless applications that often ended in a dustbin, I went on a door-to-door job search. I knocked at every office, starting from Fort Jesus all the way to the end of what is today Moi Avenue. It was a painstakingly effective way of looking for employment because at the end, it paid off. I was finally employed as a clerk at the New Zealand Insurance Company. That was sometime in April or May 1961. The company's offices were located at what is today Bima House. When the manager asked me what I expected in salary, my mind went blank. I had no idea because I had not handled big money before other than the pennies I got from relatives at Christmas.

I thought for a few seconds. Not to look like a dim-wit, I gloated that I wouldn't mind two hundred shillings a month. The manager, a heavy-set Indian fellow with a wrinkled face and a fading mole on his chick, rolled his eyes cheerily and told me: "How about two hundred and forty shillings?" I couldn't believe it. For the first time in my life I would be earning a salary. I decided at that moment that every penny of that money would go to my father to help with the upkeep at home. My father only gave me a small amount to cater for my transportation to and from Mombasa Island. My small contribution made a huge difference at home and father was happy that at least there was something small coming in on a regular basis.

Now out of politics, my father decided to look for a job in the private sector. He wrote several applications to companies and it didn't take long before he found work as chief clerk with the East African Power and Lighting Company (EAPLC). Having been a member of LegCo for Mombasa, he was highly respected by the management and other workers at the company. He was given an office that had been occupied by an Indian officer, and once when I visited, he appeared to be enjoying some of the perks that the European and Indian officers were receiving including copious cups of tea.

My father worked at the electricity company for only a few weeks before the management of the *East African Standard,* a leading newspaper then (now *The Standard*) offered him a job in Nairobi as editor-in-chief of the sister paper, *Baraza*. He had worked with *Baraza* for two years way back in 1939 as the first African editor in-charge of the Swahili pull-out edition. The weekly vernacular had now become an independent publication and he was asked to take it over from a European editor who was retiring. When he got the news, he came home early, carrying a crate of soda with cupcakes he had purchased from Seifee bakery, along what is now Haile Selassie Avenue. We celebrated and I was happy to see him smile once again. Together with my step-mother and the rest of the family, he left for Nairobi late in September 1961, to take up his new assignment.

Chapter 8

Nocturnal Tunes

My music debut at Makupa was the starting point of my intense interest in contemporary music. I wanted to play real music in a real band. I knew Joseph Silas, a very talented saxophonist from Rabai who at that time lived in Mombasa. Like most musicians of the time he had never been to a music school. He only played by the ear. He was a small light-skinned man with chapped lips and soft eyes. He had married a former schoolmate at Rabai called Kibibi. I wanted to learn more about percussions to be able to play in his band. So I wrote him a letter asking for a job, so to speak. He immediately took me on board and I started practising with the group. Soon, he put me on stage as a member of his band which was playing at the Star Night Club, opposite Ambalal House, along what is now Nkrumah Avenue. The club was a favourite joint for rowdy British soldiers, referred to as "Johnnies", who fought when drunk, at the slightest provocation. The club attracted the working class, but also prostitutes from all over Kenya and beyond.

When I joined Silas I was still in school and staying at Majengo. However, I engaged in music in the evenings during the school holidays. My father did not know about my nocturnal activities. He would probably have strangled me with a shoe lace if he had known I was playing music at the Star. Although my father didn't say it openly, I had a feeling he generally hated musicians, period. That is probably the reason why he didn't like his brother-in-law, Leones Matano, my part-time musician uncle. Matano liked to party and enjoyed his drink tremendously. He was my favourite uncle and, as I mentioned earlier, I took his name as my middle name. He had his own band and was cutting rhumba records. The years my father spent in the seminary must have convinced him that anything happening after dark was unchristian. Personally, I felt excited to be drumming with a man of Silas' calibre.

I kept the music part of my life very, very confidential, at least from my father. The only person who knew what I was doing was Charles who would carefully open the door to let me into the house in the middle of the night as father slept. We did this for a few weeks, until one night he caught me red-handed as I tried to sneak back. The following day, I got whiplashed and my short music career ended there. At the back of my mind however I knew I would be back.

There is one music treat in my childhood that gave me an adrenaline lift. Although I knew I could sing since I was a member of the church choir, I didn't know that my hidden talent could earn me a few shillings. Sometime in the late 1950s, a famous Congolese guitarist by the name of Edouard Masengo was contracted by a pharmaceutical company to promote Aspro, a medicine brand for treating headache. He was touring various parts of Kenya in a big promotional vehicle. He would play the Aspro jingle accompanied by a trombonist, and also give away free samples of the drug. When he came to Majengo, he sang the song and asked anyone who could repeat the lyrics to come forward. The lyrics were pretty simple. I memorised them with ease, then moved forward and offered to take the challenge. *"Aspro ni dawa ya kweli. Aspro ni dawa ya kweli...Aspro hutuliza maumivu siku zote..."* (Aspro is an effective medicine. Aspro is an effective medicine... Aspro will rid you of pain, always)" I sang with confidence. For that unrehearsed performance, I won five shillings. I was proud of myself. It was the first and last time I earned a professional fee for a singing gig.

Before he and the family left for Nairobi, my father gave me my Post Office savings book which had a balance of three-hundred shillings. That was the first time I knew he had been saving money for us. In excitement I withdrew the money, walked to Assanands music store nearby and bought a brand new trumpet. Of all the instruments on display the trumpet was the only one I could afford. The Indian salesman packed it neatly in a portable case which I took and jauntily walked out into the Mombasa sunshine, happy that my music career was now on course.

Almost immediately, I contacted Joseph Ngala, a prolific saxophonist who was at the time playing gigs part-time but working fulltime with the East African Railways. He happily agreed to teach me the horn and within a few weeks I was playing a few notes. Ngala, also a descendant of Freretown slaves, later became famous for his rhythmic *bango* sound. He is now populary known as "Mzee Ngala"

Not too long thereafter, I discovered that I wasn't really fond of the trumpet. It required too much blowing effort and a lot of patience which I did not have in abundance. I dumped it and took on lessons for the bass guitar with the Echo Band headed by Badi Hamisi at Buxton Mombasa. Rather diminutive with a fair skin and a happy look, Hamisi was one of the most sought after musicians at the time. It was the Echo Band that serenaded jazz maestro Louis "Satchmo" Armstrong at Mombasa airport when he came to Kenya in 1960. I didn't play, but I was there on that day too. Like Armstrong, Badi played the trumpet. At the airport tarmac where a temporary stage had been built, Armstrong listened intently to a composition especially written for him, *Karibu Armstrong*, and afterwards in his deep, hoarse voice, his unmistakable white teeth sparkling in the midday splendour, he growled: "I like your music ... especially you," pointing at Badi. I was thrilled. The music was a rumba.

Karibu kwetu Kenya
Armstrong tunakukaribisha
Hapa kwako ni nyumbani
Karibu kwetu Pwani Satchmo.

Welcome to our home Kenya
Armstrong, we welcome you
This is your home
Welcome to our Coast, Satchmo.

Although I was a fan of music, I was also a keen reader and a budding writer. I read everything I could put my hands on, everything – books, magazines, newspapers. In Mombasa, I read the *Mombasa Times* every day. The newspaper mainly covered events taking place on the island, with a lot of emphasis on shipping and European-interest activities such as golfing and water sporting. After reading and digesting a story, I would recreate it using my own words and style. A lot of people who saw my re-hashed stories encouraged me to take up writing as a career.

Soon, my writing skills became a modest source of income for me. Often, I would be hired by illiterate neighbours to write letters for them. My first customer was a woman next door called Fatuma. Before long, word of mouth had spread and I was getting customers from across the street. Each one of them knew exactly what they wanted to say to their loved ones, some of which were bizarre. "I want you to write this," the neighbour would tell me: "I love you so much that I can't sleep, I can't eat and I only dream of you." I would write that down on paper in good, readable handwriting. Then she would narrate her romantic moments and stop as abruptly as she started. "Now, tell him that my sister's wedding is coming and I need a new dress. Can he send me some money"? I would dutifully record that. After finishing, I would read the whole letter back to her. She would then go into her breast compartment and pull out a fifty cents coin. As far as I know that was my first paid assignment as a freelance writer.

I was also proficient in typing from practising on my father's typewriter. Later I enrolled at a commercial college and got a Pitmans' Certificate. I still consider myself as one of the fastest typists in the country. With typing skills, and recognising my talent in the written word, I applied and got a job as a trainee with the *East African Standard* (with the help of my father, of course), starting at the very bottom of the ladder as a copy holder. I left the insurance company and reported to work at the company offices along Standard Street in Nairobi on 7 May 1962. We worked alongside the printing machines at the basement of the building.

When I arrived in Nairobi I stayed with my parents in a four-bedroomed municipal flat at Ngara, a short distance from the CBD, on the other side of the Nairobi River. Ngara flats were quite spacious and the area was relatively safe. They were near shops, only a walking distance to Kariokor Market where we did most of our shopping for vegetables and meats. In those days, things were working well in Nairobi. Trash was collected on time, frequent power outages were non-existent and clean water was plentiful. The Nairobi River, now mucky with garbage, was then an environmental gem, with clean, clear water flowing through the city.

Often when I was free I would take long walks all the way to Majengo, a dusty neighbourhood that slightly resembled my own estate in Mombasa. Comparatively, the Majengo King'orani where I grew up was far cleaner and far less crowded. Many of the men at the Nairobi Majengo were former soldiers during the First and Second World Wars. Also resident in the estate was a large number of women from Tanzania and Uganda who had followed the soldiers to offer services of the flesh. The place was therefore a hive of activity after dark.

Once in a while I would venture into the Majengo Social Hall, in those days a popular venue for boxing practices and theatre activities. I would also wonder around the nearby Shauri Moyo for no apparent reason other than to observe people and enjoy the typical African environment.

I found life in Nairobi to be comparatively hostile compared to Mombasa. Nairobians were not as friendly as the coastal folk. While the latter were placid and hospitable, the former were irascible and instinctively occupied with chores. The phalanx of push carts, loaded with merchandise, of human traffic always in a rush, gave me a completely different perspective of human behaviour in a major town. In Mombasa, things were different. People start work late, take a two-hour break for lunch and leave early. At the Coast, haste was a foreign word. We believed that if you can't get it done today, there is always tomorrow.

After staying with my family for a few months, I yearned for independence and took a room at Eastleigh near the Pumwani Maternity Hospital. It was one of eight-rooms in a large bungalow with an open veranda. Tenants, among them junior office workers and prostitutes, shared the shower area and toilet. It was not an ideal living arrangement at all, but I tried to make the best of the situation and learnt to use my room only for sleeping. I never spent day time there because I didn't want to deal with the noise and the different strange characters coming in and out of the building.

My stay at Eastleigh lasted for two months. I relocated to Jericho in the east, where I took and shared a flat with Francis Komen, a photojournalist friend working with me at the paper. It was also at the *Standard* that I met Leonard Mambo Mbotela, then working as a machine operator. Mambo went to school in Eastern Kenya where his father worked as a teacher. Later he became a broadcaster and worked for many years at the Voice of Kenya and then Kenya Broadcasting Corporation (KBC).

The printing presses used at the *East African Standard* in those days were linotype machines that produced slugs of hot metals that were then pressed on paper to produce a dummy. The whole process of correcting proofs was done by two people: the proof reader and the copy holder. The holder held a news copy and read it aloud while the reader corrected any typo, punctuation or spelling mistakes on the dummy. The corrected dummy would then go back to the printer for correction and back again to the readers for approval. There was a standard style book with symbols; full stops, commas, etc. to direct the printer on the kind of corrections to be made.

After six months in the machine-noisy, chemical-stuffed basement, I was moved to the *Baraza* newsroom. The following year, I asked for a transfer to the *East African Standard* newsroom as a trainee reporter. Javan Chavanga and Julius Kinuthia were already on board. Chavanga was being dispatched to Nakuru to cover the whole of the Rift Valley, while Kinuthia was retained in the newsroom in Nairobi. Also joining the paper about that time was Joe Nugi.

The *East African Standard,* like many businesses at the time, was British-owned. Kenneth Bolton, a grim-faced, toothy former editor at Fleet Street in London was the managing editor. He was a stickler for perfection and always demanded a well-written, clean copy. His deputy was Eric Marsden, a short, placid man with big eyes. He was very good at mentoring young journalists like me. On the news desk was a plump man called Eric Bell who chain-smoked and drank Tusker beer like water. He would burp loudly after lunch, exhaling a foul barley smell. The rest of the newsroom, advertising and press divisions were packed with British reporters, marketing agents and machine operators. As a trainee reporter, I was often paired with a white journalist especially when it came to coverage of political meetings at Kamukunji and Tom Mboya Hall in Eastlands. I would translate the Kiswahili speeches to my English colleague who would write the story and earn the by-line.

My most memorable event at the *Standard* was when I was sent to cover a press conference called by the Kenya Federation of Labour. Normally, such an important assignment would be given to a white reporter. At the time, none was immediately available in the newsroom. I therefore went to the event and wrote a story. Bolton normally received copies of all stories filed by reporters. After submitting my story, I sat contentedly at my desk. Then I heard a burst of the editor's door. It was Bolton, furious and red-faced. He was calling my name and flagging my copy. He asked me to go to his office immediately. There he scolded me using English words that I had never heard before. I listened frighteningly, my legs shivering. Then he tore my copy into small pieces and threw them in a dustbin. I was demoralised and distressed. I almost cried. Luckily deputy editor Marsden was there to console me. We went through the copy together, and I re-wrote the story to his satisfaction. That was the baptism of fire for me. From there on I worked harder on my stories.

* * *

There were a total of three conferences at Lancaster House in London before Kenya's independence. My father was among the African LegCo members to attend the first one in January 1960 at which no agreement was reached. The second one was held between February and April 1962 at which a framework for self-government was negotiated. And the third one took place between 25 September and 6 October 1963 to finalise constitutional arrangements for independence. When Independence Day came on 12 December 1963, I was at Uhuru Gardens to witness the hoisting of the Kenyan flag. From the hand of Prince Philip Mountbatten, husband to Queen Elizabeth the II, Kenyatta also received the original copy of the first constitution of the newly independent Kenya. From Uhuru Gardens, my friends and I descended on Jeans Bar in Nairobi West where we celebrated until morning.

Soon, troubles beckoned. Before *uhuru*, Kenyans had been primed to expect immediate changes once the British rule ended. Leaders promised people jobs, good houses and big cars. Oginga Odinga confirms this in *Not Yet Uhuru*.

"Some people in the villages thought that there was lots of money in the bank and Kenya would give it all to us, that money could be printed easily enough. I told them how we had to work to accumulate wealth; that much of the wealth our work had amassed in the past had been taken out of the country. I told countless meetings of KANU and the ordinary people: 'We must be busy now with reconstruction. It is your country now, don't shake it. It will take time for the Government to fulfil its duty to the people. We must do our best to put Kenya on its feet.'"[6]

---
6   Odinga, Oginga (1967) *Not Yet Uhuru: An Autobiography,* East African Educational Publishers: 242.

That as it may be, impatient Kenyans wanted their expectations met without too much delay.

On 2 January 1964, unhappy about their terms and conditions of service, soldiers of the 11th Battalion Kenya Rifles at Lanet in Nakuru, Rift Valley, mutinied. They broke into an armoury, took up arms and demanded a meeting with Kenyatta. Soldiers wanted the Army Commander, Brig. A. J. Hardy, replaced with an African and their salaries raised. Although there appeared to have been no threat of a military coup only a month after independence, Kenyatta was jolted into realisation that Kenyans were in a hurry to take over all sectors of society. He was stunned and afraid that the army may turn against him.

At that time the military was dominated – not by his tribesmen, the Kikuyu – but by the Kalenjin from the Rift Valley and the Kamba from Eastern Province. Soldiers from the two tribes had emerged from the King's African Rifles that fought with the British in the World War II to pioneer the new independent force. Kenyatta had every reason to be afraid. Had the British not intervened to quell the mutiny, the security of the country would have been endangered. The story was front-page news in Kenyan newspapers and received wide coverage, as expected, in Britain.

I was assigned by *Taifa* to visit Buller Camp located near Nairobi Club to see whether there was any unusual military activity but there was none. Buller Camp housed the 1st Signals Squadron and the 1st Independent Transport Platoon. No other units joined in the uprising. Similar mutinies that occurred at about the same time in Tanganyika and Uganda were also suppressed by British forces.

The British were also worried about the event only weeks after Kenya got full independence because they had vast investments in the country. They owned thousands of acres of fertile land in what was then the White Highlands. They dominated everything and they were not ready to allow the country plunge into chaos. Since it was not possible to make immediate changes without a proper training programme for African officers, Brig. Hardy had to stay for two more years before he was replaced by Brig. Joseph Ndolo, a Kamba.

I apprenticed with the *East African Standard* for less than two years before moving to the rival company, the Nation Group, then situated along Victoria Street, now known as Tom Mboya Street, in Nairobi. It was housed at Nation House, a building opposite the Fire Brigade station. It was during the era of Remington typewriters, telex machines and dark rooms. While the ground floor accommodated the advertising section and at the back the printing presses; the upper floors had the management, editorial, a library and the telex room. *The Nation* had acquired a Kiswahili weekly paper, *Taifa,* from Charles Hayes in 1958. The following year it was transformed into a daily and in 1960, its English version, *Daily Nation,* was born. I joined the paper in January 1964 as a reporter and features writer. As I exited the *Standard*, my childhood friend from Mombasa, Sylvanus Nasibu, joined after finishing school at Shimo la Tewa Secondary. Another close friend, Joel Tsola, joined the Department of Information as a reporter. Tsola was later to work in senior positions at the National Assembly and at the Electoral Commission of Kenya (ECK).

I was attracted to the Nation Media Group because I felt it represented the future of journalism in Kenya. Though owned by H. E. Prince Karim Aga Khan, both *Taifa* and *Daily Nation* were run by a young cadre of African writers who were innovative and adventurous. People like Boaz Omori, Hilary Ng'weno, Joe Rodrigues, George Mbuguss, Harry Sambo and Omari Chambati were giants at the time. For a brief period, Ngugi wa Thiong'o also worked with us before he became a famous author. We also had expatriate staff to help boost quality of the paper. I worked very closely with Chambati, one of the best Kiswahili short story writers the country has had. I liked him because he always encouraged me to be imaginative. The result of my effort was a series of fiction pieces that found their way into the pages of the weekly *Taifa Kenya* edition for several months. *Taifa Kenya* was the weekly Saturday edition while *Taifa* was the daily. There was this feeling of warmth and camaraderie at Nation House that I didn't experience at the *Standard*. Journalists socialised freely regardless of position, and socialising they did.

Just behind Nation House was a popular joint called Sans Chiques. That was the watering point of *who-is-who* in the Kenyan media at the time. I was introduced to the restaurant-cum-bar by Sambo, a seasoned page-lay-out editor with *Taifa* who loved his beer as much as he loved his women. I can almost swear that he was one of those who popularised the phrase "liquid lunch". He would gulp two beers at lunch time, go back to the office to edit the front and editorial pages, and break for another round of two beers at around five, after sending the last copy down to the presses. Upon returning to check the final gulley an hour later, off he would go for yet another night of booze. Eating was not his hobby. He was my best friend, so I soon found myself following his traits. Looking around I discovered that almost everyone else in the editorial department was doing the same. However, deadlines were never missed and the papers were always on time for distribution.

Another popular place for journalists was the Press Club atop the Hotel Ambassadeur along Moi Avenue. It was so exclusive that one required a key to get in. Inside were typewriters and phone banks that allowed reporters to file stories while drinking their beers. It was so chic. However, frequent brawls among members, especially the white journalists, led to its closure.

Nairobi then, unlike now, was a relatively safe place, and cheap. Nairobi West was just emerging as a residential suburb, and Jeans Bar, located at its shopping centre was one of the more popular joints in the city. The bar was owned by Jean Armstrong, a former British soldier who chose to remain in Kenya after independence, and his wife Ruby. Later, the Armstrongs opened the Starlight Night Club, which was housed at the present site of the Integrity Centre, near the PanAfric Hotel. Rhumba music was very popular in Kenya then, and the Starlight specialised in showcasing music groups especially from the Congo. There were two other popular clubs in town: the Halians on Tom Mboya Street across from where the Standard Chartered Bank, Moi Avenue branch is, and Brilliant Hotel in Ngara. All those clubs were kept open twenty-four hours a day. Boogie sessions were featured on Saturdays and Sundays starting in the early afternoon. Sure enough my media friends and I were regular visitors to all those clubs.

In the meantime, Boaz Omori, who by that time was Managing Editor of *Taifa,* was invited by the Minister for Information and Broadcasting, Ramogi Achieng Oneko, to join the government and oversee the process of Africanising the newsroom at the Voice of Kenya (VoK). The VoK newsroom was then headed by Alistair Matheson and manned by an all-white team of journalists. I believe the events that took place at Lanet hastened the Africanisation process in the civil service, including the VoK. Omori was asked to select three African journalists from the private sector to join him. He settled on Shadrack Sikobe from the *East African Standard*, Arthur Chang'awa from the Department of Information, and myself from the *Nation*. We all resigned from our jobs and on 1 July 1964, I joined the VoK.

It was also at VoK that I got a chance to venture into news broadcasting, which happened by sheer chance. At that time, most of the top broadcasters at VoK were products of an attachment programme with the British Broadcasting Corporation (BBC) in London – people like John Ithau, Hassan Mazoa, Stephen Kikumu, Stephen Ndesandjo, Sammy Osore, Salim Juma and Daniel Gatei. They were talented, young and full of hubris. They had reached the pinnacle of their broadcasting career and thought they could afford to miss work and get away with it. But their frequent malingering allowed novices like us to get a chance to break into broadcast journalism. I was called upon to read the news whenever any one of them failed to turn up. Slowly, I found myself in the roster for news readers. That was a feather on my cap that would come in handy years later.

Within a space of one year, the newsroom had been fully Africanised. Matheson had retired and Omori had taken full charge. With the Presidential News Service and the Kenya News Agency now fully in place, we no longer had to cover stories from the newsroom. All three of us, Sikobe, Chang'awa and I, were promoted to editors, taking over from the Europeans who were leaving. Having completed his assignment, Omori returned to the *Nation* as Editor-in-Chief in 1967 to take over from George Githii who had resigned to pursue other interests.

Chapter 9

My First Trip Overseas

Up to that time, I had not received any formal training in journalism. The only course I had attended was a two-week media workshop in Moshi, Tanzania, in 1962, organised by the US Information Service for upcoming Eastern African journalists. Although the workshop taught me the fundamentals of news reporting, copy editing and photography, it did not give me a deeper understanding of the trade. Omari Chambati of *Taifa* and Jenkins Kiwanuka of the *Uganda Argus* were among those who attended the workshop. Training opportunities were rare and media houses were retaining expatriate journalists for in-house training. In the mid-sixties, the International Press Institute ran one-year training courses for journalists, in partnership with the University of Nairobi. I didn't get a chance to attend that course. I also missed out on a government scholarship to study journalism in Hungary because that arrangement, by the Ministry of Information and Broadcasting under Minister Achieng Oneko, aborted.

My opportunity finally came in mid-1965 when I was among four Kenyans selected for a nine-month attachment at the *Times of India* in Bombay sponsored by the Indian government. Two reporters from the Department of Information, Mureithi and Njeru, and one information officer from the Indian Embassy in Nairobi, Michael Kabugua, were also selected.

I had heard a lot about India from my father who had spent time in Bombay in 1947. Most of what he told me had to do with India's independence struggle and the class struggle of the Untouchables. Names like Mahatma Gandhi, Jawaharlal Nehru and the Indian National Congress kept popping up in our talks. My father always compared colonial rule in India to that in Kenya. He talked of racial discrimination and segregated facilities, and how British nationals in India were living in luxury while the majority of Indians wallowed in poverty. The same, he said, was happening in Kenya.

The trip to India was my first overseas journey ever and my first airline experience. I was therefore filled with a mixture of excitement, fear and trepidation. I didn't know what to expect in that far away country. I knew Indian culture and food were different from ours because I had attended Indian weddings and had interacted with neighbourhood Indians at Majengo when I was young. While we ate *ugali* with everything including meat, they mostly ate *chapatis*, cooked thin, with spicy vegetables.

As the Air India jet taxied at high speed towards the end of the runaway at the old Embakasi airport in Nairobi, I held tightly to my seat. My heart pounded, my head whirled and I broke into a cold sweat. I was wedged between my two colleagues and I could hear one of them breathing heavily. My mind was occupied with what could happen if, for one reason or the other, the plane nose-dived and plunged to the ground. I thought of my parents and friends and the good time we always had together. I had read about plane crashes and the many deaths they had caused and concluded I would have no chance of surviving if that particular plane went down.

My body was tight until the plane levelled off and went into a cruising mode. It was then that I ordered a cold beer and convinced myself that no such mishap would happen, at least not with that plane. The beautiful sari-clad hostesses were very courteous and made our flight comfortable. They even taught us how to say, *Namaste* (how are you) in Hindi, and showed us the right Indian way of folding our palms and bowing with respect.

The six-hour flight was uneventful until the plane began its descent into Bombay airport. The panic attack returned. My body tightened again and I found myself clutching hard on the hand rests. My ears blocked and ached discomfortingly as the engines buzzed and whistled on approach. I heard the plane's heavy rubber wheels spin furiously as the big bird touched the ground; then it taxied noisily and came to a halt at the parking bay. I sank into my seat contentedly from my shaky position and yearned to get out of the plane as quickly as possible.

Through the window, I could see the black crows gathered together in the distance as we eased slowly into the parking bay. I had seen many similar crows in Mombasa, and the story was that they had originated in India, having ridden aboard sea vessels. As I stepped out of the plane, I felt like I had been hit by a bucket of quivering coals. I could hear murmurs of protest from my colleagues about the stifling heat. The heat did not bother me much though as I had lived most of my life through almost similar conditions; between December and March, Mombasa turns into an oven. I was only happy that we had arrived safely in India, and I looked forward to what was ahead of us.

At the airport, we were met by officials from the *Times of India* who escorted us to a company guest house in a nice part of the city. Riding in a car through the terribly congested streets, and seeing the various shades of Indians, gave us the first glimpse of what we were to expect during our almost one-year stay.

The guest house was a modern four-bedroomed bungalow tucked in a *cul-de-sac* and surrounded by trees. It had a well-furnished sitting room with light blue spongy sofas, hand-embroidered curtains and a huge TV tuned to classic Bollywood movies. Two beige-tiled bathrooms and a gourmet kitchen completed the house. Contemporary paintings and frames of Indian sceneries hang on the walls. At the far corner of the sitting room was a huge picture of Indian Goddess Devi, the Supreme Being in the Shaktism tradition of Hinduism. The place was sparkling clean, and we found out why; the guest house was meant for visiting company executives and special guests like us. To keep it immaculate, two servants and one cook were in residence at the servants' quarters. After seeing many archaic residential buildings along the way from the airport, we were quite impressed with our dwelling.

We cracked jokes about our leaking flats and clogged sewerage lines back home and considered ourselves lucky. To see that we were being treated respectfully by the house servants was breathtakingly humbling. After a shower, we sat down for our first Indian meal: a splash of curries, fried rice, *chapatis*, spiced vegetables and plenty of different types of sweets, just as I had expected. Meat was nowhere in sight. There were also plenty of ice-cold drinks of different colours. The sweets reminded me of a function I attended with my father at the Patel Samaj hall in Mombasa when I was little. The Patels were celebrating some kind of anniversary and had invited my father as a town leader. I remember eating too many of those sweets and becoming sick the whole night. I decided to have none of them this time around.

If we thought the guest house was to be our abode for the rest of our stay in India, we were dead wrong. A few days after our arrival, an official from the *Times of India* informed us that rooms had been secured for us at the International Students Hostel located directly opposite the Queen's Railways Station. We moved there in utter indignation. The hostel was a multi-storied, dilapidated and rat infested building on the down side of Bombay. The kitchen had not received a good clean up for years and it smelt of stale oil and dead cockroaches. The shared rooms were small and the once light blue paint had peeled off the concrete walls, exposing a grey background and poor masonry. The only fair room was the common lounge that had a set of three old sofas, a coffee table, and at the corner a table tennis board. In the following months, we spent many hours in that room playing cards and table tennis. As its name suggests, the hostel was home to students from many parts of the world studying in universities and colleges in the city. One of the students was Gouba, a citizen of Burma (now Myanmar) who was studying economics at the University of Bombay. We became very close and talked a lot about Asian and world politics. The food was strictly Indian, heavily peppered and spiced, and our stomachs had to go through weeks of orientation.

The International Students Hostel was a walking distance to the Times of India. It took us only 20 minutes of leisurely walk to get to or from the office. The organisation had a number of publications under its management including its flagship, *Times of India*, and then *Economic Times*, several provincial dailies as well as magazines. The Group ran a training school where future journalists were trained in various disciplines. In my year of training, there were twenty students, all of them Indians, except us. Our instructor, Mehta, was a gaunt sweet-talking gentleman with a goatee. He had worked at the *Times* for years and had been seconded to the training wing to teach young, upcoming newsmen for eventual deployment to company publications. All our Indian colleagues were graduates and came from different parts of the country. In our class we had economists, lawyers, and at least one engineer. They all considered themselves lucky to get an opportunity of apprenticing with the largest newspaper group in a country with a very high unemployment rate.

We had a very tight work programme: classroom work in the morning and practical assignments in the afternoon. Each one of us was, at different times, attached to each one of the various company publications. We went to the courts to report on cases and visited the financial district to collect economic news. Each one of us also had to edit and supervise an edition of the *Training Times*.

We bonded well with our Indian friends who were curious about Africa and Africans in general. The only images they had about Africa were what they had seen in *Tarzan* movies. They wanted to know the kind of wild animals we had, and whether it was true that to qualify for marriage one had to kill a lion. We tried to explain to them the little we knew about the Maasai culture and yes, it was true, that bravery was a very key element of manhood among the Maasai, and true, to graduate to adulthood one had to kill a lion. We even tried to improvise the way Maasai *morans* jumped and sang. They also wanted to know about Mau Mau and Jomo Kenyatta whom they had heard a lot about. In turn we enquired from them about their founding fathers, Mahatma Gandhi and Jawaharlal Nehru. I was so fascinated by India's political history and Gandhi's discipline that I was inspired to write a comprehensive analysis of his *Satyagraha*, non-violence philosophy. My analysis was published in one of the editions of the *Training Times*.

Bombay was a booze-free city. Only foreigners and diplomats were allowed to buy alcoholic drinks. We requested and got permits to buy a limited number of beers and spirits every month on which we spent part of our stipend from the *Times*. We bought these drinks from a nearby government-supervised store guarded by an armed *askari* and protected by a thick wire mesh. When we could not afford to buy legally we resorted to drinking *chang'aa*, a bootleg gin, from a snuggle-toothed mama in a dingy house just a few houses behind our hostel.

* * *

India had many surprises for me. I had heard and even read about eunuchs, but never on earth did I think I would one day come face to face with them. I did. Once, as we walked to the Times we were accosted by a group of six individuals who looked like ordinary Indian girls. They wore saris and painted themselves with thick, red-coloured lipstick. They swayed their bodies and shook their behinds just like many women do. When they saw us they rushed forward deliriously uttering Indian words we didn't understand. We got scared and ran. They pretended to chase us for a while then resumed their normal walk. We looked back and saw some children on the sidewalk laughing and pointing fingers at us. It was only after narrating the story to our colleagues that we came to know they were eunuchs. From that point on, every time we saw a group of women approaching we took off in the opposite direction.

Eunuchs – people with gender identity disorder – have a long history in India. They are so many that they even have representatives in elected assemblies. They usually live in slums, and their status in society is not any better than that of the untouchables who sit at the very bottom of the social ladder; the untouchables are the lowest caste. Coming from a country that had endured years of racial and other forms of discrimination, I felt for both the eunuchs and the untouchables who are condemned to live their entire lives as forgotten human beings, tucked deep in crowded and miserable hovels. And talking of slums, one needs to go to India to find *real* slums. It is not only about the large amounts of foul matter one finds in such colonies as Juhu and Annawadi in Bombay, but the different types of garbage that finds its way there – discarded foetuses, gruesome medical waste, foul chemical residues, acrid human waste and much more grimy stuff. At the time I was in India, I thought the slums there were many times worse than our own in Kenya.

Like many developing countries, India was a nation of contrasts. When we were in India, the country was at war with Pakistan over Jammu and Kashmir border disputes. In that war New Delhi used Indian made tanks, Indian made Gnat fighter jets and Indian made guns. The government was spending billions of rupees in building war hardware, yet one out of six people in urban areas lived in slums. The gap between the rich and the poor was as wide, if not wider, as what existed in Kenya. Being the movie capital of India, Bombay had and still is home to some of the richest individuals in the world. They live in gated communities away from the slum-towns, drive big cars and often travel abroad for leisure. Not too far from their posh houses are the poor in cardboard dwellings.

Another aspect of Indian life I found strange was seeing Indians dressed in saris and kurtas attending a Catholic mass. The Indians I knew in Kenya who professed the Hindu religion kept a red dot on their forehead and wore a coloured string on one of their wrists. Seeing Indians in Bombay taking the Holy Communion was a shocker.

Unlike Nairobi where the CBD was set away from residential estates, the Bombay CBD was a cosmopolitan city with a mixture of residential units and office buildings all existing side by side. Herds of water buffalos and cows decked in colourful flowers and other adornments roamed the streets freely. Rickshaws, taxis and human traffic choked the roadways. That made me realise that Nairobi, with its unpaved streets, was still a well-organised city indeed.

However, I was taken aback by the large numbers of raggedy beggars, many of them women and children who enjoyed chasing us down the street with empty battered bowls on hand. The children were quite stubborn and would follow and pester us until we parted with something. The widespread poverty in India also contributed to the high level of prostitution. For the first time in my life I came to know about red districts. There, young girls smuggled from as far as Nepal, Bangladesh and the Philippines, were forced to sell their bodies by ruthless pimps and mamas. At night along the streets of the Bombay's red district, shining red bulbs hung from windows to signal the presence of brothels.

One of India's most popular recreations is the chewing of *paan*, a combination of betel leaves, dry areca nuts and some tobacco. *Paan*, which has stimulating and psychoactive substances is chewed and then swallowed or spat. When spat, it looks like blood. Because of its widespread use, Bombay streets were filled with millions of gooey spit spots everywhere. On the way around town we had to watch for the spits that came in different colours, sizes and texture, to avoid splattering them on our shoes. That was one aspect of Bombay I found disgusting.

We always came across curious locals who were fascinated by our thick hair. People would often approach us to get a feel of its texture. Indians – even the very dark ones – still thought of us Africans as black, but none of us experienced any form of discrimination. Later in this book, I have talked about Bombay Africans, the African slaves who were taken to India during the slave trade and the fate of those who found their way to Kenya.

* * *

We completed our training successfully at the beginning of 1966. By that time all of us were homesick. We missed our families and friends as well as our beer and *nyama choma*. We had had enough of greasy, mind-spinning peppered curries, and were fed up with the annoying, scratching, hungry rats in our rooms.

Before leaving, the Indian Ministry of Information took us on a whirlwind tour of the country, visiting interesting places including the iconic Taj Mahal in Agra, museums in New Delhi, beautiful gardens in Calcutta and historical sites in Kerala in the south-west. It was during our tour of the Indian states that Lal Bahadur Shastri, the second Prime Minister of India after Jawaharlal Nehru died. The country virtually shut down. So, as we headed home, we left behind a country in mourning.

It was not until I arrived in Kenya that I was told of Nyanya Emilia's death. My father had concealed her death from me while in India for obvious reasons. The sad news would have adversely affected me. She fell sick in Mombasa and was sent to Nairobi for treatment. She was already over eighty years old and suffering from a serious case of hypertension. My father, who was still residing in Nairobi, decided not to take her body back to Rabai. She was buried at the Lang'ata cemetery. One of the first things I did when I arrived back home was to go to the cemetery to pay homage at her resting place which even today is marked by a single tree.

Nyanya Emilia's death left a gaping hole in my life. She had nurtured me for most of my childhood and had stood by Charles and me during some very taxing moments. I remember several times when she stormed out of the house at Majengo in fury because she could not stand seeing us being punished. When she got angry her face would become taut. She would wander listlessly in the house while throwing a few nasty words at her son. Then she would pack her clothes and leave for Rabai. She was our biggest defender and her death was therefore a personal blow. I mourned privately for a long time.

Chapter 10
Kenyatta, Odinga, VoK

Not too long after I re-joined VoK upon my return from India, KANU, the ruling party, held a crucial Delegates' Conference at Limuru, forty kilometres outside Nairobi, in March 1966. Kenyatta, who had been named Prime Minister three years earlier after KANU won the May 1963 elections against KADU and became President on 12 December 1964, was facing a major political test of his rule. There was a rebellion within his government. His one-time ally did not agree with Kenyatta on a number of issues. "Oginga wanted to nationalise foreign owned corporations, to seize settler farms in the former 'White Highlands' without compensation and for Kenya to follow a non-aligned foreign policy."[7] On the contrary, Kenyatta "sought to reassure European settlers, telling them they were welcome to stay and farm without fear of the bogeyman and that his government would protect them."[8]

Oginga Odinga had been wooing the Russians and the Chinese for some time. The Russians had already built the main hospital in Kisumu and had pledged to fund some agricultural projects in his Nyanza Province. The Chinese, along other communist nations, had also contributed funds for the building of an ideological school at Kasarani known as the Lumumba Institute. Hence, Odinga was determined to give China and the Soviet Union a foothold in the country. Having been partly educated in England and married to a Briton, Kenyatta admired the European-type of checks and balances, and believed in a free economy. "Kenyatta sought aid from both East and West, but would crack down on any perceived signs of communist infiltration."[9]

---
7   David Throup, "Elections and Political Legitimacy in Kenya Africa", *Journal of the International African Institute*, Vol. 63, 3 (1993): 371-396.

8   H. Lotte, "Truth Be Told" Some Problems with Historical Revisionism in Kenya", *African Studies,* Vol. 70, 2 (2011): 182-201.

9   Mary L. Dudziak, *Exporting American Dreams: Thurgood Marshall's African Journey* (Oxford: Oxford University Press, 2008): 142.

Because of the split at the top, the country was teetering on the brink of an ethnic strife between Luo and Kikuyu fuelled by their political differences. Kenyatta had therefore called the Limuru Conference to tame the wave of Odingaism and take control of both the party and the government.

As a public broadcaster, VoK too was facing its first big test since independence. As the only broadcaster with a country-wide reach, the government found it convenient to use it as a propaganda tool against the opposition. It became obvious to us that the Permanent Secretary in the Ministry of Information and Broadcasting, Peter Gachathi, a Kikuyu like Kenyatta, and not the Director of Broadcasting, James Kangwana, a Mijikenda, was calling the shots on all major broadcasting decisions. Hence, the issue was not so much about VoK's independence, integrity or objectivity, but defending Kenyatta's political interests at all costs. Gachathi, who spent most of his evening hours at his bar in Kilimani, was a very powerful official and was part of a Kikuyu clique that was closest to Kenyatta. He was a product of Alliance High School as were many of the early top government officials such as Duncan Ndegwa and Geoffrey K. Kariithi.

Kenya was following the footpath of other African countries which had received independence ahead of it in as far as the management of the public media was concerned. Ghana and Tanzania had so monopolised their media that press freedom had become a mockery. In Kenya, the man behind the state media policies was Gachathi. Before KNA, VoK's associate in the Ministry of Information, was established in 1963, Kenya reached out to the Ghana News Agency (GNA) for technical and policy advice. The West African country had been independent since 1957, and GNA had had plenty of time to perfect the art of skewing news in favour of President Kwame Nkrumah. That was the line KNA chose to take, and since VoK depended on KNA for news, there was no way it could have deviated from the official line in news coverage.

At the Limuru Conference, the party vice presidency, which Odinga held, was abolished and replaced by eight regional party vice presidents, thus shaving off any powers Odinga had. At VoK we were under strict instructions to support the KANU's position and demonise Oginga Odinga and his group as enemies of the nation. I was one of the shift news editors at the time and stories filed by the Presidential Press Unit about the events at Limuru were openly biased, but we were under instructions to carry them without change. As a result, the Odinga group was thoroughly humiliated in the eyes of Kenyans. Almost immediately, Oginga Odinga left KANU to found the Kenya People's Union (KPU). The party lasted for only three years before it was proscribed and Oginga Odinga and his colleagues were sent into detention.

But it was during the *shifta* (bandit) war in north-eastern region that VoK's integrity as a news organisation was shattered. The war broke out soon after independence when the Somali government began a campaign to unify all Somalis in the Horn of Africa. It wanted Kenya to cede the Northern Frontier District (NFD) to Somalia, an idea Kenyatta vehemently opposed. The NFD comprised what came to be known as the North-Eastern Province and the districts of Marsabit, Moyale and Isiolo.

The crisis started in 1963 in the form of banditry attacks and cattle raids by Somalis on both sides of the border. Militarily, Kenya was not ready or even able to match the guerrilla tactics employed by the militias although it had a much bigger and more organised army. However, the Kenya Army was young and inexperienced. It had not yet fought a conventional war leave alone a guerrilla hit-and-run offensive the Somalis were applying. As a result, Kenyan troops were often ambushed and killed and their vehicles blown off by Russian-supplied landmines. Reports arriving at the VoK newsroom from sources on the ground and from international media showed Kenya was losing lives and the war.

The government, through Dawson Mlamba, then Permanent Secretary in the Ministry of Defence, admitted in July 1966 that there were "mounting casualties to the army and police" and asked the Ministry of Information and Broadcasting to mount a propaganda war against the *shifta*. There were even rumours that the government had recruited some journalists in the private media to "plant" stories that were favourable to Kenya. Such rumours were difficult to confirm, but given the desperation of the authorities over the direction of the war, it was possible that the independent media could have been roped into such a conspiracy. Mlamba sent out instructions to our Ministry that all war reports had to be cleared by his office. The government was concerned that reports filtering from the war front showing Kenya on the defensive could dim morale in the armed forces and anger Kenyans. Hence, Gachathi felt the responsibility of war reporting and any censoring should be left to his Ministry.

Seeing that Kenya could be fiddling with facts, Mogadishu upped its propaganda war by beaming Somali and Kiswahili broadcasts into Kenya and jamming Kenya transmissions. Kenya was in no position to match that propaganda assault. VoK's editorials, which were supposed to articulate the government's hard-line position and rally masses, were seamless and dense in content.

Before the Ministries of Information and Defence took over, the editorials that ran on the VoK after the news bulletins were written in the newsroom by people unfamiliar with the political and military complexities of the situation. Apart from losing the war in the field, we were also losing the propaganda war. Director Kangwana, a former broadcaster himself, had virtually ceded control of the VoK to higher authorities who manipulated it for all reasons other than nurturing it as reliable conveyer of fair and accurate news. Eventually, the *shifta* war subsided. It took the intervention of President Kenneth Kaunda for a ceasefire agreement to be reached and signed between President Kenyatta and Prime Minister Muhammad Haji Ibrahim Egal in 1967. Officially, the crisis had been overcome, but skirmishes along the border continued for many years. To me, the *shifta* war and the events at Limuru helped to spur the state's strangle-hold on the public broadcaster that continued for decades thereafter.

* * *

It was while at the VoK that I met Bob Grant, the VoA correspondent in Nairobi. Grant was a short, gentle, cowboy-type man who loved his cigarette. The American public broadcaster was, at that time, on an expansion path of its Africa coverage and wanted to increase its Kiswahili content. He asked me if I could help by translating some English material into Kiswahili and packaging it in tapes for transmission to Washington DC. I agreed. The work was part-time and me could do it during my off times. The US Information Service, to which Grant was attached, also asked broadcaster Mohammed Njuguna and me to produce a programme called "Africa Today and Tomorrow", a radio news magazine for syndication to interested radio stations in East Africa. Little did I know my meeting with Grant was the beginning of a long association with the United States of America. In 1969 when a vacancy occurred in the Swahili Service in Washington DC, Grant recommended me. I accepted the offer.

As I was preparing to leave Nairobi for Washington DC, Tom Mboya, a government Minister and a rising star in Kenyan politics was shot dead. I was off duty and having a drink at Jeans Bar in Nairobi West that 5 July 1969 when I heard about the apparent assassination. I rushed to the nearest pay phone to confirm the news with the VoK newsroom, then left for the city centre. When I arrived in town, the crime scene had been cordoned off and the body already taken to the mortuary. A lot of people were milling around outside the pharmacy along what is today Moi Avenue where he was shot.

News of Mboya's death spread fast. Flamboyant and urbane Mboya was considered a possible successor to the ageing Kenyatta. He had worked in the labour movement as Secretary General of the Kenya Federation of Labour (KFL) and had consequently forged very close ties with American labour and political leaders. His reputation soared in 1959 when he began airlifting scores of Kenyans for studies in the United States. He shared the same preferences for Western ideologies as Kenyatta, a stance that put him at odds with his counterpart from Luo Nyanza, Oginga Odinga. Mboya was married to Pamela, a beautiful and educated woman, and the couple was often likened to the flamboyant J. F. Kennedy, who later became President of the United States, and his wife, Jacqueline. In fact, it was the Kennedy family that financed the bulk of the airlift.

Tom Mboya's was the second high profile killing in Kenya since independence. Just before I left for India, Pio Gama Pinto, a Kenyan nationalist of Goan origin and a close ally of Oginga Odinga, was assassinated outside his home on 25 February 1965, along Lower Kabete Road in Nairobi. Pinto was a journalist and a socialist who participated in Kenya's struggle for independence, an effort that earned him four years in detention under colonial rule. His house was only two houses away from where my father lived. As part of my preparations to leave for Bombay, I had moved from my flat in South B to my father's company-provided house. I remember that day well. After the gunshots some of my family members and I were among the first to arrive at the scene. Although the two murders appeared unconnected, there were fears then that political killing gangs were on the loose. Mboya's murder infuriated the Luo and caused an ethnic rift between them and the Kikuyu. That combustible relationship manifested itself at Mboya's burial at Rusinga Island on 11 July when mourners scuffled, blaming Kikuyus for the murder. Two people were reported killed. Nahashon Njenga, a Kikuyu, was arrested, tried and convicted for the killing and was sentenced to death.

* * *

I arrived in America during the first week of November 1969, when the country was already shifting into winter. I travelled aboard a Pan American World Airways (Pan Am) plane over the long route through West Africa with stopovers in Lagos, Accra and Monrovia. After my first flight to and from India I was no longer afraid of taking to the skies. A few beers calmed my nerves and I slept most of the way. By the time I arrived at Dulles International Airport in Washington DC, I was tired. And because of the eight-hour difference, I was rather disoriented and had lost track of time.

What surprised me as I walked through the arrival lounge at the airport was to see white people sweeping the floors and doing other menial jobs that I thought were naturally reserved for black people. In Kenya, Africans did all the dirty jobs; they swept streets, waited on their masters, served as porters, ate leftovers, laboured in plantations and did all other demeaning chores. White people were feared and venerated. As *bwana* (master) and *memsahib* – terms used to show extreme respect and reverence – white people in Kenya were viewed by Africans as small gods who had to be worshipped; they considered them superior and more intelligent. Conversely, white people treated Africans like dogs. The whites barked orders and quivering servants carried them out without question. Thus, to see white people do menial work in America was an eye-opener. We had been independent for six years, but the superiority complex among Kenyan whites was only contrasted by the Africans' low esteem.

I was met at the airport by someone from VoA and booked at a three-star hotel just across the road from the Railway Station and a walking distance from the VoA studios at 330 Independence Avenue. From my hotel window, I could see the Capitol Building, the seat of Congress – the Senate and the House of Representatives – that I had heard so much about. Outside, the beautiful flowers and green foliage that had been dominant during summer and fall were fading into grey. The short-skirts and khaki pants were giving way to light fluffy-coloured jackets and woollen scarfs. As I walked to the office, I took note of the towering Washington Monument honouring the country's founding father, George Washington, and of museums and gardens. The official winter was still a few weeks away, but I was ready for it. I had purchased a heavy coat from a second-hand clothes shop along Kimathi Street, just a few yards from where the Nation Centre now stands.

The VoA headquarters is located in a giant grey building shared with the Department of Education, between the third and fourth streets in the south-western part of the city. Within those offices are dozens of recording and transmission studios serving different languages, music and book libraries, administrative offices and cafeterias. The Africa Service was located on the second floor, at one corner of the building, with a view of the street below. The Swahili Service was part of the Africa division which ran services in English, Hausa, Yoruba, Amharic and French. There was therefore some sort of patriotism amongst the foreign African journalists and broadcasters. We talked a lot about Africa and the politics of individual countries. We were set apart only by the way we dressed. While the East Africans almost always wore European suits, the West Africans and Ethiopians preferred their own traditional attires.

It didn't take long for me to find an apartment near the office. I found out soon that within the same apartment building was a Kenyan lady, Terry Wanjiru, a beautiful and comely lady who later became a wife of J. M. Kariuki, the assassinated Kenyan politician. For the record, it was Terry who years later stormed Parliament buildings to announce to legislators that Kariuki's body had been found after days of rumours about his whereabouts. Through her I met other Kenyans among them Jane and Christine, daughters of President Kenyatta (hence sisters to Uhuru Kenyatta) who were studying elsewhere in the USA.

Washington DC was home to many Kenyans, some students, some

professional and some just bumming around having failed in everything else. I was introduced to a number of entertainment joints one of which was the Kilimanjaro Club, owned by an enterprising old Kenyan friend, Victor Kibunja. Victor was living the American dream. He had started a motor garage in a decrepit part of Washington DC, built up capital and a few years later opened the club which became an entertainment sensation for Kenyans and locals alike. That club was like a paradise in a foreign country. Kenyans went to Kilimanjaro Club to eat *ugali* and *nyama choma* and listen to artists from different parts of Africa.

The United States can be very lonely to new arrivals. Although Africans are culturally hospitable, Americans are not known for magnanimity to strangers. When an American invites you for lunch you must be prepared to pay your part of the bill. One phrase I was forced to quickly add to my vocabulary was "going Dutch" whereby if someone invites you to go Dutch, it means the restaurant bill will have to be shared. There is nothing like a free lunch in America, which I found difficult to understand. I failed to understand because these were the same people who had opened their doors to Kenyan students, hosted them in their homes and fed them during the so-called students' airlift only a few years earlier.

Only a short walking distance from my house was the Potomac River, a long winding waterway six-hundred-fifty-two kilometre long that runs through States and pours its waters into the mid-Atlantic Ocean of the United States. Along its banks were restaurants, clubs and fish shops where one could buy live lobsters and crabs. The banks also anchored house boats and catamarans of different dimensions used for sports or even accommodation. During times of leisure I would walk along the riverside promenade enjoying the smell of barbecue coming from grills at the nearby park. The bar I loved most to visit was next to my apartment building, *The Place Where Louis Dwells*, a basement joint that featured live jazz music every Friday.

After the orientation, which included a special American Civilisation Course, I settled down to work. My work consisted mainly of translating into Kiswahili stories generated by the English Services and broadcasting them to Eastern Africa. The work was pretty routine and unexciting. Back home, I had worked on the beat, reporting events and writing news stories. For a long time at VoA, I couldn't do that. The station only trusted its citizen reporters to go out on assignments. The Americans had very strict broadcast guidelines which had to be followed to the letter. The guidelines became part of a government charter that supervised the administration and conduct of the station. Signed in 1976 by President Gerald Ford, the Charter called for accurate, objective, balanced and comprehensive coverage of news; projection of significant American thought and institutions; and presentation of US policies clearly and effectively. The Charter insisted that both government and opposition viewpoints had to be represented in news. The VoA Charter was in complete contrast to the Act of Parliament that created the Voice of Kenya on 1 July 1964. The Act mandated the station to inform, educate and entertain. It said nothing about the core principles of journalism: accuracy, objectivity and balance.

The Swahili Service was allocated only one broadcast hour per day. With five of us on staff, not to count correspondents in Nairobi and Dar es Salaam, the workload was weak. Each one of us had about one article of less than three minutes to translate and broadcast per day. Once the broadcast was over in the early afternoon, there was plenty of time left over to do other things. I liked to spend that time researching and sampling music for use in programmes. That monotony was however temporarily broken in 1970 when the VoA sent me to the Lyndon B. Johnson Space Centre in Houston, Texas, to do a feature on the first manned landing on the moon. The Apollo landing was one of the greatest American achievements of all time and fulfilled a promise made seven years earlier by President John F. Kennedy when in 1961 he told Congress that his goal was to land a man on the moon and return him safely to earth.

The visit to the space station was an extremely important and historical one for me. How many Kenyans would ever get such an opportunity? I asked myself. Apart from being away from the drudgeries of office work, I also got an opportunity to see the country. I had two choices on how to get to my destination: either fly directly to Houston from Washington DC, or combine a flight and a road trip. I thought travelling part of the journey by road was the better idea. On the way I could stop and interview rural folk about their daily activities. So I decided to fly to Austin, the capital of Texas, and from there took a self-drive car for the three-hour road trip to the Space Centre. On the way, I stopped and recorded some voices that I eventually used to produce material for the Swahili Service.

In Houston, I was impressed by the orderliness of the city and the industriousness of its inhabitants. The Space Centre was the biggest industry in the area and provided a livelihood for thousands of people working at the National Aeronautical and Space Administration (NASA) facilities. I noted that everyone around the Centre looked like an astronaut: clean shaven, marine-type, well-trimmed and brusque. I had an opportunity to interview both the astronauts and the support staff who participated in the 20 July 1969 space flight. Everyone was friendly and forthcoming with information.

* * *

When I left Kenya for the US I had two goals: one was to gain international experience in broadcasting, and the other, to further my education. I was profoundly inspired by Professor Ali Mazrui, the world-famous academic who in his earlier years did poorly in examinations but who picked himself up and advanced to Makerere University in Uganda to begin a long journey to excellence. I didn't think I would get anywhere near the famed fellow Coastarian, but I knew I had the capacity to go beyond high school. I considered myself one of the luckiest Kenyans. While others were struggling to go to the US, "the land of milk and honey," with all its restrictions, I had no such worries. My employer paid for my visa, bought my air ticket and gave me start-up money. Everything was taken care of by the US government. It was up to me to utilise the opportunity wisely and take advantage of everything good, including education. In 1959 when I was still struggling to clear my primary school, many others were registering for student airlift to the United States. Among the more famous beneficiaries were Barack Obama Snr., father of the 44th President of the United States, Barack Obama, and Wangari Maathai, the Nobel Laureate and the first woman in East and Central Africa to earn a doctoral degree in biological sciences.

Back from Houston, I looked at the various colleges in the District of Columbia area and settled on the George Washington University, a fully-accredited private institution with a high reputation for excellence. Because I had not completed my high school back in Kenya I had to take an equivalent examination as well as an IQ test to prove that I was qualified enough for enrolment. I was also asked to write an essay giving intelligent reasons why I felt I should be admitted to the university. I passed all the tests and was admitted on a probationary period. I was to be registered as a regular student only after achieving a B-plus average grade at the end of the year. I took a half load of nine credits (equivalent to three subjects) per semester and worked very, very hard through spare time and office hours. VoA was kind enough to let me attend classes during free office time and even paid for my journalism and broadcasting courses. At the end of the year, I had achieved a B-plus average and from there on the sky was the limit. I took additional credit courses at the University of the District of Columbia which had just opened. Because it was a public institution, it was far cheaper than George Washington University.

Chapter 11

The Love of My Life

On 12 December 1971, I attended the Kenya independence party at the residence of the Kenyan Ambassador to the United States of America, Leonard Kibinge, in Washington DC. As usual, many other Kenyans, US government and diplomatic officials were present. One of them was an old friend from Nairobi days, Mel McCaw, an African American, working with the African American Institute. I knew he had been transferred to Washington DC from Kenya, but I had not met him until that day. I was excited about seeing him again. However, it was the other person in his company who caught my attention. That person was a chocolate-complexioned lady in a long, black cocktail dress and a jet black afro. She was of a medium height, extremely beautiful and slender.

At that time in the American history, the Afro was a statement of pride and blackness among the African-American community. The black power movement, complete with the symbol of a clenched fist, was at its peak. People like Stokely Carmichael, who had changed his name to Kwame Toure and later married South African singer Miriam Makeba, Bobby Seale of the Black Panther Movement, and Martin Luther King, had become a thorn in the flesh of the US government. They were all fighting, in different ways, for the emancipation of the black people in the United States. The signature Afro hairstyle was a sign of militancy and with it was the popular jargon of the day: black is beautiful.

I shook her hand, and it was soft and tender. I looked at her face. It was smooth with just the right portion of makeup: not too little, not too much. My heart was saturated with excitement and my adrenaline went berserk. It was a cold December and we were indoors, but I could feel a streak of warmth in me that I had never felt before. It was love at first sight. After sweet-nothings and an exchange of telephone numbers, I left the party that night with the kind of joy only experienced by a jackpot winner.

A few days later, we met for our first date at a café along Pennsylvania Avenue in downtown Washington DC. There I fell in love with her even more. Doretha Savage was neither presumptuous nor indulgent. She ordered a simple sandwich and a bowl of soup, an indication of humility and modesty: virtues, I felt, she would carry along with her in marriage. I had been hooked big time. It was only then that I came to know she was a part-time model, something which explained the beauty, the poise and the curves. We began a year of serious dating. During that time I gave her an engagement ring. I didn't go through the traditional Westernised route of kneeling, "Can-I-marry-you" rigmarole, nor did I hire traditional African dancers, the African way. I just professed my deep love for her and unassumingly gave her a ring.

That was my happiest period in life. I was twenty-eight years old. Finally, I felt the long journey to find a perfect woman had come to a close. I had dated several women before, but I had found not a single one that had the kind of qualities Doretha possessed. It is almost impossible to describe them.

Doretha was born in a small rural town called Union. She was one in a large family that had lived through the era of segregation and cotton picking. Her parents were not middle class, but they worked hard to bring their children in the dignified Christian traditions of the Methodist Church. I was anxious to meet Ephy and Mattie Savage. One day, Doretha and I jumped into a car and travelled the 500-mile journey to her village in Union. South Carolina is in a region popularly known as the deep-south in America; pristine, rustic, with a rich culture of music, food and religion. The region was the core of slavery just like the Indian Ocean coast was.

The population of Union county was only a few thousand people when I visited, had only one major street and a few low level buildings that served as shops. Most farm houses were built with cut wood and shingles; some were prefabricated, others just mobile homes. This is an area where cemeteries are called memorial gardens and churches bear historical biblical names such as Mt Sinai, Calvary and Salem. Surrounded by walnut and cider, plum and apple trees, Union has all the characteristics of the fabled Garden of Eden, but with diversity. In summer, it is oven hot; in fall it is wet and green with thunderstorms that rattle; in winter it is cold with some snow; and in spring the kaleidoscopic mixture of colours turn the landscape into a pictorial paradise. It offers the perfect tranquillity for writers and painters.

I found my in-laws good-spirited and down to earth. They were not ashamed of their slave past. Life had been difficult for blacks in the South during the days of slavery, but they had been able to bring up ten children.

Stories of forced labour, mistreatment and killings of African American slaves were common in most places in America especially in the slave mines of the South during the 18th and 19th centuries. "Everywhere in the slave mines of Birmingham (Alabama) was death. Hardly any week passed when one or more dead black corpses weren't dragged up from inside the earth, heaped atop the mounds of coal in the railcars, or found dead in the simple infirmaries of a prison. Often no one knew or would say how a man died."[10]

Life for Blacks changed dramatically for the better after the Emancipation Declaration of 1 January 1863 by President Abraham Lincoln that promised freedom for slaves. The Savages were able to grow their own vegetables and fruits, and during fall and summer they preserved their produce in cans for use during the long winter. Mr and Mrs Savage had heard much about Africa and were anxious to know more. They were particularly enthused when they learnt that my background was not too different from their own: that my grandparents had been captured from their villages in the interior of Africa, loaded into ships to places unknown and were rescued and settled at Rabai in Mombasa, Kenya. I gave my father-in-law a Kamba walking stick with animal designs and my mother-in-law a set of *lesos* and wall carvings as gifts.

When I informed the Savages about my future plans with Doretha, they had no objection. Unlike back home where I would have been expected to pay dowry, there were no such demands and no such expectations from my future in-laws. I was happy I had impressed them enough to be allowed to marry their daughter. The following year, on 28 October 1972, two months short of a year since we met, Doretha and I walked into a small Catholic Church near the American University in Washington

---

10   Douglas A. Blackman, Slave by Another Name: The Re-enslavement of Black Americans from the Civil War to World War II, Anchor Books: XV.

DC as singles. An hour later we emerged as Mr and Mrs Joseph Matano Khamisi. It was a small wedding attended by only a dozen relatives and friends. The bride wore a long smashing white dress, and I a black tunic suit. My best man was Noah Katana, son of Ronald Gideon Ngala (the Coast politician referred to earlier). He was then a student at the South Eastern University in Washington DC.

My story of the wedding would not be complete without the following interesting backdrop. A day before the event, I drove to a farm outside the capital and bought a goat. I told the farmhand to slaughter the animal and leave everything to me including the blood captured from the neck veins. I had planned to use the blood and the intestines to prepare a local Kenyan dish called *mtura*. Not that I was experienced in cooking the sausage-type food, but I just wanted to inject some Kenyan element in the event and show my guests what was really Kenyan. What I did not remember was that inside the animal stomach was a heap of waste, which eventually would have to be disposed of. Since I was staying in an upstairs apartment, one easier way of getting rid of the smelly insides was to flush them down the sink hole. That was a big mistake. The sink clogged and I had to get a maintenance man to open up the system and get the mess down the drains. It was embarrassing. The muck stunk to high heaven. I could see the poor maintenance fellow covering his noise as he plunged the stuff down the pipes. Frustrated at the unexpected turn of events, I abandoned my cooking mission. We ended up with a normal *nyama*/rice dinner, a cake and lots of drinks. As I write these memoirs, our marriage has lasted for forty-two years. That confirms that a wedding does not have to be big for a marriage to succeed.

Now that we were a family, it was imperative that we sit and plan our future. Since I had met Doretha's family, it was her turn now to meet mine. That meant travelling to Kenya. I had mixed feelings about how my parents – still separated – would receive her. Years back, my father had cautioned me several times about marrying a foreigner. There were bad examples, he said, of Kenyans who had married overseas and had later regretted because of clashes of culture.

As much as he wanted to make a point, he had only one example to support his claim; that of one of his colleagues in politics who had married an American woman in the 1950s, then divorced her due to alleged spousal abuse by the wife. That example was hardly enough to convince me to exclude foreigners in my marriage hopes. When it came to marriage, I felt destiny should be left to take its course without any consideration to race, tribe or religion. As a matter of fact, our religious differences – she a Methodist and I a Catholic – did not feature anywhere in our pre or post-wedding discussions and neither did our separate nationalities.

My Father was a very strong character in my life. Despite everything that happened in my childhood, I was convinced he was a good, loving father. He gave us a healthy Christian upbringing and core values I have cherished throughout my life. Had it not been for his strict discipline, we would probably have strayed away and become bums. But he nurtured us the best way he could, and at the end, he was proud of us. Charles worked with Cooper Motors for thirty years and became a proficient mechanic. I went away to make my own path in life.

As for the meeting with my parents I was prepared for anything. I was certain that nothing would take my wife from me. As far as I was concerned the marriage was a done deal – till death. I had experienced first-hand the trauma of separation in my own family and I was unwilling to subject our children to single parenthood. However, I wanted my visit to Kenya to be long enough to give Doretha an opportunity of deciding whether or not she would one day want to make Kenya her permanent home. Since VoA was not prepared to give me a long leave of absence, I decided to resign. We headed home at the end of 1972, arriving in time for the Christmas holidays. By that time, I had completed only about a third of my university courses, but a visit to Kenya was very important to me at that time. Moreover, opportunities in the Kenyan media were still plentiful. I had a choice of either joining the government or working in the private sector. I chose the former. Subsequently, I applied and got a job at the Department of Information as Information Officer Grade 1. The appointment, which took effect on 11 April 1973, was on a temporary basis of one year after which I was to be confirmed depending on my performance.

Only a few years earlier, the Department had been the domain of white civil servants. The chief press officer had been Tony Hughes, a young, robust journalist with a weathered face that had seen years of writing press releases and feature articles for the colonial government. Now, the place had been Africanised with Tom Mzungu, from the rolling Taita Hills, as chief. My job as Information Officer entailed editing all correspondents' news copies coming from the regions via telex or hard copy, and re-transmitting them through the KNA wires for distribution to the VoK and commercial consumers. The Department's premises on Mfangano Street also housed the Presidential Press Service, at that time headed by Kinyanjui Kariuki. There was also a transmission room and a photographic section.

Coming from the US where public institutions worked with almost assured precision, we found life in Kenya quite challenging, especially during the first six months of our return home. Things were many times more difficult for my wife who had never been to Africa before. She had no friends in Nairobi. Sometimes when I worked late, she had to endure long periods of loneliness. VoK television, which would have provided some kind of companionship, did not have much to offer, apart from mediocre Swahili content that she couldn't understand, leave alone enjoy. She also quickly found out that while electricity and water supplies were guaranteed in the US, in Kenya, such services were erratic and unreliable. For days water would flow then all of a sudden there would be an interruption, forcing people to fetch water in buckets. At Uhuru Estate in Eastlands where we had rented a bungalow, garbage was rarely collected and many of the roads were unpaved. Eastlands was where the majority of Africans lived. And although facilities were better in the commercial business district and in areas inhabited by whites and Asians, Eastlands was not receiving the same kind of attention from the local authority. When it rained, pathways became muddy and shoes got stuck in the ground. And when it was dry, dust flew with every passing car. As if that was not enough, flies and many types of *dudus*, crawling and flying insects, and rodents and lizards often invaded our home, making Doretha quiver in fear of bites and diseases.

My salary at the Ministry was only 1,212 British sterling pounds per annum or about one thousand eight hundred shillings per month. Out of that, seven hundred went to rent and the rest to utilities, transport and food, leaving almost nothing for clothing or restaurant dining. We had to devise a survival strategy.

Doretha eventually managed to link up with a small group of American women married to Kenyans who met regularly to socialise. They reminisced about home and exchanged information about how to beat inflation. She joined them. The group had discovered that food prices at Gikomba market were substantially lower than those in many other places. So she went there for vegetables and fruits. Through an arrangement with a butcher in Kabete, the American women would order a whole cow, have it slaughtered and chopped into desired pieces for everyone to buy. Buying wholesale, they found out, was considerably cheaper than buying retail from the town meat shops. So we had meat and vegetables in our fridge at all times. We acquired the rest of our basic requirements from shops around Uhuru Estate. By following those basic survival techniques we were able to save quite a bit of food money.

That year, Doretha became pregnant, raising fresh economic issues. This meant that soon our family budget would have to go up. Luckily in those days, medical services were easily available and municipal clinics offered free pre-natal consultations. Bahati clinic was the nearest to us, so she went there for check-ups, which were then mandatory; to skip one was to invite a visit from an angry nurse. She therefore responded without fail to her scheduled appointments.

Only a short distance from where we lived was a small Catholic-run maternity hospital called Jamaa. Although it was originally meant for use by unmarried mothers, any pregnant woman was free to seek delivery services there. It was cheap. One hundred twenty five shillings included delivery services, food and a bed for three days. That was a big relief for me. When she was ready, she just walked there and delivered a bouncing baby. We named her Maria, after my mother.

Maria's arrival in the family on 15 September 1973 excited both of us. At least now Doretha had a full-time occupation in her hands. Maria drank her mother's milk for a few months, and when she was ready to feed on formula, we turned to Bahati clinic which offered free baby formula. Every week we would go to the clinic to collect our supply of milk. In those days, corruption was unknown. Had it been today, those cans would probably be finding their way elsewhere. Free milk was of great help to our young family and made our life more bearable.

Almost immediately after Maria's birth, I was seconded to the Kenyatta International Conference Centre (KICC) to assist in the coordination of press coverage during the Annual Meetings of the Board of Governors of the World Bank and the International Monetary Fund. That was the biggest meeting to be held at the Centre since it was inaugurated by President Jomo Kenyatta in 1969. Three thousand delegates from one hundred and twenty-six countries converged in Nairobi to discuss issues of poverty reduction in developing countries.

Nairobi was spruced up: beggars were removed from the central business district, gardens were replanted, and security was beefed up for the meeting, which was presided over by Robert McNamara, the World Bank President. The Mayor at that time, Margaret Kenyatta, welcomed the delegates to what was still the "City in the Sun" and hosted a big reception in their honour at the Charter Hall. Ms Kenyatta, daughter of the founding President, is still considered by many as one of the best Mayors Nairobi ever had. She headed the city from 1970 to 1976 and distinguished herself as a dedicated advocate of the homeless, street children and unmarried women. I came to know her personally through my father. When Jomo Kenyatta was in prison in Lokitaung, she was one of those who led African leaders, including my father, for a visit to the remote jail north of the country.

Although I was an employee of the Ministry of Information, my immediate boss at the conference centre was Mary Gichuru. I brought along Christopher Opiyo, a young reporter straight from the Kenya Institute of Mass Communication in Nairobi to help me cope with the coverage of the conference. Our stories were supplied to the VoK as well as to local newspapers. I was also in charge of news feeds to organisations outside Kenya. I was happy that after the conference ended I was given a letter of commendation by the World Bank for a job well done. Better news was to come.

* * *

In 1974, my name – along with three others – was recommended to the Ministry of Foreign Affairs for the position of press attaché. Four stations, namely Bonn in Germany, Stockholm in Sweden, New York in the United States, and Addis Ababa in Ethiopia, did not have press officers. I was selected to go to Ethiopia. All the selected officers moved to the new Ministry for briefings. We also toured key government institutions to acquaint ourselves with the country's manufacturing, farming and tourism industries. I also had access to correspondence files and reports that had taken place between the Ministry of Foreign Affairs and the Embassy in Ethiopia. I was therefore well prepared for the task ahead.

We took off from the Nairobi airport on a clear, sunny morning. Travelling with me to my new post was my wife, Doretha, and our daughter, Maria. After the life struggles in Nairobi we looked forward to better living conditions in Addis Ababa. At least in Ethiopia, we would be entitled to free accommodation, and I would be earning a Foreign Service allowance to supplement my income. We would enjoy diplomatic privileges and get an opportunity to explore another African culture. The thought of all those perks and new experiences kept me awake for most of the two hour flight.

The East African Airways jet banked to the left, its engines hissing like millions of attack mosquitoes. Far away, flanking the capital city of Addis Ababa were rolling hills that appeared to kiss the misty clouds. Down below snaking valleys with silver, foamy streams exposed the natural beauty of the land. The approach into Bole International Airport was uneventful and the landing just perfect. After clearing through the diplomatic immigration desk we stepped out of the building on a clear, breezy day into one of Africa's culturally rich cities.

As we joined the busy traffic along Bole Airport Road and past the buzzing Meskel Square, I could not avoid noticing the flamboyance of the Ethiopian people – chocolate-coloured women with long flowing hair, immaculately dressed in their *habesha qemis* and thick gold necklaces, and slim-fit men spotting handcrafted long shirts and matching white pants. I had read about Abyssinia and the *Habeshi* people, but seeing them in flesh in Ethiopia was fascinating. Along the winding narrow roads, the Russian-made Lada taxis and the flashy passenger minibuses were ubiquitous and noisy. The whiff of rich spices was overwhelming and smoke billowed out of houses as housewives and eating houses prepared their *injeras* and wots, confirming the good things I had heard about exotic Ethiopian cuisine.

As soon as we pulled through the big black gate of the Kenyan Embassy residences manned by an alert *askari* guard, I was immediately struck by the Chinese-like living arrangement at the Embassy. Perched on a hill in the high-end Kebelle neighbourhood along the busy Fikre Mariam Road, the Kenya mission was built in the form of a communal village. The Chancery, the Ambassador's residence and the staff apartments were all crowded in a garrison-type high-walled compound. Members of staff were accommodated in two blocks of storeyed buildings leaving little space for recreation. On the right of the gate was the Chancery with the Ambassador's office gazing out into the busy road. A few metres away on the down-slope was the Ambassador's official residence, hardly a convenient location for official entertainment.

In the Kenyatta days – as in the days of Presidents Daniel arap Moi and Mwai Kibaki – many senior government appointments were made on the basis of ethnicity and nepotism. It was not different at the Kenyan Embassy in Addis Ababa. When I got there the Ambassador was Nicholas Mugo, who happened to be the husband of Beth Mugo, the President's (Jomo Kenyatta) niece. The Third Secretary was a Kikuyu, so was the Intelligence Officer, the Ambassador's Secretary and the Ambassador's driver and cook. The only non-Kikuyus were the administrative officer, the military attaché and myself.

A typical example of ethnicity during Kenyatta's days was the appointments, on 22 November 1974, of twenty Permanent Secretaries. Eleven, including the Permanent Secretary in the Ministry of Foreign Affairs, were from the Kikuyu ethnic group. What was most interesting is that on that list, published as the Kenya Gazette Notice No. 3750, one of the appointed officials, Geoffrey K. Kariithi, was also the signatory of the Notice, which meant he actually gazetted himself.

The Embassy in Addis Ababa was conceived after Kenya's independence in 1963, and the first Ambassador was posted there in 1967. The land on which the mission was built was a personal donation from Emperor Haile Selassie, and in reciprocation, Kenyatta offered a prime property to the Ethiopian government a short walk away from the President's official residence (State House) in Milimani, Nairobi.

We were shown to our two-bedroomed furnished apartment on one of the blocks of flats. Also residing in the compound were Njuguna

Mahugu, the Third Secretary, Francis Njihia, the Intelligence Office, Lucy, the administrative officer and the Ambassador's cook and driver. The military attaché was the only one who was accommodated in a house outside the compound. Other than the fact that the location was a diplomatic mission, the accommodation arrangement was like any other one can find in any middle class location in Nairobi. The big difference was that it was relatively comfortable and free.

Unlike in Kenya where private media thrived with minimal interference from authorities, the Ethiopian media was largely government-controlled. The two main state newspapers, *The Ethiopian Herald* and *Addis Zemen* (New Era) had existed since the early 1940s as government mouthpieces. Similarly, the public radio and television stations were broadcasting monotonous pronouncements from Emperor Haile Selassie and his officials. The media were as disreputable as the VoK, forcing the majority of Ethiopians to tune in to the BBC and the VoA for news about their own country.

I knew that to be effective as a media adviser to the Embassy in a society as conservative as Ethiopia, I had to cultivate very good relations with senior government officials without stoking embers of suspicion from the omnipresent security agents. Ethiopia's intelligence service was rated as one of the most advanced in Africa. Its officers were trained mainly in Israel and Eastern Europe. It had agents posted to watch foreign embassies and the Kenya mission was not an exception. It was obvious that the sole Kenya special branch officer attached to our mission was especially targeted, and we knew all our officers were under constant surveillance. But that did not dampen my enthusiasm for work.

Within a short time, I had cultivated good relations with all the senior officials at the Ethiopian News Agency and had built enough goodwill to be allowed to enter and photocopy news items that I thought were useful to Kenya. At that time, the Internet, mobile phones and even fax machines were unknown. News was received and sent out by telex. For me to access a wide range of world news, including events in Ethiopia, I had to visit the ENA offices every morning, sift through overnight dispatches, select what I wanted and get it to the Ambassador as part of his daily brief. I also made acquaintances with the Prime Minister's spokesperson, officials in the Ministries of Information, Foreign Affairs' press and protocol divisions, local journalists, as well as foreign correspondents. I would meet some of them often for a beer or a meal in one of the many open air cafés or restaurants in the bustling capital.

Settling in Addis Ababa was not difficult. Many people, especially in Addis Ababa, spoke English and my family got around without any difficulty. One of the most interesting places we visited regularly as a family was the Markiti, Addis Ababa's biggest and most exotic market. It was considerably bigger than Kariokor market in Nairobi and sold a wider variety of goods, prominent among them being the many different shades of colourful clothing material and handicrafts.

In the meantime, famine and drought were raging in parts of Ethiopia especially in Wollo and Tigre regions. The outside world was getting worried. Up to the time I arrived in 1974, the government had refused to admit the presence of the lingering famine. It censored news on the catastrophe by tightening visa requirements and mandating stringent accreditation procedures for foreign journalists and film crews. An estimated half a million people had already perished from hunger and disease. Two regions, Wollo and Tigre, which had been producing forty per cent of the country's total food output, had now become one big desert, leaving human skeletons and animal carcasses strewn everywhere. Diplomatic pressure was on for Haile Selassie's government to appeal for food aid from the international community to avert further devastation. Addis Ababa authorities were, however, unwilling to act and chose instead to downplay the raging disaster.

Nevertheless, the conspiracy of silence did not last long. UNICEF, one of the global organisations active in Ethiopia, decided to conduct its own assessment of hunger and drought. It found that the situation in the country was extremely dire. Using that survey, several news publications overseas began to carry stories of the famine. One station produced and circulated an explicitly disturbing documentary that was to change the politics of Ethiopia forever. The documentary showed scenes of dying women and children juxtaposed with palace clips of the Emperor enjoying sumptuous multi-course dinners and feeding his garden lions with chunks of mouth-licking meat. It was now clear that the Emperor's revered regime was in trouble. There was growing restlessness in military barracks over issues of pay and conditions of service. Soon, radical civilian elements seized the opportunity and began to agitate for reforms and the enactment of a new constitution. There were peaceful street demonstrations and open defiance of law. The once peaceful feudal country, whose capital was chosen in 1972 as the epicentre of African unity, was on the brink of a civil war.

Upon Nairobi's prodding, the Kenyan Embassy began to plan for the worse – crafting for emergency evacuation, not only for the Embassy staff, but also for all Kenyans residing in the country. Information went out to all citizens directing them to take the safest routes to the Embassy if security worsened. That was not unusual because every other Embassy was doing the same. Although it was possible to reach Kenya by road from the Ethiopian capital, the overland option was considered too long and too risky, leaving the air corridor as the only viable escape route. The plan was to be activated only if the situation in the country got out of hand and posed a danger to Kenyans.

The Kenya Air Force was very familiar with the Ethiopian airspace having flown many training flights to and from Addis Ababa; hence, the Ethiopian mission was one of the luckiest among all the other Kenyan missions abroad. Thanks to the Air Force, we were able to order almost everything we wanted from home, ranging from *unga* and fresh *sukuma wiki* (collard greens) to meat and even beer. Those C-4 Caribou transport airplanes were always awaited with much anticipation and joy. We also anticipated to use them for any rescue operation.

We saw signs of danger on 12 September 1974, when several trucks full of young officers from the 4th Army Division in Addis Ababa drove to the palace in broad daylight, seized the Emperor, bundled him on the back seat of a blue VW Bettle (even as his Bentleys, Mercedes and Lincolns sat in the basement of the parking lot), and drove him away into detention at Debre Zeit military camp, forty-five kilometres south of the capital. The military coup that had been rumoured for weeks was in progress. While all that was happening, we remained blockaded in our embassy. The only person who was out on the streets to gather information was the intelligence officer. The *Ethiopian Herald*, which had only a few days earlier praised the Emperor as the Lion of the Tribe of Judah, King of Kings and Elect of God, suddenly turned tune, saying in a hard-hitting editorial that, "Ethiopia was tired of his (Emperor's) tyrant rule." As day turns to night, the allegiance of the state media had shifted dramatically to the left, painting a blissful future for the people under the new military regime. Unsurprisingly, almost all the officials who had been providing me with information were no longer reachable. They had been detained or killed. The lucky ones had escaped. Years later, I met some of them in Nairobi where they had settled down in business.

News of the military coup, though anticipated, hit Kenya hard, and brought home some excruciating memories of the refugee crisis that had visited the country after the overthrow of Milton Obote by Idi Amin in 1971. We anticipated a steady flow of refugees into Kenya (Ethiopia shares a common border with Kenya in the north). The two countries ran a Joint Ministerial Commission to ensure peace along the frontier, and they also enjoyed cordial business and diplomatic relations. With the sudden change of regime, the future of those relations could not be ascertained.

President Kenyatta and Emperor Haile Selassie, both in their eighties, had known each other for many years. It is not clear when the two first met, but records show that while Selassie was in Geneva, Switzerland, in 1936 addressing the League of Nations (the precursor of the United Nations) to protest the bombing of his country by Italy, Kenyatta, who was then a student of social anthropology at the London School of Economics, was among black nationalists demonstrating against the fascist regime at a train station in London. The country was then known as Abyssinia. During the Mau Mau rebellion in the 1950s, the Emperor reciprocated by assisting Kenyan African nationalists whenever possible.

As the Emperor's fate now lay in the hands of a group of thirteen agitated soldiers calling themselves the Ground Forces Coordinating Committee or the Derg, under the shaky leadership of Lt Gen. Aman Michael Andom, Kenya found itself in the difficult position over whether or not to recognise the new regime. Although since independence Kenya's foreign policy had been anchored on the foundation of non-interference in the affairs of other countries and on recognising governments and not individuals, the situation in Ethiopia was tricky and perhaps a little different because of the proximity factor and the close ties between the Emperor and Kenyatta. In the case of Uganda, Kenya had to put up with the brutality of Idi Amin despite its earlier strong support for the deposed Milton Obote. However, Kenyatta's friendship with Obote was not as sentimental as the one he had with Emperor Haile Selassie. Though the Kenya Government took umbrage at the events in Ethiopia, everyone knew it was a matter of time before Nairobi accepted Mengistu Haile Mariam as Ethiopia's bona fide strongman, his atrocious ways notwithstanding. It was known all along that Gen. Andom was only a figurehead. The real power rested with the Marxist hothead Mengistu. With Addis Ababa being the headquarters of the Organisation of African Unity (OAU), and Kenya being one of its most ardent backers, showing hostility towards Mengistu, however despicable his regime, would have been counter-productive and could jeopardise Kenya's stand on regional cooperation and integration. In addition, both countries were fighting a common enemy: Somalia. Hence, relations between the two countries had to be maintained at whatever cost. With the Emperor in detention and incommunicado, Kenyatta's hands were tied and had to give in to the new rulers.

Immediately after the coup, the military regime imposed an 11 pm to 7 am curfew throughout the country, shutting down major airports and ruining night life. All activities were restricted to daylight hours. Diplomatic parties began and ended before the curfew, or started just before the curfew and went on throughout the night. I remember the day when I made a potentially fatal mistake of trying to rush home at high speed just before the curfew deadline. I was chased by a police motorcycle rider and just managed to sneak into the compound before he could stop me. Had he caught up with me, I am sure I would have been executed. I told myself I would never endanger my life that way again, and I didn't, throughout my stay in that country.

During the early days of the Derg regime, security officials had no respect for the red diplomatic number plates, and treated diplomats as suspiciously as everyone else. As the country shut down at night, *kebelles* or neighbourhood vigilantes took over, combing streets and arresting curfew violators. Often, from our hilltop quarters, we could hear gunshots and loud explosions indicating either resistance or attacks on enemies; despite its apparent hold on power, the military regime faced opposition, not only from its own ranks, but also from remnants of the old regime. Armed sympathisers of the toppled regime, who had everything to lose, continued to resist the military rule, often taking sniper shots at soldiers whenever an opportunity arose. Many of them had been beneficiaries of corruption, which was rampant under the imperial regime. These pro-Haile Selassie elements knew that the game of looting was now over.

As arrests of dissidents continued so did summary executions by the new rulers. On the night of 23 November 1974, we were awoken by large explosions coming from an area near the Embassy. The explosions were so huge that they rattled our windows. At daybreak when we went to investigate, we found the residence of Lt Gen. Andom flattened. Tanks from the 4th Division had blazed their way into the General's compound, killing him and his family. Andom was a fifty-something army officer who was reluctantly recruited to take over leadership of the Derg. He was opposed to the brutal manner in which the government was treating officials of the past regime and made his position clear to the young soldiers. They decided to eliminate him altogether.

Andom's murder that night was not isolated. At the military barracks, fifty-nine former leaders, military officers, diplomats and monarchists, were lined up and executed in cold blood. A year later, Selassie's body was found dead in prison. There were a lot of rumours then that the Emperor was murdered by the military although the official explanation was that he had died of health complications. Even though out of power, Haile Selassie still commanded a lot of support from a broad section of the population, and the military junta knew that. My own view is that he was killed to end an underground build-up of pro-monarchy sentiments which, if left unattended, were to cause problems in future.

Chapter 12

Corruption Exposed

One early afternoon in September 1974, a call came to my office at the Kenya Embassy in Addis Ababa. On the other side of the line was David Ottaway, the Africa correspondent for the *Washington Post*. I had met Ottaway a number of times since my arrival in Ethiopia in May that year and had also read several of his articles on Kenya and other African countries. The articles had convinced me that he was an incisive and objective journalist. While most of his articles had dwelt on social and economic challenges in the region, none had touched on the personality of President Jomo Kenyatta. However, the article that was about to unfold in the *Washington Post* in the next few days was to be a stinger and highly embarrassing to the Kenya government.

Ottaway had called me wanting to get Kenya's side on an exposé he had written about corruption in Kenyatta's government. He told me the material was revealing and could adversely hurt Kenya's reputation abroad. He therefore felt the President needed to explain himself. Never before had any journalist – local or foreign – gone as far as criticising Kenyatta for abuse of office and power. Ottaway was about to do exactly that.

Before, journalists who had even tried to cast aspersions or who dared to accuse the government, like John Dumoga, faced serious consequences. When Dumoga, a Ghanaian national at the *Daily Nation,* faulted the Preservation of Public Security Bill of 1966, a law that was to provide for the arrest and incarceration of anti-government elements without trial, he was summarily arrested and thrown out of the country. Dumoga was an influential journalist and had worked for Kwame Nkrumah before the two fell out and he made his way to Kenya.

I met Ottaway during a diplomatic function in Addis Ababa. He was a Harvard graduate and had previously worked as a correspondent for the United Press International (UPI) in Algeria, among other things. While

I was a government functionary with a propaganda mission to fulfil in a monarchical country known for its widespread class disparities, Ottaway was an independent collector and conveyor of news in a continent beset with turmoil. From a professional point of view we needed each other.

At the time of our meeting, the region was embroiled in internal strife. In Uganda, the brutal despot, Idi Amin, was on a killing spree. In Tanzania, Julius Nyerere was struggling to implement his utopian socialist ideology of *Ujamaa*. He had moved thousands of reluctant Tanzanians from their farms into collective villages, but all indications were that his policies were failing. In Kenya, a cabal of greedy individuals, mainly close to President Kenyatta, was on an orgy of looting the country. Scandal after scandal appeared: charcoal was being smuggled to Saudi Arabia; huge consignments of Zanzibar cloves were being traded on the black market; maize and rice were being carted illegally to Uganda aboard tankers; and, the benign *harambee* campaign initiated by Kenyatta to raise funds for construction of village development projects had turned into a cash cow for the rich. At the same time, wildlife poaching had become a pastime of influential people. Despite a ban on ivory exports in 1974 following the killing of more than five hundred elephants the previous year, state-compliant individuals, some close to the President, continued to carry out the illegal business.

My job at the Embassy was to foster cordial relations with both local and international journalists and to protect my country's image. But here I was: helpless. Kenya was under threat of an unprecedented media attack by the *Washington Post*, one of the world's most influential publications. Relations between Kenya and Washington were wavering. The American government had for weeks been expecting such adverse publicity on Kenya. In fact, the US State Department had informed its Ambassador to Kenya, Anthony D. Marshall, months earlier, to expect a media bombshell. In a cable dated 30 June 1974, the Ambassador was informed that an "unfavourable story possibly critical of high level GoK (Government of Kenya) officials will be breaking in US press soon."

I tried to convince Ottaway to postpone the release of the story to give us more time to respond and to allow us put in place a damage control mechanism, but he too was under pressure, not only from his editors, but also, I believed, from the authorities in Washington. Our Ambassador in Ethiopia, Mugo, was a quiet, soft-spoken man. A graduate of Warren Wilson College, a Presbyterian institution in the United States, he often came out as a disinterested, docile individual. But behind that persona was a strong-willed individual. Beth, a former television producer at the VoK was outwardly friendly but assertive.

In the rankings of Kenya embassies at that time, Ethiopia was close to the top. A rumour circulating among Kenyans in Addis Ababa then was that Kenyatta and Selassie had entered into a secret pact that would have Ethiopia give refuge to the former, and Kenya to provide similar hospitality to the latter, in case of a coup in either country. No one I knew could confirm that story. Kenyatta hated flying, so a coup in Kenya would have forced him to take the long, torturous road journey to Ethiopia. The route would have been too dangerous, and at his age, too risky. That version of the story was tested when Haile Selassie got into trouble with his military. It was not put into motion. In any case I don't think the Emperor was convinced a coup was in the offing.

Immediately after the call from Ottaway, I informed Ambassador Mugo about the impending story and tried desperately to persuade him to meet the journalist and offer a response. I warned him of the serious damage the article could cause to the image of the First Family and Kenya in general, but Mugo wanted to hear nothing of it, preferring instead to let the matter go. Disappointed and concerned about the consequences to Kenya's image, I tried once again to convince Ottaway to wait a little longer. He declined. I therefore informed the journalist not to expect any comment either from the Ambassador or from higher authorities in Nairobi, effectively giving Ottaway the go ahead to publish the report.

In previous months, there had been a series of signals from Nairobi that led Washington to believe that Kenyatta's government was up to no good. Since independence in 1963, America had viewed Kenya as a strategic partner in the region. Other than a brief period in which the Soviet Union attempted to set a foothold in the country through Vice President Jaramogi Oginga Odinga, Kenya had emerged from the Cold War as a firm friend of the West. US business in Kenya was doing well and had more than doubled within two years to one-hundred-seventy million dollars. But when an American citizen, James Skane, was deported at short notice, allegedly for security reasons, relations between Nairobi and Washington soured. The expulsion was unexpected and rattled ties between the two countries. The US Ambassador, Anthony D. Marshall, made it clear that the treatment of Americans by the Kenyatta government had become a matter of major concern. As it turned out, the then chief executive of Esso Standard Kenya Limited had not breached any security protocols to warrant his banishment. He had been sent packing only because he had dared demand seventy-thousand Sterling Pounds for petroleum services his company had provided to Kenyatta's companies.

Whispers in the Kenyan business community then was that Kenyatta rarely paid his bills. Those who persisted in demanding payment, like Skane, were either thrown out of the country or their businesses were blacklisted never to be awarded state tenders again. Attempts by the US government to get Skane's deportation rescinded failed. Instead, the Kenyatta government, as if to rub salt in the wound, followed a few months later with two other deportations of American citizens in an incident that followed an alleged grabbing of a mine field in the Tsavo area by one of Kenyatta's relatives.

I was at the bookstand when the 27 September edition of *Washington Post* hit Addis Ababa. Perusing the paper, I knew immediately that the Kenyatta family was in for a big international roast. The *Washington Post* article accused the Kenyatta family of grand corruption and dwelt extensively on the issues surrounding the controversial ruby mine adjoining the world famous Tsavo National Park. The exposé was as devastating as it was shocking. Ottaway said in his article that although Kenya had one of the most efficient and least corrupt civil services of any African country, the situation at the ministerial level was another story, with officials wheeling and dealing in outside business ventures with the approval and encouragement of President Kenyatta. Ottaway also berated a senior minister for trying to solicit a huge sum of "harambee" money from a local Columbia Pictures TV producer ostensibly to help a children's school. The producer declined to contribute.

The *Washington Post* article was followed almost immediately by another one in the *London Times* which categorically alleged that Kenyatta was behind the ruby affair. The *TIME* magazine called the whole scandal a Ruby Rip Off even as the Foreign Minister, Dr Njoroge Mungai, dismissed the allegations as "malicious and a gratuitous insult".

The leading star in that saga was John Saul, a graduate of the prestigious Massachusetts Institute of Technology (MIT) who had arrived in Kenya in the sixties to engage in mineral prospecting. He registered with the Ministry of Natural Resources and immediately left for Garbatullah, a town in northern Kenya, intending to search for sapphires. It was there that he met an artisanal prospector who showed him a glittering piece of ruby. He claimed he had found it in an area near the Tsavo National Park. After ascertaining that the piece was genuine and of high quality, Saul abandoned his mission in Garbatullah and rushed to Tsavo where, after only a few weeks of prospecting, he reportedly stumbled on the biggest ruby mine in the world that had high quality, clear, bright and purple pink rubies. That is when his troubles started.

When Saul, now joined by a fellow MIT graduate, Elliot Miller, went to register a management company for the mine at the Ministry of Natural Resources, he encountered corrupt officials who wanted a piece of the cake. Officials told them in no uncertain terms that their application would not be approved unless they were willing to share the company. The request came from two cabinet ministers who during Kenyatta's time commanded tremendous clout. For fear of losing everything, Saul and Miller agreed to a deal that was to give fifty per cent of the shares to three top officials. However, as soon as the agreement leaked out, some of Kenyatta's relatives came forth demanding a much bigger share – complete ownership of the project.

As the two sides haggled over the deal, security officers visited Saul at Tsavo and bundled him into a van, deporting him the following day. Miller who had gone into hiding emerged two weeks later and he too was expelled. Soon thereafter, Kenyatta issued a decree directing that no foreigner would be allowed to engage in trade involving the country's natural resources. That decree was said to have been directed at the two American prospectors.

When finally the Kenyan Embassy in Addis Ababa commented on the matter, it said the two Americans had been sent home because they smuggled gemstones and ivory, an explanation everyone knew was nothing but a cover-up. I was unable to know who in the Embassy actually made that comment, but it was certainly not me as Press Attaché.

A lawyer who was involved in this matter confirmed details narrated by Ottaway in the *Washington Post*, but lay most of the blame on George Criticos, a Greek wheeler dealer, who, he said, was then close to the President's wife, Ngina. "George was well known to the Kenyattas and was a partner of Mama Ngina in a trading company," he said. The lawyer told me from his Nairobi home that it was Criticos who colluded with Mama Ngina for the takeover of the mine, and it was him too who took the police to Tsavo and had Saul arrested. But Ottaway's story quoted Saul as saying he had "no evidence" that Mama Ngina was responsible for his expulsion. The fact that Criticos – father to a former Member of Parliament – was given the mine to manage on behalf of the Kenyattas after that debacle proved further that there had been some form of high-level connivance. He continued to manage the mine even after a court injunction stopped him from digging.

George Criticos came to Kenya in the 1950s and bought a large sisal plantation in the area adjoining the park. He became friends with the Kenyattas through a land deal on a farm at Ruiru. The lawyer said he tried to get the State Law Office to intervene and sort out the ruby mine affair, but the effort did not bear fruit because of high level interference. Two years later, Beth and her husband, Mugo, founded Beth International Aqua Mines Limited and became the sole producer of Micah ruby in the country with exclusive outlets for the products at both the Nairobi and Mombasa airports. I could not ascertain from where exactly Beth International was sourcing its ruby to sell at its high end shops, but it is widely known that the mine is now known as "Aqua" mine.

What is interesting about this story is that while much credit had been given to the Americans for discovering the mine, later to be known as the "Penny Lane Mine", one Kenyan individual stands out as the first one who stumbled on the precious gem at Tsavo. He is described by Swala, a gem traders' publication, as "a suave former tour guide who sported a Stetson and carried a 'John Wayne' demeanor, spoke in slow American accented English, and had a potbelly and a squeaky voice." It is not known if the man, whose name was published, benefitted at all from the discovery.

From where I was in Addis Ababa, I could see that the damage to the Kenyattas was profound. Immediately after the article appeared, the Special Branch went on a search for Ottaway. They thought he was in

Nairobi since the story was datelined Nairobi, but Ottaway was holed up in the Ethiopian capital. Had he been in Kenya at the time of the story release, he would have faced the same fate as Dumoga, the Ghanaian journalist. Ottoway was not to set foot in Nairobi again for the remainder of Kenyatta's rule.

Meanwhile, Ambassador Mugo found a scapegoat in me. He blamed me for not doing enough to stop the publication of the story. Mugo and I had not been in good terms anyway, though I could not point out any one single incident that could have triggered the bad blood. An incident in 1975 however gave me a hint. I had applied for a job as a public relations officer in the Ministry of Tourism and Wildlife and was one of several candidates shortlisted by the Public Service Commission (PSC). A letter was sent to me in Addis Ababa inviting me for an interview. The letter never reached me. In fact, I didn't know anything about it until I received a call from the Ministry of Information and Broadcasting asking me to confirm my attendance at the interview two days later. This is when I realised for the first time that something was not right. When I asked the Ambassador about the letter he feigned ignorance. I decided to take matters into my own hands. I turned in the keys of the office to the Ambassador's secretary and booked the next available East African Airways flight to Nairobi.

Upon arrival in Nairobi, I discovered there was a telex message from the Embassy in Addis Ababa at the PSC offices asking that I be disqualified on account of absconding from duty. The PSC ignored the request and interviewed me anyway. In the meantime, the Permanent Secretary in the Ministry of Information, Darius Mbela, told me to stay put in Nairobi to await the outcome of the interview. Two weeks later I got a letter informing me I had passed and was instructed to report to my new job. I immediately left for Addis Ababa to collect my family and personal effects. As expected, I found Mugo in a foul mood. He refused to authorise shipment of my personal effects. With my wife and daughter Maria in tow, we booked tickets and headed for the airport to return home. It was not until one year later that I took possession of my personal belongings. I had to travel to Addis Ababa to fetch them.

* * *

I was cleared at the gate of the Eastleigh Air Force base at 7 am sharp and directed to the take-off point where I found four airmen, clad in light green jump-suits, making final flight preparations. The flight crew was in the cockpit while two others were loading food items intended for the Embassy staff at Addis Ababa. The DHC-4A Caribou cargo lifter, had been introduced in the Kenya Air Force in 1966. It was a very useful aircraft which could carry up to two Jeeps or similar light vehicles in its belly. Kenya used the twin piston engine Canadian-designed aircraft extensively as a cargo and troop carrier, taking off and landing in bush airstrips in the remotest of places in the country. It was also used as a training aircraft for new recruits. During the course of my stay in Addis Ababa, the cargo plane had made several training trips to Ethiopia.

When configured into a passenger plane, the Caribou can accommodate thirty-two people, but on this flight the passenger cabin was empty except for one seat, mine, bolted on the floor and placed almost at the rear of the plane. The two extra airmen were pitched on jump seats behind the flying crew. As we lifted into the open sky over the sprawling Mathare slums with its labyrinthine streets, my mind went to Kachene, a crowded slum colony in Addis Ababa where, like Mathare, houses were of mud and wood, and sanitary conditions were some of the worst anywhere. I could see smoke brimming from hovels, and from innumerable *nyama choma* joints at Kwa Maiko, and the Outer Ring Road snaking its way through crowded Eastlands neighbourhood. In the distance, planes were landing and taking off at the Nairobi International Airport.

The high wings of the heavy plane banked to the right and headed towards Mt Kenya. We must have been flying not too high at that point because I could pick up tiny figurines of human beings below and spot huge plantations which, from the sky, looked like well-arranged match boxes. Soon, there was a noticeable thrust of the two three-pointed blades. Then the noisy engines settled into a smooth roar, and we sliced through the silver coated skies like a champion diver splashing into calm waters.

I knew we had to cross the Equator and we did. We flew over the tourist attractions of Buffalo Springs, Shaba and Samburu National Reserves and into the rugged, semi-deserts of northern Kenya. We crossed the border at Mandera and entered the Ethiopian airspace. All along, as I sat quietly contemplating what to expect from the Ambassador, I could hear the cracking of the radio from the cockpit and the exchange of communication between towers. Then the familiar site of tall, majestic hills appeared far away. At that point I knew we were approaching the Ethiopian capital.

The plane eased downwards and then landed with a thud while shaking violently, before careering smoothly on the hard, dry runway and coming to a near stop in the middle of a long mirage-filled runway. Slowly it made a U-turn and – at the direction of a marshal – headed to an isolated part of the airport away from the parking area of commercial planes and came to a shaking halt. An airman opened the rear hatch and let down the ramp. I walked out without much difficulty.

As expected, an officer from the Embassy was at the airport as we landed at Bole, and had brought with him an extra car for our crew and the limited cargo. Whenever an Air Force plane flew into Addis Ababa, the Embassy would write a diplomatic note to the authorities for clearance indicating the type of the aircraft, its cargo content, time of arrival, purpose of visit and duration of stay. Although this information is then routinely sent to immigration and customs officials at the airport, our embassy staff was always present to facilitate clearance. This time, unlike during normal training flights when planes often turned back the same day, this particular plane was to stay overnight for reasons I will explain in due course.

As I pointed out earlier, Ambassador Mugo had adamantly refused to authorise expenditure for shipment home of my personal effects. There had been long correspondence between him and the Permanent Secretaries in both Foreign Affairs and Information and Broadcasting, and a long stalemate had emerged. Some felt Mugo had been unfair to me and had overstretched his authority over a niggling issue. Unable to get Mugo to agree to facilitate shipment of my personal effects, the Foreign Ministry wrote a letter to the Department of Defence requesting for a special training flight. Permission was granted and that is how I found myself aboard that flight, my first in a military plane. I was instructed by Nairobi to bring back all my belongings from Addis Ababa including a red Renault saloon car I had bought from the diplomatic store. Mugo was adequately informed about the purpose of that mission and I saw no reason to engage him in any form of discussion upon my arrival.

That same day, I assembled my things and arranged for their transportation to the airport. I drove the car, and was present when the crew took it over the rear ramp door and into the main cabin, fastening it with thick, braided rope. I got a lift back to the Embassy, and as we passed through Piazza, a popular shopping area in Addis Ababa, I could hear Tilahun Gessesse's calming golden age music of the 1960s playing from a store. I felt an inner peace in me. Ethiopia is a very musical nation with different tribes each having its own variety of music. Early the following day we were airborne once again on our way back to Nairobi.

The above incident showed how hubris and power fixation can blind individuals – even those with a high degree of education and knowledge – into behaving irrationally and with little regard to common sense. Such behaviour is, more often than not, borne out of ego or, in extreme cases such as this, super-ego. Many years later when I read an article in *The Standard* newspaper in Nairobi about how Captain Edwin Smith of the RMS Titanic ignored all safety advice and caused the sinking of the passenger ship in the North Atlantic, I thought of Mugo. The writer of that article surmised that the skipper had chewed too much pride. Mugo too, because of his high connection in government, had done the same.

It has been close to forty years since I met or talked to Mugo. As for Beth, his wife, I had the privilege of serving with her in the Ninth Parliament when she was the MP for Dagoretti and I for Bahari.

* * *

Early in March 1975, news came in that J. M. Kariuki, one of the most popular politicians in Kenya at the time and who had become renowned as the "voice of the poor", had disappeared. I knew Kariuki during my years as a reporter. Always jovial, always willing to help, the Member of Parliament for Nyandarua was a great friend of the media, available at all times to comment on issues of the day. The report of his disappearance disrupted normal activities in the country. Kenyans wanted answers on the mysterious disappearance and the people he was last seen with at Hilton Hotel in Nairobi. One of the people named along with senior security officials was a character I knew called Peter Kinyanjui or Mark Twist, who was known in the Nairobi nightclub scene as a playboy.

With the government unable to control the crescendo of public outcry Daniel arap Moi, who was then Home Affairs Minister, told Parliament that Kariuki had travelled to Zambia on a business trip. The report, given credence by the *Nation,* was rubbished by many and soon thereafter Kariuki's badly decomposed body was found in Ngong Forest, a victim of an apparent murder. Up to now, no one has been arrested for that killing.

Chapter 13

The Poaching Menace

I began work at the Ministry of Tourism and Wildlife with gusto in late 1975. My boss was a young, cheerful Minister called Mathews Ogutu, an engineer by profession. Ogutu was a smart dresser, handsome and a good public speaker. His hero was Charles Njonjo because of the latter's English mannerisms, his conservative suits and his strict time-keeping habits. Njonjo was the powerful Attorney General in Kenyatta's government who always sported a fresh rose bud on the lapel of his well-tailored black-striped suits. He looked everything like a typical British barrister with a persona that smelt of wealth. In an attempt to look like Njonjo, Ogutu in fact did buy a couple of dark striped suits. The Permanent Secretary was Yuda Komora who hailed from the minority Pokomo community in the northern Coast region. Komora had a thick tongue so that whenever he spoke, the words came out in a belligerently gabbled manner exposing heavy Pokomo overtones.

Officially, I was the public relations officer, but I was also the Minister's *de facto* personal assistant, speech writer, travel consultant and companion. We bonded so well that in a short period of time I became his most trusted aide. He consulted me often on delicate political and personal matters. He was also a social maniac who enjoyed the night life. Several times during our visits to Mombasa we would end up at a local night club, drinking and dancing the night away.

At the time of my arrival at the Ministry, a huge controversy was raging over the delicate matter of wildlife conservation. Elephants were being massacred by poachers in their dozens, especially in the Tsavo National Park. Flamingos were dying of poisonous chemicals emitted by offshore fish factories in Nakuru, and at the Nairobi National Park animals were perishing from hunger following a prolonged drought. The government had banned sport hunting and rich white hunters – supported by influential global organisations – were hitting back with serious accusations of wildlife mismanagement by the government.

The state-run Game Department, which had existed since before independence, was in the process of being merged with the National Park Services, a body controlled by an independent Board of Trustees. At that time the Parks Services controlled only five per cent of the national reserves, while the Game Department controlled the remaining ninety-five per cent. Individuals and groups, beneficiaries of poaching, resisted the merger and wanted the Game Department to remain independent even though everyone knew the department was the driving force behind decimation of animals. Even Parliament – dominated by the ruling party KANU – rejected the merger when a motion was first presented in Parliament. Minister Ogutu was therefore under pressure from the World Wildlife Fund and the World Bank, which were the main financiers of conservation programmes, to do more to stop the destruction or resign.

In an attempt to diffuse the uproar, Ogutu fired all honorary game wardens – many of them Kenyan whites. He also banned officials from the Ministry from talking to the media. Ironically, opponents felt Ogutu's actions were intended to shield a well-organised clique within government that was engaged in widespread poaching and export of ivory. The involvement of some senior officials in poaching – some directly connected to the President – was well known within the government, but no one, including the Minister, was in a position do anything about it. As a matter of fact, Ogutu's hands were tied as orders came from high up for the Ministry to provide security and storage for tons of illegally acquired elephant tusks and rhino horns. Warehouses were therefore leased at several locations and guarded round the clock by armed wildlife wardens.

Accompanying the Minister on visits to National Parks – many times aboard an aircraft piloted by the organisation's director, Peres Olindo – and to some warehouses in Mombasa, I saw with my own eyes lots of animal trophies complete with tags on who owned them. The names read like who-is-who in government and politics. An influential publication[11] reported at the time that the elephant population in Tsavo had declined by forty-five per cent between 1974 and 1976 from thirty-five thousand

---

11 Joe Coogan, "Sundowner Tales: Kenya's 35 year Hunting Ban – For What?" *African Hunting Gazette*, Vol. 17, Issue No. 2 (Winter 2011): 143.

nine hundred to twenty thousand, and reiterated views that the slaughter "involved people at the highest levels of government...facilitated by the complacency, if not connivance of high-up game department officials ..."[12]

As the Ministry's media guru, my job was to control the massive fall-out arising from an aggressive media offensive overseas. I issued press releases and organised press interviews for senior officials to defend the government position. It was not an easy task given the obvious facts on the ground that some of Kenyatta's close relatives were implicated. It was my duty to defend the status quo even though down in my heart I knew the whole process was evil. Kenyatta, like Moi who followed him, was intolerant of any form of criticisms or resistance so I just followed the order.

Other than cautiously refuting the allegations, the Ministry also vigorously embarked on a marketing strategy to reverse a slow-down in tourist visits. G. N. Macharia, probably the most effective Director of Tourism the country has ever had, tendered for and printed marketing material – folders, posters, sales manuals, brochures and calendars – in almost all the major and not so-major languages of the world. He also ordered his officers abroad to step up promotional campaigns through seminars and meetings with key tour operators, and told them to get involved in as many international fairs as possible. Senior Ministry officials were also dispatched to key tourism generating countries in Europe and in the United States to control the fast-spreading damage to the country's image.

Wildlife is Kenya's biggest selling tourist attraction. Without animals, Kenya ceases to be a destination of choice. Beaches, as someone told me, are beaches and can be found in many parts of the world. In fact there are better beaches – with sugary white sand, clean shores, free of beach boy's menace – in Tanzania, Mauritius and Seychelles, all along the blue waters of the Indian Ocean. Compared to beach hotels in other countries, our hospitality facilities do not stand anywhere near the top, regardless of how much Kenyans brag about them. The decline in wild animals was therefore the main reason why tourists were running away from Kenya and going elsewhere.

---

12   Ibid: 143

One person who was deeply pained by the indiscriminate destruction of wildlife was Ras Makonnen, a diminutive, soft spoken, one time political firebrand. Ras Makonnen was not really his birth name. He was born George Thomas N. Griffiths in Buxton, Guyana. He had assumed part of Haile Selassie's name, Ras Tafari Makonnen, because of his sentimental attachment to Ethiopia, a country of his paternal grandfather, who was said to have been taken to Guyana by a Scottish national. Ras Makonnen was in Kenya courtesy of President Jomo Kenyatta who had appointed him advisor in the Ministry of Tourism and Wildlife. He was an extraordinary individual with an extraordinary history. He was with Kenyatta in London when a group of Africans protested against Italian atrocities in the then Abyssinia. And together with West Indian George Padmore and Ghana's Kwame Nkrumah, they formed an anti-colonial lobby to agitate for the freedom of British-held colonies through published works called *Ending British Rule in Africa*.[13]

Makonnen was the treasurer of the fifth Pan-African Conference in Manchester, England, in 1945 which was chaired by Dr Peter Milliard from British Guyana. Kenyatta was the conference secretary while Padmore and Nkrumah were joint political secretaries. The conference discussed the plight of black people in Africa, America, West Indies and Britain. It was part of a series of Pan-African conferences started in 1919 by W. E .B. Dubois who came to be known as the grand old man of Pan-Africanism. The reason why Manchester was chosen was partly because that is where Dr Milliard and Makonnen lived. The latter owned several restaurants where Africanists met away from the racial discrimination in white-owned establishments. "He was a very good businessman, managing his restaurants and a bookstore and editing the journal *Pan-Africa*."[14]

Eventually, Makonnen moved to Accra when Ghana became independent under Nkrumah, but upon Nkrumah's overthrow in 1966, he was arrested and spent time in prison. It was Kenyatta who negotiated for his release, gave him Kenya citizenship in 1969, and appointed him to the nominal position of advisor on tourism.

---

13 Carol Polsgrove, *Ending British Rule in Africa* (Manchester: Manchester University Press, 2009).
14 George Shepperson and St Clare Drake, The Fifth Pan-African Conference 1945 and the All African People's Congress 1958: Contributions in Black Studies 1986, A Journal of African and Afro-American Studies, ScholarWorks, Vol. 8, Article 5: 9.

Although Ras Makonnen was a graduate of Cornell University, a reputed hospitality training institution in the United States, he did not have any new ideas on how the country could grow tourism in terms of numbers and revenue. At his advanced age, he did have strong, personal views, about what Kenya needed to do to curb runaway poaching, and how to rein in officials implicated in illegal wildlife trade. He loved Kenya and always talked emotionally about his admiration for Kenyatta. But he often complained that officials in the presidency were blocking him from seeing the President on a regular basis. He yearned for an opportunity to tell Kenyatta personally that some of his relatives were letting the country down by engaging in wildlife destruction. In his opinion, he believed Mbiyu Koinange, who was Kenyatta's closest friend, was blocking the meetings. Once in a long while he would be called to State House for a meeting with the President, but to him that was unsatisfactory since Koinange was always present in the discussions. He was constrained when it came to expressing his honest opinion freely and frankly to his friend.

The Ministry of Tourism and Wildlife did not value Ras Makonnen's advice either. He was not included in the meetings on strategic planning and was not consulted on anything to do with tourism. Most of the time, he sat in his cluttered office at Kencom House reading documents and chatting with visitors. I left him there when I was posted to Paris, France, in 1977. He died and was buried in Nairobi in 1983.

* * *

I received my posting to Paris, France, on 21 July 1977, through a letter signed by the Deputy Secretary, J. D. Wandera, a sharply dressed, always cheerful career civil servant. It was part of a comprehensive deployment of tourist officers abroad. Peter Muiruri was already in New York. Catherine Kimura was sent to Los Angeles, Sammy Okungu to Stockholm, and Titus Muya to Germany. These were just few among others.

My family and I landed at the Charles de Gaulle Airport in Paris in the middle of the European summer to begin a tour of duty as Tourist Officer for France, Spain, Luxembourg and Belgium. I had been to

Europe several times before while working at the headquarters, mainly accompanying Minister Ogutu on promotional tours for Kenya. On arrival we were met by a Kenyan Embassy attaché and driven directly to our rented house, a three-bedroomed upstairs flat on Rue Lalo in the 16th District. The District, which was considered up-market, had at least a dozen foreign embassies within its zone at the time, and was home of some very high ranking government officials. On our way there we took a peak at the Eiffel Tower, perhaps the most famous edifice, shooting up into the heavens like a skyrocket, and marvelled at the spectacularly wide Champs-Elysees and the majestic Arc de Triomphe, a landmark honouring fallen soldiers. I could see immediately why Paris is touted as the fashion capital of the world: small boutiques displaying trendy clothes and shoes were everywhere along the main thoroughfares; huge billboards at street corners showcased slender models promoting everything from cars to beverages; and, multitudes of well-dressed people either milled around cafés or rushed to their various chores. Veranda bars and brasseries selling freshly-brewed coffee in small cups featured at every corner; the sweet smell of fresh baked baguette floated in the air; and, small family butcheries selling rabbit meat conflated with perfume worn by beautiful women pedestrians, to lend the area an exquisite Parisian atmosphere. *Palais des Congres*, a popular concert hall, was only a short distance away from our flat, so was the Bois de Boulogne, one of the most popular parks in the city for outdoor games. Once many years ago French Kings hunted deer in that area.

My first impression of Parisians was that they deeply loved their pets just as Africans loved their goats, but for different reasons. Pets are for patting and company, while goats are for food. I saw small dogs the size of dik dik and big dogs the size of calves. The French either cuddled them under their arms or dragged them on leashes; and drivers sat them on passenger seats, car windows slightly open, tongues and ears flapping in the wind. Unlike in Addis Ababa and Nairobi, I found Paris to be a well-organised city. The nation's pride – Peugeots, Citroëns and Renaults – was ubiquitous. I did not see anything that resembled *matatus* or minibus taxis – just orderly traffic, colourful flowers on street islands and on window sills and many signs of opulence. Once in a while I could hear the rambling vibrations of metro trains crisscrossing each other and disappearing into tunnels like giant snakes on a hunting mission. Our landlord was a former French Foreign Minister who was at that time serving as Ambassador to London.

Rue Lalo is along a row of storeyed flats built in the 1930s featuring marble fireplaces, hand-crafted panels and art deco from the past. When our landlord went for his assignment abroad, he left behind a fully-furnished flat with furniture and deco that were far from our taste. We had expected simple, contemporary furnishings, but what we found there were walls adorned with huge pictures of scenes and personalities we knew nothing about, chairs and tables embellished in fake gold plates, and kitchen gadgets that should have been retired years ago.

The Kenya Tourist Office in Paris – like all the others in the world – is an appendage of the Embassy. Both the office and the home-based officers who serve in it enjoy diplomatic immunity. The only reason tourist offices are located away from the Embassy is because they operate like any commercial business. They allow free movement of people unlike the Embassies which exercise strict security precautions. That is the reason why our office in Paris was located far away from the Mission.

Settling down in a non-English-speaking country was challenging. Neither my wife nor I spoke a word of French. We knew that adjusting to French life would provide some hurdles. The pressure was on when we realised early enough that the French were particularly proud of their language. They despised those who didn't understand or speak it correctly and had no time for those – like French-speaking Africans – who tended to infuse their own tribal tongues in the language, thus distorting the tone and delivery immensely. My wife and I had to take language lessons to be able to somehow function on a day to day basis.

I have always had difficulty learning foreign languages. Years back, I took German at the Goethe Institute in Nairobi, but failed to complete. To me, all foreign languages are difficult to learn. In French, the gender nouns always puzzled me. For example, *le village,* a village is masculine, while *la maison,* a house is feminine. I found it difficult to understand why one thing would be masculine and the other feminine. We enrolled Maria at the International School of Paris, the only English-speaking school in the French capital. Pili, who had been added to our family two years before, was still too young to go to a regular school and instead attended a nursery. To help with house chores, I brought from Kenya a niece, Selina, daughter of my cousin Anthony.

In the early days of our stay in Paris and because of the language difficulties, I came across many embarrassing moments. As I mentioned earlier, the French loved animals. I didn't realise how deep that love was until I stumbled on animal munchies displayed next to human food in a supermarket. I almost fell into a trap when I picked up a reasonably priced can of food labelled "la pattee du chat." The price was good and I thought I had found a bargain only to be told by the cashier that I had picked a kitten dinner. My mistake would have cost me many years of memories and a lot of distress. Why didn't they separate the food counters? Luckily, I got away with that. Another embarrassing moment came when I got a farewell card from a foreign tourism colleague who was leaving France. "*Je vais bientot partir,*" it said, meaning I am leaving soon. My God! I thought I had been invited to a party, until my assistant saw my jubilation and cut it short.

France was a relatively new tourist destination for Kenya compared to the traditional markets like Britain, Italy, Germany and Switzerland. I was only the second Tourist Officer to serve there. The first one was Sammy Wafula who had done a wonderful job of awakening the French to the varied holiday possibilities in Kenya. My job was to take the promotion a notch higher; to get large masses of French people to stop dreaming about Kenya and to get into planes. To do that I had to get to know tour operators and airline personalities, to listen to them and discern why Kenya was not yet a favourite holiday destination for many French people. Big tour wholesalers like Kuoni and Nouvelles Frontières were already selling Kenya in a moderate way, but there were many others that did not feature Kenya at all in their travel brochures, preferring instead to send holiday-makers to South Africa, Tunisia and the Seychelles, among other places.

The "poaching menace" was apparently one of the reasons why French tourists were shying away from Kenya. The French are very passionate about animals and conservation. Press reports and television documentaries in the French media showing increased poaching activities had hurt Kenya's image. The media was not shy to say that the destruction was perpetuated by very senior personalities in government. That publicity over dwindling animal numbers and impunity in government had stunned and angered the French. But there was another reason why Europeans in general were not responding to Kenya's promotional initiatives.

In 1973, Kenyatta had launched a programme of Africanising wholesale and retail businesses owned by Indians. Notices had gone out to hundreds of Asian businessmen to vacate their shops and give way to Africans. The campaign, while widely cheered by Africans, caused tremendous discomfort to the Asians, most of whom had been in Kenya since the early nineteenth century, some having been brought in as indentured workers by the British government to build the Kenya–Uganda Railway (which was built from 1896 to 1901). After completion of the railway line, many of them settled in different parts of the country and started running retail shops.

When I left Kenya for Paris in 1976, the Kenyanisation programme, which had started in the 1960s, was still causing ripples within the Asian community as well as in Europe. Thousands of Asians had already left the country mainly for Britain, Australia and Canada. Asians denounced it as racial discrimination, and their complaints were carried as news around the world. In essence, Kenya was portrayed as a racist country that had uprooted the British racist regime only to replace it with its own home-grown form of prejudices. In 1972, military dictator Idi Amin had expelled thousands of Asians from neighbouring Uganda. So, when Kenya began to talk about Kenyanisation, Asian business people got worried. Also seeing the programme as racially-motivated were Europeans. Potential European tourists were therefore holding back their plans for Kenya and in the meantime choosing other destinations.

Threats of terrorism were also to blame for the disinterest in Kenya. In July 1976, an Air France plane carrying 248 passengers on a flight from Tel Aviv to Paris was hijacked in Athens and diverted to Entebbe by militants of the Popular Front for the Liberation of Palestine (PFLP) and the German Baader-Meinhof gang. A major night-time operation was undertaken by the Israeli Army to rescue the hostages from the hands of Idi Amin, and although no French tourist was killed, the incident left a bitter taste in the palate of Europeans. The French were particularly

Joe Khamisi

With SWAPO leader, Sam Nujoma and SWAPO Secretary General Toivo ya Toivo at the former's Katutura home in Windhoek, Namibia, prior to the country's independence, 1989.

My father, Francis Khamisi, with Kamuzu Banda who later became the first President of Malawi during his visit to Kenya, 1960.

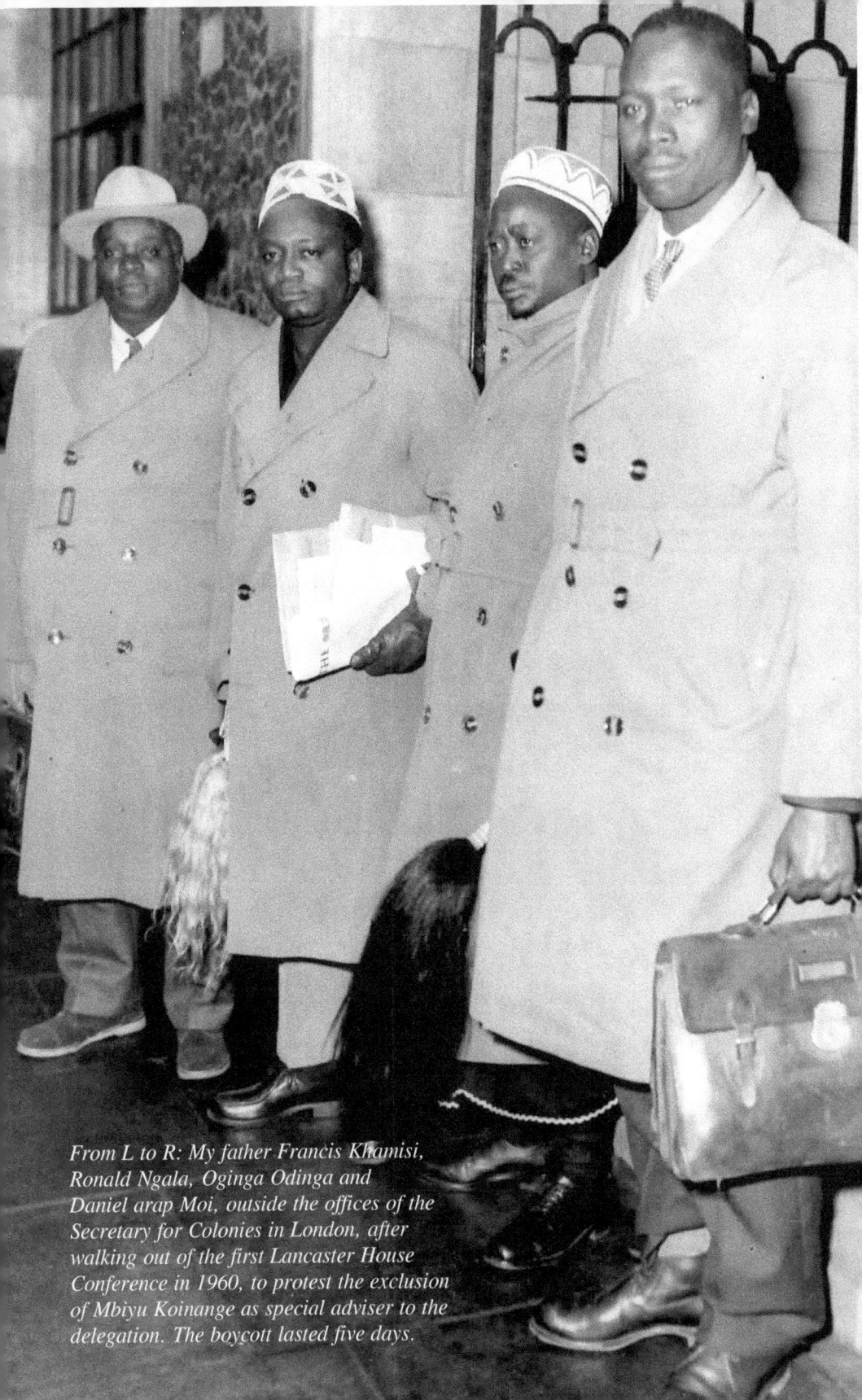

From L to R: My father Francis Khamisi, Ronald Ngala, Oginga Odinga and Daniel arap Moi, outside the offices of the Secretary for Colonies in London, after walking out of the first Lancaster House Conference in 1960, to protest the exclusion of Mbiyu Koinange as special adviser to the delegation. The boycott lasted five days.

With Raila Odinga (right) and Denis Kodhe, founder of the Liberal Democratic Party, in Nairobi around 2004.

Myself (in a jacket and tie) with my father (on the right). On the left is my elder brother Charles, younger brother Fred (on the scooter) and other siblings, at Ngara Flats, Nairobi, around 1962.

Nyanya Pauline Stephen and some of her grand-children at Kinyakani village, Rabai.

My father, Francis Khamisi as Editor of Baraza newspaper around 1961.

With my wife, 2010.

At our wedding in Washington DC: Front row, L-R: Virginia (my sister-in-law), Katana Ngala (best man), myself and Doretha. At the back are Ben (brother-in-law) and Millie McCoo, a friend.

During my younger days.

Myself (front row, second from left) with fellow students at VOA after being awarded a certificate of excellence in broadcasting and production, 1986.

My mother, Maria Faida in 2011.

Auntie Mesalama, daughter of Juma Sadala, my great uncle.

With future wife Doretha in Washington DC, USA, 1972.

With my family (L to R): Pauline, Noa and my wife. Standing at the back (from L to R): Pili, Luka, Chiza, Sydney, Maria and Bryan.

With my wife, Engineer Otieno and Head of KBC Television, Joseph Murema, at the Great Wall of China during an official visit, 2001.

In a pensive mood.

On a visit to the Great Wall of China as Managing Director of Kenya Broadcasting Corporation, 2001.

With my wife and daughters Pili and Maria after returning from Namibia.

St. Paul's Church Rabai, built in 1846 by Dr. Ludwig Krapf, a German missionary of the Church Missionary Society of England.

The bell tower at Kengeleni, Mombasa. The bell was rang to warn freed slaves to hide to avoid re-capture by slave raiders.

Original chains used to secure slaves, now on display at the Rabai Museum.

With President Mwaki Kibaki and Kisauni MP Karissa Maitha at the Mombasa Show Grounds, 2003. Here, I was presented with a Lamu chair for winning the Bahari Parliamentary seat on a NARC ticket. James Kanguana is on the left.

My different faces.

With former Mombasa Mayor, Taib Ali Taib, and Kisauni MP, Karisa Maitha, during a consultative meeting in Mombasa, 2003.

Addressing the Coast Parliamentary Group legislators as their chairman, with fellow Coast MPs Suleiman Shakombo (Likoni, left) and Lucas Maitha (Malindi, right).

The entrance of Kilindini Port, a major theatre of activity during the slave trade.

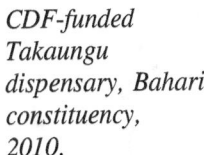

CDF-funded Takaungu dispensary, Bahari constituency, 2010.

Laboratory Block at St Thomas Girls Secondary School, Kilifi: one of the projects built with CDF funds during my term as MP for Bahari, 2010.

Fort Jesus, now a museum, was built by the Portuguese for defense purposes.

A view of Rabai and its palm trees.

Pili with husband Chiza after receiving her law degree at the City University of New York, 2011.

Pili and Maria leaving the graduation ceremony, 2011.

After graduating with a BSc degree in Mass Communication at the University of Maryland, University College, Maryland, USA, 1988.

concerned about their safety after that incident since the plane was France's national carrier.

My job was to rebuild confidence of potential tourists and assure them of their security in Kenya. I told them Kenya was not a racist country and was trying to correct the injustices that had been cemented by a long period of colonial rule. That effort to persuade the French to view Kenya positively was not easy and results came slowly. In our office at 5 Rue Volney, a location near the Opera district, I found dozens of boxes containing thousands of promotional materials in French, Spanish, Dutch and German awaiting distribution. I decided to get the material out as soon as possible. I drew a schedule of work to take me into the interior of France, Spain, Luxemburg and Belgium. I planned workshops with tour operators and travel agents and organised press conferences with the travel media.

In the following few months, I toured those countries by road using the office Volvo station wagon. Wherever I and my assistant, Elizabeth Muema, went questions of security and wildlife conservation arose. We answered them to the best of our ability. Within a year I had convinced a large group of tour operators and travel journalists to tour Kenya on a promotional visit. I got airlines to offer complimentary tickets, hotels and lodges in Kenya to provide free accommodation, and tour operators to volunteer vehicles. I organised discussion sessions with their Kenyan counterparts at the Hilton Hotel in Nairobi, and took them on an extensive tour of our tourist attractions. After our return to France, the visiting journalists wrote glowing stories about their experiences, and from that moment we began to see a gradual growth in tourist numbers from my region of representation. That year, the Ministry entered into an agreement with a French video specialist to produce a multimedia show as an added promotional tool. It was not highly digital like today's Adobe Flash or Microsoft PowerPoint presentations, but it was a well-crafted platform nevertheless, using half a dozen projectors, hundreds of slides of Kenya attractions and six huge mobile screens. Two officers from Nairobi, John Maliti, a tourist officer, and Boaz Mugalo, who had taken over from me as public relations officer, joined me in Paris for training on how to operate the system. The training took one week after which we assumed control of the multi-vision show from the French operators.

In the following twelve months we toured many countries in Europe and elsewhere staging the show. The slides represented a cross section of our country, from culture to wildlife, topography to the beaches, urban to rural life. The equipment – mixers, sound equipment, loud speakers and slides – was bulky, and was stored in five huge metal trunks. We carried the equipment in planes, trains and trucks from one place to another.

The most memorable presentations to me were in Israel where we were invited as guests of the Tourist Board and tour operators. They had heard of the multimedia show and wanted us to visit and showcase Kenya in a number of cities including Tel Aviv and Jerusalem. The shows were well attended by industry players and received good media coverage. Many Israelis were surprised at the richness of our natural resources and the beauty of our landscape. While in Israel, I got a rare and unique opportunity to tour the Holy sites and relive the teachings of the Bible. We visited the Church of Nativity, the place of Jesus's birth in Bethlehem, the Via Dolorosa (the route that Jesus took on his way to crucifixion), the Wailing Wall built by King Herod in 20 BC and the open air synagogue next to it, all popular sites for pilgrims. We even had an opportunity to visit a restaurant along the Sea of Galilee where we ate the same type of fish said to have been used in the miracle in which Jesus multiplied two fish and five loaves of bread to feed more than five thousand people. I was left spiritually uplifted.

Our visit to Israel pioneered a steady stream of Jewish visitors to Kenya culminating in the building of the Paradise Beach Hotel in Kikambala outside Mombasa, a facility catering exclusively for Israeli visitors. Unfortunately, despite taking comprehensive security measures, the hotel was bombed and extensively damaged by Osama bin Laden's Al Qaeda terrorists in 2002. Thirteen people were killed in the explosion which happened only a few months away from the general elections. Kikambala, a small but growing locality north of Mombasa, was part of Bahari, the constituency I intended to contest then as a parliamentary candidate. It is also only a few kilometres from our family home at Kanamai and my rural home at Mtepeni. Thus, the attack affected me personally, and I arrived there fast enough to witness the mangled reception area still emitting flames. My presidential candidate, Mwai Kibaki of NARC, together with other leaders who were campaigning elsewhere at the Coast, was compelled to make a detour to the scene of the explosion. It was a grisly scene with villagers, who had lost their loved ones, wailing in pain and Israeli visitors in shock.

On our return from Israel, we took our multi-vision show to Florida in the United States at a place called the Busch Gardens, a theme park where visitors can take the Serengeti Safari to see various types of wildlife. The shows we had in the auditorium of Busch Gardens attracted large crowds of Americans, some of whom had not even heard of Kenya. They had only heard of Africa and thought it was one single country like America. We explained Kenya was one of approximately 50 countries with its own president and its own jurisdiction.

Every year, the Paris Tourist Office participated in major tourism fairs. In France, we exhibited at the Salon De Mondiale du Tourisme, the largest travel exhibition in that country. In Spain it was Fitur, and in Belgium it was the Salon des Vacances. Those fairs gave us an opportunity to display our tourism resources and our cultural heritage. We also had the participation of Kenyan cultural, agricultural and manufacturing sectors. We gave out samples of our famous coffee brands and distributed small handcraft mementos to visitors.

***

My stay in Europe gave me a completely different perspective of life and opened my eyes to differences in lifestyles between Europeans and Africans. Culinary habits are a good example. While Africans view eating as an exercise in survival, Europeans treat eating as an artistic experience and a valued part of their culture. From a very young age, French children are taught to appreciate food, starting from the point of purchase where they are taught to identify fresh produce, to the table where proper eating etiquette is observed. No meal, whether it is *Coq au Vin* (chicken in wine) or *Steak Tartar* (raw ground beef), is complete without a glass of fine wine and a cut of the finest cheese. Every cutlery and every plate and glass on the meal table is meant to serve a particular purpose. To the French, dinner in particular is supposed to be a feast of various different types of foods. The French take time to eat and during that period they talk a lot about everything in their lives. In France, vineyards and wine factories are found in every corner of the country and these produce hundreds of different wine brands and flavours.

On their part, Africans, regardless of their location in the continent, have no such refined culinary habits. Wine or any other type of beverage, if and when available, is drunk either before or after the meal, not as part of the meal. There are no defined courses and no table settings. An African meal is one complete serving; no starters and no desserts. Cutleries are foreign gadgets and table arrangements are reserved only for the rich. The rituals of *"cheers"*, or *"santé"* or *"salud"* or *"prost"*, do not exist in most of African languages. I have heard Kenyans say, for example, "chakula chema" (good food) as a Swahili equivalent of *"bon appétit"*, but this phrase is grossly off the mark! In general, most Africans – because of poverty – do not take food for granted and have no reason to wish anyone *"bon appétit"*. They just eat. Also, in many parts of Africa, meat – or even fish – is considered a delicacy, eaten only on special occasions. Worst still, even during special occasions, it is the men, not women or children, who enjoy the choicest of pieces and the largest of portions, making eating in an African homestead a socially unbalanced experience.

The only aspect of the French culture I did not like was the way they allowed dogs to litter everywhere with no concern for hygiene and the environment. The footpaths of Paris were as hazardous as the mine fields of Angola. A false step and your shoe soles would be plastered with all manner of gooey, smelly stuff that could be both embarrassing and annoying. I didn't mind the French dressing their pets in winter clothes and cuddling them like human babies, but letting them defecate everywhere and leaving the walkways with droppings of faeces left me with the most disgusting memories of life in France.

One thing I enjoyed was hanging out at street cafés and bars during my leisure time, watching people come and go and listening to the nuances of the French language. What shocked me however were the different prices that were charged for customers who sat on stools at the bar counter and those who stood. I had not been anywhere else in the world where the price of a beer was calculated on the basis of whether you drank it standing or you swallowed it sitting at a table. But that was what I found in Paris.

I also discovered France was one of the most intolerant societies in the world based on the way the French treated African immigrants from its former colonies of West Africa. The way the police harassed and chased African hawkers from the streets – compared to immigrants from other parts of Europe – was most debasing and racist. In France, Africans, even those who were born in the country, often complained of being subjected to maltreatment.

If my experiences in France were a mixed bag of exhilaration and deep reservations, my encounters in Spain were more tolerable, made so perhaps because of the glitzy flamenco dances, the gaudy bull-fights and the gut-shattering sangria cocktail drinks. Flamenco, which comes from southern Spain, is a genre of music that combines the sound of guitars, singing, handclapping and a titillating expression of arms and stamping of feet. I had an occasion to experience these highly sensual dances in restaurants in Madrid and Barcelona as I sipped my sangria, a wine punch that includes chopped fruit and brandy. It's very potent. Bull-fighting is another aspect of Spanish culture I thoroughly enjoyed. I admired the audacity of the matadors and the ferocity and determination of the charging bulls.

There is one incident that took place in Madrid that I will never forget. It was normal for the office to play host to Kenyans visiting the area on tourism-related activities. In this particular instance, the visitors were from the Ministry of Tourism who had come for the Fitur exhibition. Unbeknown to us, one of the officers had a serious drug habit, and that manifested itself in an almost fatal way. After the officer failed to show up for breakfast, I got concerned and asked to be allowed into his room. I found him sprawled on the bed unconscious. On the side table was a bottle of Valium, a prescribed medication used to control anxiety and a big bottle of alcoholic spirit. I was convinced the officer had mixed the two, a dangerous combination indeed.

Valium is safe when taken as prescribed by a doctor, but when abused it can cause hallucinations or even harbour thoughts of suicide. It took a while before we could bring the officer to his senses. In disgust, I flushed the tablets down the drain. The officer confessed to me later that he had taken to drugs to fend off depression. The man had been married for years, but the couple had not been able to get a child. That had sent him into a state of depression bordering on suicide. I encouraged him to get medical help which, I am glad to say, he eventually did upon his return home. The couple divorced, he quit drinking and stopped taking the pills. When I met him ten years later he was sober and healthy.

What I also liked about Spain is that they had night courts. Once, one of our visiting officials became unruly in a bar. He was arrested and taken to court past midnight. The judge, the attorneys and court *askaris* were all there. I had to spend hours waiting for the hearing of his case in a court that was full of drunks and prostitutes. He was slapped with a small fine which he paid and was released. We did not get back to the hotel until five in the morning, ready for a brief rest, breakfast and back to work. I thought night courts could be introduced in Kenya to deal with the backlog of cases. It would ease congestion in remand cells and provide quick justice.

* * *

Sometime in September 1979, towards the end of my tour of duty, I received a notice of posting to Stockholm, Sweden. By that time I had been in Europe for two-and-half years. I was already tired of the harsh winters and was unwilling to take another tour of duty. But the main reason was because I desired to leave government to go into the private sector. So, I opted for a posting back to Nairobi.

Before I left Paris for Nairobi at the end of my assignment, my family and I took one last look at the French capital, this time from atop the Eiffel Tower, the tallest structure in Paris. Observing the city from 300 meters above and seeing River Seine snaking its way into the horizon carrying on its head hundreds of river vessels was a fascinating experience. The view was many times more fascinating than what one experiences looking down from atop the 345 feet high Kenyatta International Conference Centre (KICC) in Nairobi.

Headed to the unknown, I bundled my family for a return journey to Nairobi in September 1979. While in France, my extended family at home got smaller. Sepetu, my uncle, the other mosquito catcher who had remained a bachelor all his life, died suddenly at his farm in Malanga, Malindi. He had retired, got married and, as if to catch up with life, had sired seven children in quick succession. He considered himself "born again" and had married an equally religious wife. They had moved to the farm and were growing subsistent crops like maize, cassava and vegetables. I missed the actual burial, but my wife and I arrived in Kenya before the mourning period ended and were able to pay our last respects at the grave.

Out of the family of five siblings in the ex-slave Stephen Sepetu's family, only Matano, the musician, and my mother Maria, were alive. Their mother, Nyanya Pauline had long died having succumbed to old age diseases. Matano was living in Dar es Salaam, Tanzania, where he had retired after the collapse of the East African Community. He was married and had a number of children. Mother Maria was in Rabai. She had stopped drinking and had raised her own children with a man I never wanted to know. I re-established close bond with my mother, but we never discussed the tribulations each of us went through in all those years of separation. We decided to leave that pain behind and forge on with our lives.

Chapter 14

Business Attempt

I had made a lot of business and personal contacts in Europe, which came in handy after I decided to start my own tour business in Kenya. I left government as the 1980s started and registered a company called Jetset Africa Tours and Safaris with offices in Mombasa. I chose Mombasa, and not the capital Nairobi, for three reasons: one, because of low operating costs; two, the coastal town offered less competition from big tour operators; and three, Mombasa was my home town. I could count on support from both family and friends. Consequently we rented a bungalow in Chaani, west of Mombasa Island, and enrolled Maria and Pili at Loreto Convent Mombasa.

One of the first business actions I took was to renew my local and overseas contacts and spread the word around about my new company. I found a suitable street-level office along Moi Avenue, which was being vacated by the *Nairobi Times*, a publication owned by Hilary Ng'weno, my one time editor-in-chief at the *Nation*. Ng'weno had resigned in 1965 to start the *Weekly Review*. In 1977, he established the *Nairobi Times*, first as a Sunday paper and later as a daily, and opened a bureau in Mombasa. However, due to dwindling advertising revenue, he sold the paper to the ruling party, KANU, and closed the office in Mombasa.

My wife, Doretha, managed the company, and I did what I knew best: promotion and marketing. We installed a telex machine at the office and sent out many notifications. I also joined the local chapter of Skal, a global association of travel and tourism leaders, and became a member of KATO, the leading tourism trade association in Kenya.

Jetset's main target was the European market with focus on France, Spain, Belgium, Luxembourg and Netherlands, my former areas of operation. During a promotional visit to Netherlands a year earlier, I had met a group of farmers who wanted to visit agricultural projects in Kenya. I contacted them and they agreed to sign up with Jetset as their ground operator in Kenya. Nineteen farmers made the first group. We took them to coffee and tea plantations and arranged meetings with small-scale farmers in various parts of the country. Those activities were interspersed with safaris to Masai Mara and Amboseli National Parks. The following year, we hosted yet another group of Dutch farmers.

As we continued to cultivate the European business, a smaller, lucrative market was emerging in the Middle East involving American expatriates working in the oil fields of Kuwait, Saudi Arabia, Abu Dhabi, Dubai and Bahrain. The expatriates were highly paid in their jobs and preferred individually-arranged tours offering a high degree of comfort and quality products. After exhausting the beautiful beaches of Tunisia and Morocco, they wanted something different and looked to Kenya, Tanzania and South Africa for exotic wildlife experiences.

The expatriate business started with one request for information from an American couple in Bahrain. The family eventually visited Kenya and thoroughly enjoyed the attractions and the personal service we offered. When the couple returned to the Middle East, they spread the word and inquiries started pouring in. Although we had employed a qualified safari guide, a few times my wife and I took visitors around the parks.

In 1982, I booked a promotional booth at the Fitur International Tourism Fair in Madrid. Usually, the fair attracts thousands of people hunting for new holiday destinations. I took with me posters, business cards and brochures and spent four days selling my company services. My participation at Fitur paid off. I returned home with a contract for a back-to-back arrival/departure arrangement. That meant for every fourteen Spaniards who arrived, fourteen would be leaving. It was going to be a profitable three-month deal for my company. We obtained the best hotel rates around the country, made transport arrangements and waited for the first group to arrive. It never did.

* * *

In the dawn hours of 1 August 1982, a group of Kenya Air Force soldiers broke out of their barracks outside Nairobi, went on a looting spree, and took over the VoK station. They announced they had overthrown Moi's government and had imposed a military leadership. The unexpected event shook the country and sent the government in a panic mode. It was a Sunday and we had gone to church unaware of what had happened in Nairobi during the night. The news spread quickly around the world. We stopped briefly at the office to check incoming messages and were shocked to see the number of tour cancellations, including the much awaited Spanish back-to-back arrangement. I was disappointed. All the money we had put in the European promotional tour had gone to waste. But worst still, the whole tourism industry was now in jeopardy.

The coup attempt lasted for only a few hours. Loyalists recaptured the VoK station, rounded up the rebels and restored Moi to power. I dropped the family home and drove through the Nyali barracks to see if there was any activity there. It was all quiet. In the following weeks, suspected plotters were court martialled and sentenced to long prison terms while their leaders were condemned to die. In the lingering political instability, the entire tourism industry came to a standstill. Dozens of tour companies, including mine, collapsed and several hotels closed down. Never before had I felt as insecure as I was during that period in my life. I had two school going children and a wife who depended on the tourism industry for survival.

The collapse of the company meant we no longer had an income to meet our daily expenses. We had very little savings and no investments. Whatever we had accumulated in Europe we had invested in the company. We were desperate. Yes, we were expecting a few payments from our overseas agents, but how long would those payments sustain us? We had to come up with Plan B. I felt there was no time to brood, but plenty of time to ask myself questions. Had I made a mistake to resign from a stable job in government to go into private business? Yes. Did I regret the brief adventure in tourism? No! Maybe I was not made for business anyway. In business one had to have a bucket of perseverance and a large dose of tolerance. I was not good in persevering and I was not tolerant. If I had been tolerant perhaps I would not have changed jobs so many times. I always wanted to do many different things as if the world was coming to an end tomorrow. Perhaps, I thought, I could go back to journalism, a profession I was most familiar with. And that is the direction I took.

We remained in Mombasa and the children continued with their studies, but we had to cut down on expenses while waiting for the next opportunity. For the first time, I looked back at my life in America with refreshed nostalgia. I had a steady though dreary job at the VoA that was paying well. Why couldn't we just go back there? I asked myself. I had worked with the VoA for three-and-half years and had left without a blemish. While there I had won two awards for excellence in broadcasting and production. I was convinced VoA would take me back. I remembered also that I had some unfinished business: the matter of completing my university studies.

I made contacts and found the people in the Africa Division would be quite happy to have me back. Luckily, there was a position soon to be vacant. Within a few weeks I was filling forms and completing formalities in preparation for our clearance. A year later, my family and I were on a flight to the United States for another stint at one of the world's most listened-to international radio stations.

* * *

We arrived in America on 25 August 1983. I had been away for almost ten years and a lot had changed in Washington DC. When I left, the Metro rail system was still in its early stages with only a few stations open. I returned to find the system extended further into the suburbs. K Street, the equivalent of Koinange Street in Nairobi and teeming with strip clubs and seedy bars and casinos, had been transformed into a decent thoroughfare with skyscrapers and trendy restaurants. Public parks looked bigger and the number of loafers who sat on benches in parks with their trollies loaded with life belongings had gone down. They had been driven out to less prominent areas of the city.

Settling back in the city was much easier this time around. We boarded in a hotel for a week and soon found an apartment in the south-west part of the city, within a walking distance from the office. Maria was now ten and Josephine Pili eight. We enrolled them at a public school, Amidon Elementary School, only a few metres from our apartment building. With Doretha initially at home, we began a new phase in our busy, adventurous life.

At VoA I found old friends and made new ones. Alex Chemponda, Emmanuel Muganda and Athanas Maijo were still where I left them earlier in the Swahili Service. During my first stay in America I was a bachelor with few responsibilities other than an eight-hour work schedule. Life then was one continuous party. This time around things were different. I had a family to look after. I was earning a good salary, but not enough to give us the extra amenities of life we desired. I needed a car to get around and money to take my family to restaurants, museums and other entertainment places. I wanted my children to have a Christian-based education. I therefore moved them from the free public school to Our Lady of Perpetual Help School, a private Catholic institution. I also re-enrolled for my degree course.

Education in the US is costly, but I was lucky that I got the support of my employer who paid for all courses that had to do with my writing and broadcasting career. When I was ready to buy a car, we travelled to the dealership in a train and drove home in a brand new vehicle. The only money I was required to pay was for the number plate and registration fees. The rest I was to pay over a three-year period. That was how easy it was to purchase goods in the United States.

Before I arrived in the USA, there was one horrifying incident. A friend at the VoA, Y. B. B. Mushala, had been shot and killed by robbers who stormed a private party in an apartment in the north-western part of the city and ordered everyone to empty their pockets. Mushala, a Tanzanian, was a lecturer at the Howard University and a part-time broadcaster at the VoA. Stubborn as he always was, he refused to comply and was shot and killed instantly. Mushala's sudden death angered and bothered the tight East African community in Washington DC. He was a very popular individual who had helped a lot of his countrymen to access education in America. In order to meet demands of his growing family, he was engaged in several undertakings including running a laundry. He was married to a pleasant Ugandan lady and the two made a loveable couple.

The manner in which Mushala was killed galled me. The 1960s, 1970s and early 1980s were particularly dangerous in the US. America was still going through the hippie and black power revolutions. Dr Martin Luther King had been assassinated in April 1968, and blacks were still bitter. People were smoking marijuana freely and openly. The moral fibre had disintegrated and young people were engaging in free sex. With its liberal gun laws weapons' shops were not inconspicuous like in the case of Nairobi. They operated, and still continue to operate, in plain sight;

anyone can walk in unarmed and come out holding anything from a small calibre gun to an assault rifle such as an AK-47. Despite my hurt over what had happened to my friend, I decided to soldier on albeit carefully.

In order to live comfortably I decided to take a second job. Working two or even three jobs is not unusual in America. Many do that to supplement regular incomes and achieve the American dream. So, I ditched my night studies and took a job as a waiter at a private members' club. That meant I could only attend classes at certain times of the day. No one else knew of the night job except my wife. The pay was minimum wage, but I looked forward to receiving a cheque at the end of the Friday shift. The additional income made a lot of difference in the household. In the meantime, I used every available free time to schedule classes. I went to class at 8 am in the morning, returned at lunch time for one more, and squeezed at least two classes every evening before dashing across town to wait on the rich and the mighty.

This second job was both interesting and demeaning. I had no experience in waiting tables before, but it didn't take long before I learnt how to balance – on my right shoulder – a huge round tray with six dinner plates of food on it. During a period of about two months that I was there I had only one serious accident. This was when the tray tipped over as I unloaded the plates, and driblets of greasy gravy splashed on a lady's sparkly dress. I knew right away that my short career as a restaurant helper had come to an end. I dashed back to the kitchen and hid behind a desk to await the sacking order from the supervisor. Luckily, the woman noticed how nervous and contrite I was and did not press for punitive action. When the supervisor, a plump Caribbean national with an amusing and jaundiced look found me, he only had words of comfort and caution. When I got my cheque that Friday I quit.

By that time Doretha had found a job at a bank and life had started to look somehow rosier. It was then that we managed to buy a three-bedroomed house in Maryland, on the outskirts of DC, with a basement and a bar I christened "Joe's Bar". Other than the lesbian couple opposite our house who was unabashed about cuddling and kissing on its porch, in full view of our children, many of our neighbours were friendly.

* * *

One of the highlights of my stay in America was a visit to the country by President Daniel arap Moi in March 1987. The four-day tour, though official, was marked by protests by a section of Kenyans and extensive negative publicity over deteriorating human rights situation in Kenya. American authorities, including President Ronald Reagan, Secretary of State, George Shultz, and Defence Secretary, Caspar Weinberger, underscored the excellent relations between the two countries, but the officials also raised issues of police torture and other abuses.

Describing Kenya as a "model for political and economic stability" in Africa during initial talks, American officials quickly changed tune at subsequent meetings by issuing a statement asking President Moi to allow more freedoms. The visit turned out to be a major embarrassment to the President who refused to answer media questions about the allegations on violations of human rights. Seeing my President being embarrassed in a foreign country was hard, but I thought of the victims of torture and felt an obligation to speak on their behalf, at least in terms of covering the story.

Up until then, Kenya had been one of America's biggest allies but reports of mistreatment of dissidents were received badly in Washington DC. That visit was in complete contrast to the one the President had made in February 1980 when he held useful discussions with President Jimmy Carter on a variety of issues including East African regional cooperation, the political situation in Zimbabwe as well as the Soviet Union's invasion of Afghanistan.

In the meantime, I was rippling through my university studies and earning accolades at work. I no longer just prepared material for Swahili broadcasts. I was going out on reporting assignments for the English Service and preparing scripts for house use. I covered Congressional hearings and interviewed visiting African personalities. In addition, I researched and wrote radio features that earned me a lot of respect from my professional colleagues. I had transferred my academic credits from George Washington University and the University of the District of Columbia to the University of Maryland, College Park, which was nearer to my house and more convenient for night classes. I chose to major in journalism and selected government as my minor specialisation. I also decided to take science-related courses to give me a more broad-based understanding of diverse issues relevant in today's world, so I registered for a Bachelor of Science degree. That meant I had to take a load of science subjects including astronomy, clinical psychology and computer sciences, among others. That period was one of the most hectic in my life. Driving a long distance to work, being able to attend classes, getting time to study and spending time in the library were taking me away from my family. However, I tried to spend whatever little time I could with my wife and children.

Finally, my years of struggle to acquire a university education finally came to an end. On 21 May 1988, at the commencement ceremony, University of Maryland, University College, presided over by Chancellor T. Benjamin Massey, I was awarded a BSc degree. As I moved forward to collect my diploma amid the soothing graduation music – the Pomp and Circumstance – I thought of the journey I had travelled from that nursery school at Isaac Nyondo and the troubles I went through as I worked hard to chart my future. I thought of the slashes and frustrations of living in a single parent home, and of the challenges I faced in trying to provide a decent livelihood for my family. A dream had come true. I was convinced beyond doubt that everything was possible. Without a Form Four education, but with a strong determination to succeed, I was able to plough through well-paying jobs and live a decent life. For the first time, I felt "educated". And I managed to do that through hard work and a lot of personal sacrifices. I could have bought a certificate from the many diploma mills in America and pretend to be educated; or I could have squandered the opportunity of obtaining a decent education, but I didn't. I took the hard route. My achievement also set an example to my children that dreams are there to be realised; that a failure can be transformed into a success.

Many years later when I saw my colleagues in Parliament rushing to universities to seek higher education, I felt a sense of satisfaction that I had not been the only one to miss out. I could see in the legislators the same kind of enthusiasm that ran through my body and mind as I shuttled from class to class in search of knowledge. At that time aspiring MPs were required to have a degree from a recognised institution to qualify as candidates. That is why it was embarrassing for Bishop Margaret Wanjiru, the MP for Starehe, when it was discovered that her Doctor of Theology degree she purported to have obtained from a little known institution called the Vineyard Harvester Bible College in the United States in 2003 was fake. I was proud of myself when I presented my diploma certificate for verification at the Ministry of Higher Education in September 2012 in readiness for the general elections. It was checked and promptly stamped as genuine.

However, the fact that I was able to hold fairly good jobs without a degree for such a long period of time was a show of personal determination and hard work. I have come across many people who have done well in life without a higher diploma. The best example is Richard Leakey. He dropped out of the Duke of York Secondary School (now Lenana School) at the age of sixteen, set up a business of trapping and selling animal skeletons, later becoming a world renowned palaeontologist and wildlife conservationist. With a low level of education, Leakey became the Head of Civil Service in Kenya and supervised thousands of civil servants, some of them with PhD degrees. I was however not prepared to take a chance.

In April 1988, the VoA sent me on an assignment to Sweden to cover the Fourth International Conference on AIDS. It had been seven years since the first case of AIDS had been diagnosed in the United States in 1981. Scientists agreed the cause virus – the Human Immunodeficiency Virus – had been present in the US since the late 1970s, but it was not until 1982 that the term "Acquired Immunodeficiency Syndrome" was used to describe the opportunistic diseases accompanying the virus. Debates had been going on for several years about its original form with a controversial conclusion that it had originated from chimpanzees in Africa, which hunters had killed for food. The virus was then transmitted to humans and eventually spread from Africa to the rest of the world.

Three similar conferences had been held before the one in Stockholm: in Atlanta in the US, Paris in France, and Washington DC. The four-day Stockholm conference attracted scientists, researchers, clinicians and health and community practitioners from all over the world – over seven thousand of them. Those series of conferences were intended to promote global solidarity in the fight against HIV/Aids, coordinate research, and fight off discrimination against those infected with the virus.

I had applied for leave so that after the Stockholm conference I could fly to Kenya to visit relatives as it would be cheaper for me. The VoA paid for the sector, Washington-Stockholm-Washington, and I paid for the remaining sector, Stockholm-Nairobi-Stockholm. From the conference I sent daily feeds to VoA on issues of interest to Africa and a few times went live through a telephone line. After the meeting ended, I left my colleagues to return to the US while I flew to Nairobi. I spent two days in the city then took a train to Mombasa where my brother Charles waited for me at the railway station.

Charles was particularly special to me. We had been through so many events together. He was the only person who knew me better than anyone else. The same was true of me to him. We did everything and went everywhere together. When we were growing up, our father always bought us look-alike clothes. We seemed to be wearing uniforms at all times and a lot of people thought we were twins. So when we met again after several years apart, we wanted to spend as much time together as possible.

From the train station Charles and I went straight to his municipal-rented house at Likoni, dropped the suitcase and immediately hit the bars. We drank and ate until late at night. In the morning we crossed the Likoni ferry and took public transport to our family home at Kanamai on the north-coast. We spent several quality hours talking to my father and step-mother without bringing up the past. Later that evening Charles, in good health and jovial as usual, bid us goodbye and returned home, leaving me to spend a few days at Kanamai.

Early the following morning, Charles's son, Francis Khamisi, came to say his father had fallen seriously ill at night. Together with my step-mother Tabu we rushed to a doctor's clinic at Bima House where he had been taken for treatment. His blood-pressure had shot to two hundred and six. He was asthmatic and had difficulty breathing. The doctor also found he had malaria, a fatal combination indeed. We decided to have him admitted at Pandya Memorial Hospital. His condition did not improve. He looked wasted. His once confident eyes had sunk in giving his face a calm, sorrowful posture. His wife, Bahati, sat on his side throughout the day and night, fiddling with her rosary and maintaining a façade of hope.

In the meantime, my return date to the US was drawing near. My ticket was restricted and I could not change it without paying a lot of money. After considering all options and consulting with the family,

I decided to travel back to work. I left some money and tearfully bade Charles goodbye. The day I arrived in Washington DC, I received a message that he had passed on. I just cried and prayed. I wished I had stayed back to see him in his last dying moments, but it was too late even to think about that. He was buried at the family farm at Kanamai. He left behind his wife and six children, Salama, Faida, Khamisi, John (now deceased), Nasibu and Nicky.

For me, it was difficult to fathom how life would be without Charles. Although I have step-brothers and sisters, they are much younger and a little removed from my experiences. They spent their growing up years in Nairobi and did not share my joys and sorrows in a village environment. By the time I left the family home, my father had lost interest in corporal punishment, and my siblings were therefore saved from lashes. In other words, my siblings lived a normal life that permitted them to pursue education in a congenial, familial environment. Two girls, Dorothy and Margaret (now deceased), went all the way to the university and Dorothy became the principal of Kibondeni College, a girls' catering and hospitality training institution in Nairobi; Christopher finished school and joined an oil firm where he has risen to a management position; Josephine went into teaching; Alice and Rose are happily married and raising their children; Fred, Gregory and Austin are engaged in various activities at the family compound in Kanamai; and Christine, who was married to Walter Mbotela, has since died and was followed to the other world by her husband only in 2013. Although we live apart, family issues always bring us together.

Chapter 15
Namibia Surprise

With a degree in my pocket, doors were now open for many bigger and interesting things ahead. As much as I wanted to advance to a Master's degree, I could not resist the hunger of returning home. I had now been in the US for five years. My children were doing well in school and my wife was working. Although I had acquired a green card and was officially a resident of the United States, I knew down in my heart that there was something better out there for me to do than working on Kiswahili translations.

Towards the end of 1987, Bethwel Kiplagat, the Permanent Secretary in the Ministry of Foreign Affairs, visited the United States on official duty. He had been my Ambassador in France for a while when I was working there as the Tourist Officer. During a reception at the Ambassador's residence, I informed him of my desire to join the Foreign Service. He was quite receptive. He suggested that I write him a letter which I did that same week. On 7 March 1988, I received a response in which he gave me a choice between the Department of Information and the Foreign Affairs Press Section. "I would like...to know from you what, precisely, your expectations are, to work in the media or in the Diplomatic Service," he said in the letter.

After having worked in the media for years, I thought the Foreign Service would be a better option. I remembered how I used to walk along Harambee Avenue, stop outside the Ministry's building, and dream of the day when I would become a real diplomat, not just a press attaché, not just a tourist officer. I would peep through the wire fence and admire the big cars on the parking lot. Once in a while, I would see a diplomat-looking smartly dressed man or lady emerging from the building and I would imagine how it felt wearing foreign-tailored suits instead of the ones I was wearing, outfitted at a shop near Jamia Mosque.

A few months after I received the letter, I started making preparations to depart the United States. I felt my presence in Nairobi would help expedite the process of clearance through the Public Service Commission (PSC). I resigned from the VoA and left for home late in 1988. The PSC called me for an interview early in 1989 and I was immediately appointed Senior Assistant Secretary in the Ministry of Foreign Affairs. I was assigned to the Asia Division as deputy director under Chrispas Muema who later became our Ambassador in Nigeria. Our division was responsible for the whole of Asia plus all the islands in the Asia Pacific. I was tasked to handle student issues in those countries, maintain a roster of all their national days, draft messages of goodwill as required, and follow up on reports and analyses from our envoys.

One depressing issue I had to deal with on almost daily basis involved many unexplained deaths of Kenyan students in India. The frequency of deaths among our young people, mainly through road accidents and suicides, was mind boggling. I had the unenviable task of conveying sad news to parents and relatives, a role so difficult I could not get used to. Each tragic event was as hurtful to me as it was to the kin. Then, I had to coordinate the arrivals of bodies at the Nairobi airport and help the families cope with their grief. At one time, I was processing an average of two bodies per month. Unfortunately, consumption of illegal drugs and excessive drinking played a significant role in the destruction of Kenyan lives in India. When I thought about India and what was happening to our students, my mind went to that *mama* at the back of our hostel in Bombay who sold us *chang'aa* and wondered whether she was responsible for some of those deaths. What I enjoyed most was reading situation reports from our envoys in Asia. The political and economic analyses and briefs on bilateral relations taught me a lot about how diplomacy worked. For the first time, I came to know a little more closely such islands as Vanuatu, Papua New Guinea, Nauru and dozens others.

The Asian Division was much smaller compared to the African or European Divisions because it had fewer countries to cover and that meant a smaller share of work. But good fortunes were ahead. One morning, the director of political affairs, Francis Kasina, called me to his office. As I climbed the stairs one floor up, I wondered about the reason for the summons. Normally, the director dealt directly with heads of divisions.

But here I was, second in command, being asked to go to see the political boss. From his body language as I got into his office, I knew whatever the matter it wasn't anything bad at all. He looked relaxed behind his big desk. He was a short, greying individual who was serving his last few years in government before retiring. He had worked as a diplomat for years serving in many stations abroad. He welcomed me with a broad smile, put down his cigarette and said he had an assignment for me. "Mr Khamisi, we are sending you to open the Kenya Liaison Office in Namibia." I looked at him unbelievably. My skin prickled. What? For a second, I thought my heart had stopped. It hadn't. It started beating faster and faster like the foot sounds of a tap dancer until my face brightened and I released a subtle smile. Inwardly, I was thrilled only that I didn't want to show it. I had been in the Ministry for less than a year. I was not even in the Africa Division where such an offer would normally have been directed to. I was in the wrong division.

The only thing I knew about Namibia then was what I was reading in the papers: the liberation struggle, the UN resolution and the fact that Kenya would be sending soldiers there for a peacekeeping mission – nothing more. I was still new in the business of diplomacy. True, my minor specialisation at the university dealt with how governments worked under different systems, how democracy compared to communism, how monarchs and imperial kingdoms functioned, and so on, but I had no clue about real diplomacy, that art of negotiation and persuasion. Yet I was being called to do a job that was customarily reserved for more experienced officers. "You should prepare to leave within the next few days," he said, taping his half-smoked cigarette on a round ash tray choked with small disfigured butts. I rose from my chair, shook his hand and thanked him profusely for giving me an opportunity to serve. As I opened the door, I looked back and saw he had disposed of the half cigarette and was fishing for another stick from his pocket. His job had ended. Mine was about to start.

I walked slowly down the stairs and went back to my office. I knew my posting to Namibia would generate apathy from senior colleagues, and sure it did, but I really didn't care. A few felt I deserved it, many wondered how I could have been picked ahead of them. No one could talk of political connections because I had none. Namibia was not yet independent, and in any case, I was not going there as an Ambassador but as a liaison officer, a relatively junior position even though I was going to be in charge. I figured out that, the fact I had been chosen from the Asia Division to take up an Africa assignment, meant my bosses at the top had confidence in my ability to deliver. Moreover, the decision to send me to such a sensitive station during a delicate period of that country's independence struggle could not have been taken at the level of the director of political affairs. It had to have come from much higher up. How high I didn't know, and it did not concern me then.

* * *

Kenya had been selected by the United Nations as one of several countries to play a peacekeeping role in Namibia, then known as South-West Africa. The territory was still controlled by the apartheid regime of South Africa despite international protests. A UN Security Council Resolution 435 of 1978 had put forward proposals for UN-supervised elections; hence the country would come under the authority of the United Nations ahead of expected general elections.

I had only one week to prepare for my departure to Windhoek in April 1989. Since the notice was short, I spent the next few days sorting out my personal issues and getting ready for the trip. My assignment was for an unspecified period of time. I decided to travel ahead of my family, which would follow later. On the appointed day, I travelled aboard one of several chartered flights carrying the Kenyan peacekeeping soldiers. The transportation of the troops lasted few days between 7 and 19 April and involved a total of one thousand men and women of different ranks. Since the troops were going under the United Nations flag, a prior clearance had been obtained for them from Pretoria. Sadly for me, no such clearance was sought. The Kenya government refused to apply for a visa because it did not recognise the apartheid authority there. My Ministry only informed the British High Commission in Nairobi hoping it would use its influence to facilitate my entry but the British refused to be dragged into the affair. Lack of travel documents however did not stop me from travelling to Namibia.

Our plane was packed with eager young soldiers who had replaced their jungle green hats with blue berets of the United Nations forces when we took off from Nairobi. They were the lucky lot. In Namibia they would gain peacekeeping experience and earn allowances far beyond their monthly earnings. As the plane rose above the Kenyan skyline on its way south, the soldiers were animated, jovially exchanging jokes and anecdotes of all matters of interest, but as we entered the South African territory, the only sound rippling through the cabin was that of jet engines. I could only imagine what was going on in their minds. For most of them this was their first trip outside Kenya, and they knew that, after Namibia, life for them would never be the same. They would be transformed from mere foot soldiers trained to kill to keepers of peace; from Kenyan to international soldiers.

I tried to sleep as I always do in planes, but I couldn't lure a wink however much I tried to count sheep. My mind was spawning questions about how I, a rookie junior officer in the Ministry, could have been chosen to undertake such a challenging assignment. As I tried to close my eyes for the umpteenth time, the words of my political affairs director repeated themselves in my mind over and over again like a broken record. "Mr Khamisi, we are sending you to open the Kenya Liason Office in Namibia... You should prepare to leave within the next few days." The practice in the Ministry over the years was that whoever was sent to open a new mission abroad was almost always appointed the first ambassador to that country. In my case, this hypothesis was hollow. There were far too many senior diplomats in the Ministry with training and better qualifications waiting for just that kind of appointment. As I tried to find an answer to that puzzle, I heard from the belly of the Boeing airplane the flaps snap and the wheels coming out in readiness for a touch-down.

We landed at the J. G. Strijdon airport (named after a former Prime Minister) on a nippy day. While the soldiers were welcomed by senior UN officials, I was met by a duo of mean-looking Boers. They had been informed of my impending arrival by the British High Commission in Nairobi from whom we had sought intervention. The British government already had a diplomatic mission in Windhoek. We had thought the British intervention would soften the minds and hearts of the South Africans. Instead it did the opposite. I was directed to the airport lounge by ruddy-faced, burly heavyweights, one with an intimidating moustache and a cynical expression, and the other with a menacing look and a husky drawling voice, which sounded like it was coming from an angry warthog. Other than my passport, I had nothing in my possession resembling a visa or a temporary pass. When the person with a rolled-up moustache asked me to produce a letter of authority from the UN I said I had none. I reminded them that Kenya was a member of the UN and since Namibia was under its authority, Kenya had every right to be part of its transition without unnecessary red tape.

I don't think they liked my snide remark. I could see one of them fiddling with his walkie-talkie and showing signs of disgust. They kept on insisting over and over again that I could not enter Namibia without a visa, and I kept on telling them I had done nothing wrong. After a gruelling one hour of back and forth as they consulted with their higher-ups, the one with a drawling voice suggested that I travel with them to the capital Pretoria to get clearance. There was a plane at the airport ready for the journey, they told me, and that they would bring me back to Namibia after the matter was cleared. They didn't think there would be any big problem. I found that idea unacceptable and I could not do that without permission from Nairobi.

Since Lt Gen. Daniel Opande, the Deputy Forces Commander of the UN Transition Assistance Group (UNTAG) and Commander of the Kenyan troops, was at the airport to meet his men and women, I decided to consult him and both of us agreed that the Pretoria visit would be too risky. There had been too many killings of black Africans by South African terror groups. One such case was when President Samora Machel's Topolev Tu-134 plane was bombed off the air as he flew home from a meeting in Zambia in 1986. Although nine survived, twenty-four were killed including the President himself and senior government officials. South African agents were suspected to have planted the bomb. In 1961, a plane chartered by the Botswana government to fly ANC liberation movement officials to Dar es Salaam went up in flames as it stood on tarmac at an airport in Botswana only minutes before take-off. One of those who escaped death in that botched murder attempt was Hage Geingob, a South-West Africa People's Organisation (SWAPO) operative who later became Namibia's Prime Minister. Again, South African agents were blamed for that explosion. There had been so many such gruesome incidents, and we were not going to take a chance.

The South Africans questioned me relentlessly about what my activities in Namibia would be and I responded by insisting that since the territory was under the UN supervision, Kenya had every right to be present. I was going to open a Kenya Office and ensure the comfort of our troops, I added. Upon seeing that I was unwilling to go with them to Pretoria, they threatened me with prosecution and detention. I told them I was only following orders from my government and they were at liberty to do whatever they wanted. One of them went aside and made a call I suspected was to a much higher honcho in Pretoria. When he joined us and after talking to his colleague in Afrikaans, he told me permission had been granted for my entry on condition that I reported to the immigration office in downtown Windhoek within forty-eight hours. I had no problem with that. We shook hands and I jumped into Lt Gen. Opande's white four-wheel drive vehicle for the drive to Safari Hotel, just off the highway on the way to the downtown.

Like South Africa that ruled it, Namibia was an unequal and racist territory where Africans and the Coloureds were segregated away from whites. There were different schools for blacks, coloureds and whites. Blacks were also restricted to overcrowded designated hospitals that lacked drugs and qualified staff. The situation reminded me of Kenya before independence and took my mind back to the Native Hospital in Mombasa. When in 1961 the Boers wanted to take over the more attractive hilly part of Windhoek, they chased away all the blacks and created a sprawling black satellite town called Katutura north of the city. Katutura is like most slums found in other parts of Africa; dirt roads, uncollected garbage, neglected schools, limited and erratic water and electricity supplies, poor sanitation, poverty and rampant unemployment. In fact, Katutura in the Herero language simply means "the place we did not want to go". Life in this slum was depressing; during the day the town appeared unassuming, but once night fell, armed gangs roamed the township terrorising and robbing inhabitants.

The deployment of Kenyan troops in the centre and south of the country coincided with an incident earlier in April when SWAPO fighters crossed the borders from Angola ostensibly to set up camps inside northern Namibia, The idea, I was told, was for the fighters to be in place in case of an all-out offensive should South African authorities continue to filibuster efforts towards independence. The news was disturbing. Immediately after the incursion, South Africa unleashed its brutal might by dispatching platoons of the paramilitary counter-insurgency group Koevoet, and by launching air attacks along the Angola-Namibia border region without permission from the UN (it was required that any such attacks had to be cleared by the UN representative in Windhoek). By the time the UN representative acquiesced to the deployment of a limited number of South African troops to dispel the insurgents, close to three hundred SWAPO guerrillas had been killed.

Although Kenyan forces were nowhere near the theatre of incursion, they were readied – just like all the other infantry battalions – to peacefully intervene in case things got out of hand. The deaths of the guerrillas was a major political and military blow to Sam Nujoma, the SWAPO leader, who immediately invoked the support of the UN for the South African Defence Force (SADF) to clear the way for his troops to return to their bases in Angola. It was only after everyone retreated to their bases that the march towards independence picked speed once again.

There were two almost parallel governing authorities in the territory: one administered by the UN Special Representative and head of UNTAG, Marti Ahtisaari from Finland, and the other by South Africa's Administration General, Louis Pienaar. The former was supposed to supervise the latter, but that was not always the case as Pretoria desperately tried to hang on to power by sabotaging and frustrating the UN work. However, Ahtisaari had the troops and the mandate of the world body to lead the country to independence. He was out to specifically implement the UN Resolution 435: creating a suitable environment for free and fair elections and for a Constituent Assembly to draft a new constitution. The military head of the peacekeeping troops, and Lt Gen. Opande's boss, was Gen Prem Dewan Chand, a former career soldier in the Indian Army, while Ahtisaari was deputised by Legwaila Joseph Legwaila of Botswana.

My immediate job was to open avenues of communication with the Ministry in Nairobi which meant I had to acquire a post office box number, lease a telex machine, and register Kenya with the Ministry of Foreign Affairs in Windhoek as one of the observer missions. We also had to get clearance for the diplomatic bag and secure other protocol services. The telex and telephone lines were installed in my room at Safari Hotel which now served as the Kenya mission in Namibia. From that modest room, I observed the political and diplomatic trends and reported the same to Nairobi, maintained contacts with SWAPO and other political leaders, and attended UN briefings. I also visited our troops and police officers to ensure their well-being, and comfort those who, for one reason or another, were admitted in hospital. There were at least two soldiers who were admitted in hospital with serious ailments during my stay in Windhoek.

As mentioned earlier, I had attended a HIV/Aids conference in Stockholm in 1988, but I had not personally seen a HIV infected person until I visited some of our troops in hospital. Two of our men had been found to be HIV positive and had sores all over their bodies. The sight was pathetic, and for the first time, I came to realise how devastating the disease was. Both soldiers had served in border areas, I was told, and I suspected that was where they picked the virus. What I knew from my general knowledge of HIV was that the virus could go undetected for months after exposure. It was possible then that any medical tests done in Kenya prior to departure did not detect the virus. The soldiers were eventually evacuated to Kenya.

My diplomatic work in Namibia kept me busy, but whenever I had free time I played golf with Lt Gen. Opande at the Country Golf Club. I had leased a Nissan saloon, and on top of the bonnet I had perched a mini Kenyan flag. I flew that flag whenever I went on official duties. That gave Kenya a semblance of diplomatic presence in the country.

I was directed by the Ministry to open an official bank account for the mission, which I did, with the first disbursement of six hundred thousand Kenya shillings. I knew very little about accounting. The only training I had was a course in booking-keeping, which I had taken at a commercial school in Mombasa many years earlier. To make things easy for auditors, I opened a "daybook" where I recorded all the monies received from Nairobi and all the official purchases. My record was so meticulous that when auditors came for a routine inspection months later they found that every penny had been accounted for. In fact, I had underpaid myself, and for that, I received a substantial refund.

Chapter 16

Kanu Membership by Force

At home, the ruling party KANU had, from way back in 1986, embarked on a vigorous membership recruitment campaign. Two years later, the membership had reached eight million, according to some estimates. A directive had been issued that all civil servants must be KANU members. When I joined Foreign Affairs, I had to acquire and wear on my lapel a badge with President Moi's image. Whenever I changed clothes, I also had to transfer the badge. That was in compliance with a dubious directive from some KANU stalwarts as a show of loyalty to the party and the President. I didn't apply to be a KANU member, but one day in the diplomatic bag came a certificate and a receipt to show that the membership fee had already been deducted from my salary. I had been recruited as a KANU Life Member No. 20068. I remained a member of KANU until 2002 when I resigned.

It was important for me in Namibia to maintain good relations with SWAPO, which my government and the ruling party KANU fully supported. I therefore interacted closely with such senior party leaders as SWAPO founder and Secretary General Andimba Toivo ya Toivo, Hifikepunye Pohamba, who was the party's publicity secretary, Theo Ben Gurirab and Hage Geingob, two key advisers to Sam Nujoma and who later became Prime Ministers after independence. SWAPO was formed on 19 April 1960 in Ovamboland by Nujoma and Toivo as successor to the Ovambo People's Congress (OPC) established in 1957. Initially, it represented the Ovambo people of northern Namibia but later co-opted other groups including the South West Africa National Union and the Namibia African Peoples Democratic Organisation to become a national party in 1962.

Occasionally, President Moi would dispatch, through the diplomatic bag, a letter to Nujoma, which I would then deliver personally to his house at Katutura. After a few days Nujoma would call me to his house to collect a response. Through those visits, I learnt a lot about SWAPO and what made Nujoma such a magnetic leader to his people.

In public, Nujoma was a fiery defender of his peoples' rights. He spoke with a lot of emotion about what apartheid had done to his people. Privately, he was nonchalant and gentle, quite uncharacteristic for a man who had spent many years in the trenches of the liberation struggle. Almost every time I visited him at Katutura I found him in the company of Toivo or other freedom fighters, always appearing to strategise on the next move towards freedom. On one occasion, I took along my children, and a picture showing Nujoma and Toivo and three of us remains a treasure in my household. I did not only meet with SWAPO officials, but I also dialogued with opposition personalities such as Mishake Muyongo and Katuutire Kaura both of the Democratic Turnhalle Alliance, and Moses Katjiuongua of the Democratic Coalition of Namibia. Because I did not want to be seen to be according the whites undue recognition, I avoided them except when it was absolutely necessary.

I operated from the Sahara Hotel for six months before moving to a house the Kenya government had bought in an upmarket area of Windhoek. There, I flew the Kenyan flag, proudly hoisting it up in the morning at 6 am (just like they do at home) and bringing it down at 6 pm in the evening. A rambling bungalow near town, which the Kenya government had also purchased, became the Chancery. In due course, two officers, an accountant and an intelligence officer, were posted to Windhoek to join me.

We received the diplomatic bag from Nairobi every week and we sent it back every week. The national carrier, Kenya Airways, was not flying on this route in those days of apartheid and we had to rely on British Airways and its southern African subsidiaries. I wanted to believe that our bags were safe at all times, but after reading Antonio J. Mendez's book, *Master of Disguise: My Secret Life in the CIA*,[15] our diplomatic cargo was vulnerable to official tampering as it passed through South African airports. Mendez talks of the activities of spy agencies including snooping and printing of near perfect replicas of foreign documents, and wondered whether our enemies did not intercept our letters, carefully

---

15   Antonio J. Mendez, *The Master of Disguise: My Secret Life in the CIA* (New York: William Morrow, 2000).

opened, photocopied and resealed them in their original envelopes. There was no way of knowing.

After about nine months, my family joined me in Namibia. Soon after arriving in Windhoek, Doretha got a job at the local UN office. At that time Maria had completed two years of secondary school. Since there were no English language secondary schools in Namibia, we sent her off to Moedin College, a boarding school in Botswana. Located on a picturesque valley shielded by hills and indigenous vegetation, the school was built in the early 1970s jointly by the Botswana government and the London Missionary Society. Its secluded rural location provided a perfect setting for serious learning. Pili stayed with us in Windhoek and attended the English School.

Among the African countries involved in Namibia's march to independence were the Frontline States (FLs) comprising Tanzania, Zambia, Mozambique, Zimbabwe, Botswana, Lesotho and Angola. Those countries had the biggest influence on the direction an independent Namibia would take. They held regular consultations with SWAPO leaders on issues as wide as the formation of the constituent assembly that was to draft a new constitution, the future of the guerrilla movement and the integration of the guerrillas into the regular Namibian army, and regional cooperation. At times it appeared envoys from the seven states were jostling among themselves for Nujoma's attention. Because they offered camps to SWAPO, the states had suffered years of attacks from the South African Defence Force (SADF).

As far as Kenya was concerned, not much had been recorded in terms of it helping significantly in the Namibian bush war. Other than one four-wheel drive vehicle, a Land Rover, Kenyatta contributed to SWAPO way back in 1964 I could find nothing on record to suggest that Nairobi had actively and materially participated in the liberation of South-West Africa. This explained why the Frontline States were so protective of their role, pushing Kenya as far away as possible from the centre of diplomatic activities in Windhoek. What was left was for us to cultivate post-independence bilateral ties centred on business, education and the military. We did that and the effort paid off when, at independence, Nujoma requested a segment of Kenyan troops to remain behind to train

Namibian soldiers. A large number of Kenyan technocrats were also recruited to help build the country's economy.

The presence of Kenyan troops was reassuring to Namibians most of whom were aware of Kenya's armed struggle for independence. To many of them, Kenya's struggle was no different from their own. Both countries had repressive colonial regimes with almost similar tenets of colour discrimination. In South Africa they called it apartheid, while in Kenya we called it colour-bar. In both countries, the war for liberation was fought from two fronts – in the bush and from exile. The militias in Namibia and the Mau Mau in Kenya went through similar experiences, enduring regular air raids, killings, destruction of property and mental anguish. And both Kenyatta and Nujoma spent many years in exile using travel documents issued by friendly countries. Perhaps the only major difference is that Kenyatta was incarcerated by the British colonial rulers while Nujoma was free throughout the struggle.

Dozens of countries had offered to assist Namibia during the transition period. Some had donated medical personnel, others provided monitoring teams, and yet others offered military and police contingents. Of the three countries that supplied infantry battalions, Kenya was the only African country. The others were Finland and Malaysia. Kenya also had a small but effective team of police officers under the leadership of Inspector Jonathan Koskei. For the first time I was able to interact closely with our fighting forces and I found them to be professional, disciplined and highly trained. As they say, discipline is everything in the military. Soldiers who are disciplined win wars; those who are unruly lose. If you don't believe this, try what happened to Benito Mussolini's troops in Italy in 1945 when they refused to obey orders. Lacking discipline, disoriented and disjointed, the Italian army surrendered to the Allied Forces and Mussolini himself was executed by Italian fascists.

In the Kenyan camps those who flouted rules were summarily punished. I will never forget a scene where a young officer who had gone AWOL (Absent without official leave) was made to carry a heavy combat gear on his back and forced to slow jog as a colleague hosed him with cold water. The drama took place at the Okahandja airport as he waited for a plane to fly him home. I can still see the humiliated officer, still obviously drunk, his uniform drenched in water, hobbling and wobbling to near collapse in front of his peers. It was perhaps the most humiliating experience I have seen an individual subjected to ever. I was later informed the twenty-something-year-old officer was dishonourably discharged.

* * *

It had been almost a year since my arrival in Namibia, but I hadn't found time to tour the country. One long weekend, I decided to take my family to Swakopmund, a sea resort town west of Windhoek that serves as one of the country's prime holiday destinations. Also travelling but in a separate car was Lt Gen. Opande. It was a road journey that took a few hours, traversing some of the most picturesque sand dunes I have ever seen. We could have chosen a route that would have taken us through the Namib-Naukluff national park, but we decided to head directly west through Okahandja and into the resort town known for its rich German history and palm tree-lined seaside promenades.

Don't think because Swakopmund is along the sea it is hot and humid like Mombasa or Dar es Salaam. The cool winds from the Atlantic Ocean keep this place cool, sometimes cold, throughout the year, contrasting the harsh conditions prevailing in the nearby Namib Desert and indeed most of the country. German culture and historical monuments were visible. However, the beach at Swakopmund did not impress. I come from the shores of the Indian Ocean where the waters are warm and calm. At Swakopmund, the waters of the Atlantic Ocean are cold and rough and, in my opinion, dangerous to swimmers. But there is more to Swakopmund than just touristic and historical beauty. Within reach from the town are significant industries, one of them being the world's fourth largest opencast uranium mine at Rossings providing hundreds of jobs to the locals, and hence boosts the country's economy.

About thirty kilometres from Swakopmund is Walvis Bay, another major tourist attraction and a popular landing place for sea vessels that are attracted there by its natural deep-water harbour. As Namibia approached independence, Walvis Bay was the subject of a bitter territorial dispute between the South African government, which wanted to keep it as its enclave, and SWAPO, which insisted that it remains part of a free Namibia. At the end of the day the latter won, and as I write this book, the mayor of that town is a black man. The visit to Swakopmund and Walvis Bay offered a well-deserved holiday for me and my family.

As the elections approached, the United Nations asked Kenya, among other countries, to send in election supervisors and observers. From Kenya, Joseph Mwangovya, the man who oversaw the 1988 controversial queue voting polls that got Moi re-elected unopposed, was chosen to assist in preparing for the first multiracial franchise elections taking place from 7 November to 11 November 1989. The polls were to elect leaders for a constituent assembly that would in turn draft the country's constitution. The elections went on without a hitch and SWAPO won 57 per cent of the votes making Nujoma the undisputed president-in-waiting and opened the way for the drafting of the constitution. The first meeting of the 72-member Constituent Assembly was held on 21 November 1989. SWAPO had 41 members in that body while the Democratic Turnhalle Alliance had 21. The other ten seats were shared among five small parties. On 9 February 1990, the Assembly adopted the first constitution of what was to become an independent Namibia.

It was around that time that I received news from home that my stepmother, Tabu, had died. That was a big blow to my father. They had been together since 1952 and, as far as I knew, they had a loving marriage.

Early in 1990, Achieng Adala, who was now director of political affairs at the Ministry of Foreign Affairs, called to inform me that an Ambassador had been named for Namibia. His name was John Likoko Odede, a career diplomat, who had served in several missions abroad and whose appointment as Deputy Secretary – an Ambassador level status – had been made on 1 March 1989, along with seven other officials. For months I had been searching for suitable premises to serve as the Ambassador's residence in readiness for such an appointment. I finally identified one, which was approved by the Ministry of Works. I chose to name it "Nyayo House" but was told permission for use of that name had to be obtained from State House. The approval finally came, and I placed at the gate of the premises a gold plate that said exactly that. Because of the upcoming independence celebrations and the expected visit by President Moi, Odede was instructed to travel quickly to Namibia to supervise preparations for the President's official schedule.

The first thing I did after being informed of the ambassadorial appointment was to write a Note Verbale or diplomatic memo to the Ministry of Foreign Affairs in Windhoek informing them of the arrival of the Ambassador-designate and asking for the necessary protocol assistance. Odede was known by his colleagues as a thorough and intelligent diplomat, whose analyses of issues had formed the basis of Kenya positions in various international conferences. He was now at the very prime of his long career in government. I wanted him to be absorbed into the local scene as quickly as possible, so I scheduled appointments for him to meet key people ahead of the celebrations. We paid a courtesy call at the Ministry of Foreign Affairs, I introduced him to all the leading SWAPO and opposition leaders, I took him to the Speaker of the Constituent Assembly, I arranged meetings with the UN representative, and I accompanied him to meet the UNTAG leadership as well as Kenyan peacekeepers.

Since Namibia was not yet independent, Odede could not present his letters of accreditation to Nujoma, but we went to the Ministry of Foreign Affairs and presented a letter from the Kenya government stating he was the Ambassador-in-waiting. By that time, Namibians had been integrated into various government institutions to understudy their white incumbents. For weeks, Kenya military officers had been drilling young, rookie Namibian soldiers – some coming directly from SWAPO camps – on parade formation in preparation for the Independence Day celebrations. The training went on well and senior SWAPO officials were quite happy with the results.

We had agreed with Nairobi that President Moi would occupy the official residence for the duration of his stay in Windhoek. Odede did not therefore move into the house upon his arrival and stayed at the Kalahari Sands Hotel in the city centre. An ambassadorial Mercedes Benz had been delivered, which was now going to be used as the presidential vehicle. Adequate security had been arranged by the host. However, the President's advance team did not like the furniture which had been bought and ordered its replacement with new, mostly red velvet seats. We had to incur additional expenses of re-furnishing the house, which to me, was completely unnecessary given the fact that the President was to be in town for only three days. The rejected pieces were distributed to staff.

The President and his entourage arrived in Namibia on 20 March 1990, one day before the independence celebrations – to a colourful welcome at the airport. He was then driven to the Ambassador's residence. The Chief of Protocol, Njuguna Mahugu, took over the coordination work, liaising closely with the Namibia officials attached to the Kenya delegation.

President Moi had a busy schedule in Namibia. He held formal talks with President Sam Nujoma, President Joaquim Chissano of Mozambique and the US Assistant Secretary of state for African affairs, Dr Herman Cohen. He also visited the Kenya battalion headquarters for a meeting with Kenyan soldiers.

Moi's visit came at a time of national grief and high tension at home. Less than a month earlier, on 13 February, his Foreign Minister, Robert Ouko, had gone missing from his rural home in Koru, western region of Kenya, only for his badly burnt body to be discovered in a thicket not too far from his house. Ouko's death drew a dark shadow on Moi's government, which many people believed had a hand in the Minister's disappearance and death. Most of the African leaders who met President Moi in Windhoek knew the Minister well through the OAU. He had also represented Kenya at the United Nations and other world forums. Moi's presence in Namibia therefore provided an opportunity for them to commiserate with Kenya and personally convey their condolences.

The independence celebrations in Windhoek were attended by representatives from one hundred and forty-seven countries including twenty Heads of State. They all gathered at the Independence Stadium to watch dances, a colourful military parade and befitting speeches by the South African President F. W. de Klerk and UN Secretary General, Javier Perez de Cuellar, who jointly conferred the instruments of independence to the new President, Samuel Daniel Shafiishuna Nujoma. Also present to witness the occasion was Nelson Mandela who had been freed less than two months earlier on 11 February from twenty-seven years in a South African jail. After the colourful independence celebrations, Moi went to the Windhoek State House for private talks with the new President before departing on 22 March.

With Namibia now independent it became necessary for envoys to present their credentials to the new Head of State. Odede did exactly that, becoming the first Kenyan High Commissioner to Namibia.

Being in Namibia at that time felt like being in a miniature United Nations. There were people from all over the world. Some were from governments and others were from non-governmental organisations all eager to offer services to the new country. Hotels were full and night clubs, real estate agencies, car dealers and local traders made booming business. That experience cannot be duplicated anywhere and I consider myself very lucky to have witnessed a new, vibrant nation being born. Namibia was a very enchanting place and the people were friendly and hospitable, which made our life in Windhoek pleasurable.

In theory, my assignment in Namibia had come to an end. Kenyan troops were leaving – except for a small contingent that remained behind for three months to train Namibian soldiers. Other UNTAG troops too were packing their bags. The Kenya mission that I had been sent to open was now fully operational and an Ambassador was in place. Namibia was now a free country. So what next for me? At least I had a choice. While in Namibia the Permanent Secretary, Bethwell Kiplagat, offered me two options: stay as number two to Odede or return to headquarters. I picked the latter and chose Protocol as my preferred division. I felt I had done my bit in Namibia and needed to move on.

When I sent a note to President Nujoma informing him of my impending departure he swiftly invited me and Doretha for a farewell lunch at State House. Foreign Minister Theo Ben Gurirab was there too. The President and his wife, First Lady Kovambo Katjimune, hosted us to a sumptuous mixture of English and traditional Namibian dishes. Nujoma informed us they had enjoyed my company in Namibia and wondered, with a laugh, whether I wanted him to intervene with President Moi to have me stay longer. I respectfully said it was not necessary.

By mid-year in 1990, my family and I were on our way home.

Chapter 17

Protocol

Any relocation takes a toll. This time around however the burden of relocation was lifted because we did not have any furniture or heavy personal effects to carry with us from Namibia. We moved Maria out of Moedin College in Botswana and enrolled her at Braeburn School in Nairobi to finish her last year of secondary education. All in all she had attended twelve schools since she started her journey for knowledge, but she was coping just fine. She was not complaining, at least not to us. Pili was ready for high school and we found a place for her at the International School of Kenya. Doretha had to quit her job at the UN in Windhoek, but on arrival in Kenya she was hired to work in a UN Project.

I had always been fascinated by protocol work. The whole idea of meeting and rubbing shoulders with VIPs was to me breathtakingly seductive. I reported for work at the Ministry of Foreign Affairs along Harambee Avenue within days of our arrival. The internal postings were out and at my level of Senior Assistant Secretary I was to deputise for the Chief of Protocol. Since my work was to involve dealing with international state visitors, I acquainted myself with how the division worked: about planning and organising official visits abroad for Kenyan VIPs; about coordinating arrivals and departures of foreign dignitaries; about hospitality, including taking charge of ceremonial events involving diplomats and foreign state visitors; and, about preparing guest lists, invitations and seating plans.

Njuguna Mahugu, the Chief of Protocol, was not a stranger to me. When I was the Press Attaché in Ethiopia he was the Third Secretary at the Embassy, a position equivalent to that of an Assistant Secretary in Kenya's bureaucratic hierarchy. Our relationship in those days was neither friendly nor adversarial, but I was convinced we could leave the past behind and cultivate a fresh working relationship. President Moi was a very active president and was constantly on the move. One day he could be at State House meeting diplomats, the next he could be travelling abroad on official visit. It was important for officers to work as a team. There was no room for conflict in a division as critical as protocol. It required collectivity and cooperation at all times.

Apart from his sometimes combustive nature, Mahugu was hardworking and result-oriented. He was respected and had a lot of influence in the high echelons of government, so much so that senior government officials had to come begging to get their names included on the list of VIPs accompanying President Moi on overseas trips. Although the President had the final word on everyone on his entourage, especially non-civil servants, Mahugu's word carried a lot of weight. For example, a visit to Asia would generate a scramble from within government and parastatal organisations. Mahugu's recommendations could be crucial. During his tenure as Chief of Protocol, Mahugu raised the bar too high for any of his successors to follow. The division became the face of the Ministry and the media invariably mentioned its presence during high-level state functions.

Protocol work is a twenty-four-hour assignment. I remember spending many hours at the Jomo Kenyatta International Airport VIP lounge either waiting for or seeing off foreign officials. The protocol officer on duty at the airport is required to clear arriving VIPs through customs and immigration inspectors, collect luggage and whisk them out through a special VIP area. They must be at hand all the time to ensure the comfort of official visitors. During national days or international meetings in Kenya when visitor traffic peaked, this process was repeated many times over and over throughout the day and night. For the safety of visitors, protocol must work closely with the police to ensure VIPs were facilitated in their travels around the city.

Preparations for presidential trips overseas were more involving. Once information arrived at the Ministry that the President had accepted an invitation to travel abroad, a careful planning process was devised. The Kenyan Ambassador or High Commissioner would start preparations and, in collaboration with the Ministry, schedules of meetings would be prepared and approved, hotels would be booked, invited guests to Kenya functions identified, list of the Kenya delegation drafted, and the mode of travel arranged. Security agencies would be involved in a big way and media coverage would be planned through the Kenya Broadcasting Corporation.

President Moi liked to travel abroad with huge delegations of between ninety and one-hundred officials, friends and business associates. There would be youth representatives from local universities as well as women leaders. Unlike his predecessor, Mzee Jomo Kenyatta who abhorred air travel, Moi was a consummate traveller who seized every opportunity to board a plane. He rarely turned down an overseas invitation. Almost always, he used the Kenya Airways planes for his travels. In many cases, the airline had to surrender an entire plane for presidential use, which sometimes inconvenienced passengers and resulted in huge financial losses to the airline. If the President was visiting Addis Ababa for three days, for example, the plane and its crew would have to be on the tarmac there for all those days. Heavy expenses would be incurred for the crew as well as for parking fees at the airport. But Moi was not a person who cared about details. Issues of finances were left to appropriate officers, and that is why an accountant was always included in presidential delegations.

Our biggest challenge in protocol was in the crafting of delegates' lists. Every Tom, Dick and Harry among politicians and government officials scrambled to be on that list. Ministers and Members of Parliament believed travelling with the President would give them political mileage and afford them private moments with the Head of State. So there was a lot of jostling ahead of presidential visits. Names would be included then cancelled, then included; people would call in and claim presidential clearance only for us to find out the claim was false, and many such intrigues. We made a lot of enemies with people in high places.

In hotel room allocations, preference was given to the Foreign Minister and the Comptroller of State House who were always placed in rooms closest to the President. This was done to facilitate access and communication with the President. Of course there were others who insisted on being accommodated near the presidential quarters. The decision as to who was booked where in hotels was the prerogative of the Chief of Protocol. The second tier of preference always included cabinet minister Nicholas Biwott and politicians Mark Too and Ezekiel Barngetuny who were the President's closest allies. As much as possible they were accommodated near the presidential suite. Also the President usually took along his private doctor, Dr David Silverstein, a consultant cardiologist at Nairobi Hospital who checked his blood pressure and pulse several times a day. He too was allocated a room nearby. Another regular passenger in the presidential plane was Mohamed Aslam, now deceased, a shrewd wheeler-dealer who had endeared himself to the leadership and became a close friend of the President. Aslam was the Chairman of the Pan-African Group of Companies and was one of the few people who were allowed into the presidential cubicle in the official plane. Aslam's name was later mentioned adversely in a number of reports, including the one prepared by the commission that delved into the mysterious death of Foreign Affairs Minister, Robert Ouko, in 1990. The fifty-five-year-old Asian businessman himself died in unclear circumstances on 8 August 1992, two days after he was rushed to hospital. Another regular companion was Hosea Kiplagat, a politician and businessman.

Usually, about one week before the President departed for an overseas trip, an advance team of one protocol officer, several Special Branch operatives and a crew of journalists and cameramen from KBC would leave to link up with the Kenyan envoy in the receiving country. Once the team got to the destination, the security agents would take charge of the presidential floor while the protocol officers liaised with their host counterparts on meetings and seating arrangements. I was on such advance parties several times and I found that part of the work exciting.

From the time the presidential plane landed in a foreign country, officials in the host country took charge, leaving our protocol officials the coordination tasks; ensuring every delegate was housed, transport was available and invitations to various functions were distributed. There were those official functions where all delegates were invited to and then there were those that were exclusive for the President and a few selected delegates. At the end of the visit, all delegates – including those in the advance party – returned home in the presidential plane.

Back at the Nairobi airport, President Moi would always be welcomed by traditional dancers. There too, because of the presence of foreign envoys, protocol officers would be deployed to work on seating arrangements based on seniority. The Vice President's chair was always placed on the President's right; on his left would be the Foreign Minister.

The Dean of the Diplomatic Corps (one who had served longest in the country) would be seated nearest the top officials in a special area, while the rest of the envoys would be seated in one diplomatic area.

Apart from participating in presidential functions I came across many fun moments as I went about my duties. One memorable moment was a luncheon organised by the Speaker of the National Assembly for visiting British legislators at Parliament Buildings. It was a small affair, about a dozen visitors and about the same number of Kenyan MPs. I was there to assist in the seating arrangement and in meeting the visitors upon their arrival. One of the MPs invited to the luncheon was Mulu Mutisya, a nominated legislator who spoke very few English words. Mutisya was more than a nominated lawmaker. He was a very close friend of former President, Mzee Kenyatta, and the incumbent President Moi, and a highly respected Kamba tribal leader with a rib-cracking sense of humour. Mutisya was among a few non-Kalenjin leaders that Moi came to like a lot. The others were Sharif Nassir, the popular Coast Arab politician, and Kariuki Chotara, a Nakuru-based Kikuyu KANU kingpin. This group provided comic relief to the President, sending him into a paroxysm of laughter and joy during stressful moments.

Worried that his language deficiency could embarrass Parliament and Kenya, as an English-speaking country, I decided to ease possible damage by wedging myself between Mutisya and a British MP. The idea was for me to intercept any question directed at Mutisya without exposing him to humiliation. That meant I had to hijack any comment from the British MP that could leave Mutisya in a state of confused shock. "Have you been to Britain?" the visitor asked Mutisya amid clicking of table-wares and gulps of thick tomato soup. Before I could intercept, Mutisya blurted out words that vaguely translated into something like: "Tomaato sup very sweet," then he let out a deep ha! ha! ha! To rescue the situation, I responded quickly: "No, Honourable Mutisya has not been to Britain, but he is looking forward to visit your beautiful country someday." "That's interesting," the gentleman replied nodding. From there on the Briton realised my neighbour on the left had a language problem, and the visitor became more interested in talking to me directly. The two of us ended up conversing over Mutisya's face while the Kenyan legislator grinned and ferociously attacked his plate.

Apart from all that, the protocol section had a role to play whenever a new envoy arrived and was scheduled to present their credentials to the Head of State. It was mandatory for them to escort the Ambassador from the respective residence to State House and escort them back to their residence after the ceremony.

In 1991, Njuguna Mahugu was appointed Kenya's High Commissioner to Australia and his place was taken by Harry Mutuma Kathurima who was brought in from the Office of the President. Having deputised for Mahugu I thought I would be in line for a promotion to Chief. That did not happen and I felt offended. I did not wait for Kathurima to report to the office; I resigned from the Ministry to return to private practice. The Permanent Secretary, Bethwell Kiplagat, who was on official duties in Mombasa, only came to learn of my impending departure upon his return to the Ministry.

* * *

After resigning from the Ministry of Foreign Affairs I accepted an offer from the Safari Park Hotel as Public Relations Manager in January 1991. The hotel, situated along Thika Road, was owned by a South Korean group whose chairman was also Kenya's Consul General in Seoul. The previous year, President Moi had visited South Korea to attract investments and promote tourism. As usual, a large group of Kenyan businessmen accompanied him, and arrangements had been made for them to meet their South Korean counterparts. The country, which only five decades earlier had been classified as underdeveloped, was at the time of our arrival in Seoul one of the fastest growing economies in the world. It had been almost at par with Kenya on economic indexes at the latter's independence, but was now a major international trader. It belonged to the group of the so-called Asian Tigers along with Singapore, Hong Kong and Taiwan. Nairobi was looking at Seoul as a potential partner in business and investment.

I had arrived in Seoul a few days earlier as part of the advance party. Also on the trail of the President was the Safari Park Hotel's Managing Director. One evening as we sipped vodka on ice, he offered me the job. I made no commitment at that time and I let the matter rest while

I pondered over whether or not to accept the offer. I was certainly not ready to make a move at that time. But when the time came and I saw no prospect of getting a promotion at the Ministry of Foreign Affairs, I decided to make a quantum leap.

I joined the hotel at a time of massive re-building and expansion programme. The transformation of the former Spread Eagle Hotel, at a site once occupied by the British military barracks, was meant to upgrade it into a luxury resort offering a number of ethnic restaurants, a modern casino, an entertainment ring and many other facilities. I sat through management meetings that gave birth to names such as Café Kigwa, The Chiyo, the Nyama Choma Ranch, and all the others. My job was to promote those facilities both in Kenya and internationally. I communicated with tour operators all over the world. By the time the hotel was officially opened by President Moi, we were getting bookings not only from South Korea, but also from all over Europe.

To capture the local market, I produced a number of commercials and ran them on KTN television every day for several months. Our conference facilities were well equipped with modern gadgetry and offered direct competition to amenities in more established five-star hotels in and around Nairobi. The casino was a hangout of some senior government and business people who, at the height of the gambling fever, would offer personal items as collateral to sustain them for just a few more minutes of gambling. The only drawback to marketing the hotel was the distance from the airport and even downtown Nairobi. Thika Road was chaotic and unreliable while the Outer Ring Road that would have provided an easy access from the airport was prone to traffic jams. We had to provide free transport from the city centre every evening to clients wishing to dine and gamble, but even this arrangement was not satisfactory since clients found the bus schedule too confining. The hotel had therefore to rely on wedding parties and conferences, and for a long while these were the main sources of income. There was also some business from airlines for accommodation for their crews.

PR work at the hotel was mainly a management function; it was not a nuts-and-bolts, hands-on, controversy-ridden, rough-and-tumble occupation. Yet, it could also be smooth and alluring. There was one thing I enjoyed most. For several days every month I was required to perform the functions of the Resident Manager, which meant I had to take charge of all facilities, guest relations and personnel up to midnight when most restaurants – excluding the casino – closed down.

At one time the management wanted me to attend a two-year hotel management course at the Roche International School of Hotel Management in Switzerland, one of the top hospitality training institutes in the world, but I declined. At over forty years of age and with a family properly settled in Nairobi, I could not see myself being away for that long period of time. Moreover, I did not want to have to start a new career. After a while though, I concluded good money and perks were not the only reasons for me to cling to the job. There were other equally important things such as job satisfaction and just the pure fun of asking tough questions and getting rude answers that journalism provided. After a little over a year at the job, I resigned.

In the meantime, the Somali President, Siad Barre, who was overthrown by a coalition of opposition forces crossed the El Wak border with over one thousand supporters on 27 January 1991, to seek asylum in Kenya. Barre and his Supreme Revolutionary Council came to power in a coup d' etat on 21 October 1969 a few days after the assassination of President Abdurashid Ali Shermarke.

Although President Moi welcomed him, a crescendo of protests followed. Opposition groups protested against the government footing hotel bills for the deposed leader and his entourage of top officials. Two weeks later, Barre flew to Lagos, Nigeria, where he died of natural causes on 3 January 1995.

Chapter 18

I Thrive on Africa's Chaos

The decade of the 1990s was a period of devastating political upheavals in sub-Saharan Africa. It was a decade of military coups, assassinations and ethnic strife. It was also a decade in which one of Africa's biggest and richest countries, South Africa, took the hard decision of dismantling apartheid in favour of radical democratic reforms. All those events brought a conflation of joy and misery to the Africans. The occurrences also rejuvenated the media industry across the region and opened new avenues for journalists and cameramen.

In Somalia, north of Kenya, President Siad Barre, who had taken power in a bloody military coup in 1969 from Dr Abdurashid Ali Shermarke, was himself overthrown by a coalition of armed clan militias, triggering an immediate power struggle that led to a bitter civil strife and the secession of a part of the country to be known as the Puntland State of Somalia.

Next door in Ethiopia, the revolution tempo had peaked, and after thirty years of an armed liberation struggle, the Eritrea People's Liberation Front (EPLF) finally freed itself from Ethiopian control and declared independence in 1991. Two years later, that independence was legitimised following a UN-supervised referendum on independence, bringing Isaias Afwerki, to the presidency of the Red Sea nation. South of Kenya, Tanzania was struggling to define the Ujamaa (collective villagisation) philosophy of President Julius Nyerere, which was intended to increase agricultural productivity. The idea failed and led to increased poverty and starvation in a country with a great agricultural potential. In the Democratic Republic of Congo, President Mobutu Sese Seko was not sitting easy, thanks to massive corruption, nepotism, embezzlement of state resources and uncontrolled inflation – factors that contributed to his overthrow by Laurent-Desire Kabila in 1997. And in 1994, as Rwandan President Juvenal Habyarimana and his Burundi counterpart Cyprien Ntaryamira approached Kigali from a meeting, their plane was bombed out of the sky and triggered long ethnic atrocities as anti-Tutsi militias, the *Interahamwe,* murdered Tutsis and their Hutu sympathisers.

But the most dramatic event was recorded in South Africa where President F. W. de Klerk began a process of dismantling the brutal apartheid system, which for many years had left the Africans and the Coloureds in a disadvantaged and marginalised state. He lifted a long standing ban against the African National Congress and other political organisations, released Nelson Mandela from twenty-seven years of incarceration, and began talks intended to bring freedom to the majority Africans.

In Kenya, President Moi went through two general elections in 1992 and 1997, both marred by tribal clashes. Corruption and human rights abuses became a matter of grave concern to Kenyans and the international community. At the end of 1991, he abolished the one-party system and allowed formation of opposition political parties to his Kenya African National Union (KANU), but the country remained a powder-keg waiting to explode. Foreign journalists and camera teams flooded Kenya like flies setting up bureaus in downtown Nairobi and in residential areas.

Stories on Rwanda, Somalia and DRC were filed and datelined Nairobi, giving Kenya a leadership role as Africa's communication centre. There was plenty of news to cover. As a journalist I took advantage of the proliferation of news events and set up a bureau at Chester House in Nairobi, a building made famous for its concentration of international journalists. While many hotels refused to host press conferences called by political activists, Chester House provided a forum for anyone who had something to say. The centre was run by the Foreign Correspondents' Association and when I became a member; Horace Awori was Chairman.

I made contacts with various media organisations around the world that were unrepresented in Kenya. One of them was the Argus Group of Newspapers, the largest newspaper stable in South Africa. That contact started off a very fruitful relationship that lasted for a decade. I was appointed the group's correspondent for the whole of Eastern Africa. My stories were carried in the *Johannesburg Star, The Cape Argus, The Mercury, The Daily News, The Pretoria News* and *The Sowetan,* among others. South Africans were hungry for news from Kenya. They wanted to consume everything from a country that had alienated them for decades

– from politics to human interest stories, business and sports. Until then Kenya and South Africa were poles apart. Kenya abhorred apartheid, and its foreign policy was one based on complete isolation of the Boer-led regime. Specifically, President Kenyatta did not want to have anything to do with Pretoria even though in 1978 when he became ill, it was to South Africa that he ran for a surgeon, Dr Christiaan Barnard, a heart specialist. Dr Barnard was the eminent cardiologist who performed the world's first human-to-human transplant. It was reported then that President Kenyatta declined the course of treatment suggested by the South African surgeon. A few months later, while holidaying in Mombasa, he died.

The deep-seated illwill between Kenya and South Africa ended when de Klerk repealed all apartheid laws and the international community lifted sanctions it had imposed in 1961. It was in this year that South Africa left the Commonwealth and declared itself a republic. The release of Nelson Mandela and other political prisoners, and the talks that followed to broaden democratic space and end apartheid, helped to open South Africa to the rest of the world.

I also covered stories for the South African Broadcasting Corporation (SABC) and Radio 702, both based in Johannesburg. I registered a media firm – Copy Deadline Ltd – and equipped it sufficiently. I brought in Edmund Kwena, a seasoned journalist and former foreign editor at the Nairobi-based Nation Media Group, to help me. From our Nairobi bureau we monitored breaking news in Kigali, Mogadishu, Addis Ababa, Dar es Salaam and Kampala, and conducted a lot of phone interviews with newsmakers in those capitals.

Although not on a war path like Rwanda, Somalia and the DRC where people were butchering each other on a large scale, Kenya was nevertheless attracting a lot of attention because of Moi's bad governance. The discovery of a gold export fiasco popularly known as the Goldenberg scandal spotlighted the rot and shamed the regime. The Goldenberg debacle involved a government programme of compensating gold exporters for every foreign exchange brought into the Treasury. The irony was that Kenya did not produce any gold of commercial value and the precious stones were actually smuggled in from the Congo. At the end of the day the country lost through the scandal an equivalent of ten per cent of its GDP.

Like many other locally-based news organisation, the Copy Deadline covered extensively the twin issues of corruption and human rights abuses in Moi's government. We reported on the suppression of the media, the detention of political activists, the tribal clashes in the Rift Valley, and the destruction of the forest cover by unscrupulous loggers, among many other subjects. Many of those stories were considered critical and against the regime. At one time, Information Minister, Johnstone Makau, made it clear that the government would be strict in applying sedition and subversion laws against media groups and individual journalists who abused the freedom of press. I took that warning seriously, although in one report published in South Africa, I wasn't afraid to say that newsmen and women were being arrested for the flimsiest of reasons, physically and verbally abused by politicians, and publicly ridiculed at political rallies.

In 1991, South African Foreign Minister, Pik Botha, visited Kenya. That visit was followed by de Klerk's and reciprocated by Moi the following year. It was during those two visits by the South African leaders that an agreement was reached to open a South African liaison office in Nairobi. The office was promoted to a full embassy when South Africa became independent. Kenya then followed with its own embassy in Pretoria. During all that time, our stories were used widely in South Africa and I suspected being monitored closely by the Kenyan Embassy in Pretoria.

By mid-1990, I began to get feelers that the Kenya government was not happy about my critical write-ups. I confirmed that when I attended a presidential function one evening at the Norfolk Hotel. A senior official confronted me accusing me of being among those who wanted to destroy Moi's regime. She made those allegations within a hearing distance of security officers. That made me very uncomfortable. That was the time when a group known as "February 18 Movement" was allegedly planning to overthrow Moi's government. For the first time in my career, I felt afraid and in danger. That was during the time when journalists were being arrested and detained under the Preservation of Public Security Act. Printing presses were also being destroyed by security agents. In those days, Special Branch agents were known to pounce at night. Sometimes, they would kidnap their targets in broad daylight, some never to be seen again. I was therefore afraid that anything could happen.

The following day I informed my editors in Johannesburg about my fears. I also met with a senior diplomat with whom I was in regular contact and told him of my concerns. Within a day or so, the diplomat had prepared a contingency plan that would have seen me take refuge at one of their unoccupied premises in Muthaiga. I was given the address of the residential premises and a telephone number, which I was to use should I find myself in danger. That assurance however did not stop me from working on an escape plan of my own.

My own Plan B was to take a night bus in disguise, plough through the bush into Tanzania and from there fly to South Africa. My choice of Tanzania was deliberate. I had relatives who could have hidden me in places Moi agents would have had difficulty tracing. Luckily, it did not get to that point. The official who threatened me remained in Moi's government for the whole period of his rule. She was later elected a Member of Parliament in the Grand Coalition government led by President Mwai Kibaki.

* * *

On 13 August 1997, violent attacks occurred at the Coast, which diverted the attention of Kenyans. An estimated two hundred youths raided a police station and a police post at Likoni in Mombasa, killed six police officers, stole guns and burnt buildings. Before the police mobilised support, the raiders had disappeared into the forests further inland. Their target was upcountry people they blamed for grabbing land and taking over jobs they thought should be given to locals. Among those killed and over one hundred injured were Kikuyu, Luhya, Luo and Kamba. According to human rights groups an estimated one hundred thousand people were displaced from homes. The surprise attack disrupted tourism and attracted fresh travel advisories from some Western countries. It also kept news bureaus like Copy Deadline busy for weeks.

For people who had been closely following the brewing tension over land issues at the Coast over the years, the raids did not come as a surprise. The problem of landlessness and squatting had been a powder keg waiting to explode since before independence when Arabs – through the Sultan of Zanzibar – were allocated huge parcels of land to the disadvantage of locals. After independence, many of them left the country earning themselves the title "absentee landlords" but left their holdings in the hands of agents who charged locals rent for use of the land. The land grabbing continued in a big way after independence when President Kenyatta took personal control of prime beach plots and dished them to relatives and cronies. The locals became squatters. Even those who had managed to hold on to their ancestral land had no title deeds to confirm ownership. The Coastals also complained about being short-changed on jobs and educational opportunities.

The witnesses who appeared at the Judicial Commission of Inquiry on Tribal Clashes, which was commissioned on 1 July 1998, by President Moi to investigate tribal wars in the Rift Valley, the Coast and other places, blamed politicians for the violence. Many named Members of Parliament and Councillors from the region as people who had instigated youths to attack up-country people as part of a plot to extend the KANU rule. The witnesses reported that politicians had given the youths money, food and even arms. In fact, prior to the Likoni attack, reports had circulated for weeks that youths were taking oaths in the forests to make them stronger and unafraid of bullets. They were also amassing crude weapons for the attacks.

During the 1992 elections when Kenyans voted in a multiparty set-up after years of one-party rule, the Coastals voted overwhelmingly for KANU. However, there were worries in government that up-country people were about to turn against President Moi in the 1997 polls and a plan was hatched to scare them to leave so as to provide a smooth win for the ruling party. In effect, thousands of up-country people, afraid for their safety, did leave and eventually Moi won another term in office.

The violence at the Coast coincided with an initiative by some regional leaders to form a Coast-based political party. Two months to the 1997 elections, Shirikisho Party of Kenya (SPK) was registered with the objective of championing the same issues raised by the Likoni raiders. The idea of forming the party came from Digo leaders in the South Coast led by Hamisi Jeffa and Mbwana Warrakah who later became Chairman and Secretary General respectively. I took an active part in that initiative and eventually became the Organising Secretary. Leslie Mwachiro from Rabai, who played a key role in the writing of the party constitution, became Treasurer. We also had Omar Kalasinga from Tana River and others from Taita Taveta. Because of the euphoria generated by the Likoni raids, our candidate in Likoni, Suleiman Shakombo, won the parliamentary seat. The following year, in February 1998, I officially resigned from Shirikisho and left for Tanzania.

I now believe that the Likoni raids and the push for equal distribution of resources by the SPK may have contributed to the formation of the Mombasa Republican Council (MRC) in 1999. The MRC had been talking about political and economic marginalisation the same way we did in SPK. The difference was that the MRC was a radical organisation that went beyond the popular common Coast agenda in demanding the secession of the whole province under the slogan "*Pwani si Kenya* (the Coast is not part of Kenya)". Also, while the SPK was a duly registered organisation planning to follow the legal path in resolving the region's issues, the MRC had been adjudged to be an illegal organisation, which was linked to several attacks where ordinary people and police officers were killed and injured. So, as much as many Coastals sympathised with the issues at hand, they disagreed with the methods used to achieve change. Moreover, the Coast is, and the Coast will, always remain part of Kenya.

In the meantime, I began to think about building a home for my family. During all the time of our transient life, we did not have a permanent abode. I thought time was right for us to settle down. I set out to find a small farm somewhere at the Coast where we could build a house, keep a few goats, chickens and ducks, and once in a while, when time permitted, relax with the rural folk. I finally found a piece of land at Mtepeni village, twenty kilometres north of Mombasa, and seven kilometres west of the buoyant Mtwapa township. Mtwapa is known for its twenty-four-hour economy with lots of bars, prostitution, illegal drugs and *nyama choma* (roast meat) joints. But in the common language of city planning, Mtwapa is just a big slum town trying to look chic; parading its women in skimpy dresses and playing ear-shattering music at every corner.

The land was a four acre property on a flat land right in the middle of Mtepeni village owned by a person from the Central region. It had tall but aged cashew-nut trees, several mango and coconut trees, and possessed great potential for vegetable and maize farming. I loved the place at first sight and wasted no time in closing the deal at seventy-five thousand Kenya shillings per acre. Many upcountry people were now afraid of staying in the interior and the low selling price reflected the panic that had gripped non-Coastals. Villagers helped me clean it up and within weeks we were laying the foundation for a three-bedroomed house, a spacious sitting room, a gym area and two bathrooms. We manicured the grounds and planted exotic trees and flowers. Since we didn't have enough money to build the house all at once, we began with one room and a toilet. It took nearly ten years to achieve the level of comfort we wanted in a rural setting.

At my office in Nairobi, the United Press International, one of the leading news agencies in the world, had come on board, and the Argus Group had changed its name to the Independent Group of Newspapers. The war in Rwanda was raging furiously. In Somalia, the American government had intervened with soldiers to fight the self-proclaimed government of Mohamed Farrah Aideed. In subsequent battles, Somali militia downed an American plane. US soldiers who were captured following that encounter were dragged along the streets of Mogadishu, a scene condemned by many nations and organisations including the UN. That incident in 1993 compelled President Bill Clinton to withdraw all US forces Somali in May 1994. Copy Deadline thrived on those events and for several years the business was good.

But that boom in business did not last long. The Internet, which by now had made a splash into the corporate world, the media and homes, became the new medium of communication. The telex, the fax machine and the popular tape recorders, instantly became obsolete as tools of news dissemination. Now people could access information from any part of the world much faster and more efficiently through the use of laptops and desktop computers. The characteristics of news collection and dissemination had changed forever.

Around 1997, we began to notice a slow-down in business. It was much easier for news organisation to scan the Internet for on-time information and use that information to compile news reports than to maintain a correspondent with a monthly retainer. The Independent

Group informed me they would no longer pay me a retainer although they would continue to accept analyses, while the UPI slowly reduced use of my copy. With the virtual loss of those two major outlets, the business became untenable. In February 1998 – more than seven years after I ventured into independent journalism – I closed down the company and sought fortunes elsewhere.

Chapter 19

Journey Across the Border

In June 1998, I was approached by the Dar es Salaam-based Media Holdings Ltd to become chief editor of its weekly newspaper, *The Express*. The owner of the tabloid was Riyaz Gulamani, an Indian tycoon with extensive interests in insurance, banking, public relations and marketing, among others. Gulamani was affiliated to nineteen companies – as chairman or director. He was a suave and shrewd middle-aged entrepreneur with wide contacts in and outside Tanzania. The offer from *The Express* was quite attractive. I was to relocate to the Tanzanian capital and direct the editorial team from its Raha Tower offices along Morogoro Road.

Dar es Salaam was not entirely new to me. I had worked there briefly in the 1960s on relief duties when Robert Makange, editor of *Mwafrika*, a Swahili daily run by the Nation Group went on leave. Since then I had made a number of personal trips to Tanzania to visit relatives and friends. I was therefore returning to familiar grounds. Moreover, Dar es Salaam and Mombasa have almost similar characteristics. They are both Swahili-speaking towns, have almost similar slave trade experiences, are along the Indian Ocean coast with beautiful, sugary beaches, and share similar cultural values. So in many ways, it was like going to another home.

After receiving a one-year work permit I settled down to familiarise myself with the editorial policy and the market. I had a small team of journalists that, though not well trained, was nevertheless eager. The paper had a very small market share compared to the other English weeklies in Dar es Salaam. It had a vague editorial policy and a weak and poorly paid editorial team. The editorial policy needed to be re-defined and the journalists motivated. That proved to be difficult due to the management's fixation for cutting corners. They felt more comfortable hiring untrained writers and correspondents and paying them meagre salaries than investing in quality personnel and improving the value of the paper. For advertising revenue, the paper relied heavily on government institutions and friendly Indian-owned companies and little was done to build a more broad-based business clientele. The twin presence of a weak editorial policy and a narrow advertising base stifled the paper's growth.

Every week the general manager, the head of the group's public relations company and I would attend an editorial meeting chaired by Gulamani at his offices not too far from our own. As is in any such editorial meeting, I, the chief editor, would brief the meeting on the major stories we were working on, and the general manager would give circulation and advertising figures of the past week and prospects for the following issue. We would also discuss staff and logistical matters.

There was one other problem. The difference between my salary and emoluments of my juniors was quite big and that created animosity. I was paid handsomely and my salary was in the bank on time. Conversely, my junior colleagues were poorly remunerated and their salaries were always late. As expected in such situations, jealousy kicked in. I was no longer referred to as the "chief" by my staff but as "that Kenyan". My instructions no longer mattered and a silent go-slow campaign emerged, jeopardising deadlines and creating a not too conducive office atmosphere. The management did not see that as a problem so I continued to work with the team the best way I could.

The Express was more of an entertainment tabloid directed at the Indian community in Tanzania. I tried to transform it into a bold, news publication with a strong editorial position, but this did not work. The management did not want to tread into uncharted waters. English newspapers were fewer compared to Kiswahili papers. Apart from *Business Times* and *The Express*, there were the government-owned *Daily News* and *Sunday News*, *The African* edited by veteran journalist Jenerali Ulimwengu, and the *Guardian*, which was part of Reginald Mengi's IPP Empire. Mengi is one of the most enterprising businesspeople in Tanzania. Apart from owning a big stable of newspapers and television stations, he is also an industrialist with investments in soft drink and mineral water production, among others. In 2013, the prestigious Forbes Magazine listed him at number 34 of the 50 richest Africans. He also chairs a number of boards in the public and private sector.

The working environment at *The Express* was bearable but not excellent. Because the editorial policy was undefined and only dependent on prevailing events at any given time, it was difficult for me as editor-in-chief to take chances with political commentaries. The owners had vast investments in the country and, understandably, wanted to protect those investments. I therefore left it to the management to write the editorials.

I had fallen in love with Zanzibar and every so many weeks I would board a ferry for the ninety-minute water journey to the Stone Town. The islands of Zanzibar (also called Unguja) and Pemba have a special meaning to me given their long, sad history of slavery as well as their attachment to my own ancestry. A walk through the narrow roads, visiting the holding cells, seeing chains bolted on hard, concrete walls, and studying the poignant goodbye messages scrawled on the walls by slaves on their way to the unknown, overwhelmed me with emotions. They gave me a deep feeling of inexplicable indignation and hatred for the people who, for years, traded, tortured and humiliated my people. At one time I went to Bagamoyo, the Zaramo country of my grandparents and presumably great grandparents. I visited the station and saw, in a register, names of tens of thousands of slaves who had passed through the town on their way to Zanzibar and across the ocean, and wondered whether or not some of those names could belong to the ancestors I never got to know about. It was profoundly poignant.

* * *

In September 1999, after one-and-half years at *The Express*, the management of Business Times Ltd – a rival publication – asked me to join them as chief editor of its English flag-ship, the *Business Times*. I accepted without a second thought more so because the company was bigger and offered better opportunities. The terms and conditions of service were about the same as those at *The Express* except that the salary was to go up by a third over what I was getting from the Media Holdings Ltd.

The Business Times Ltd was an African-owned company started in 1988 by Richard Nyaulawa, an American-educated management and financial analyst. Apart from the *Business Times,* it had three other publications in its stable, all in Kiswahili: *Majira, Dar Leo* and *Spoti*

Starehe. Unlike *The Express*, which outsourced its printing works, the *Times* had its own plant situated along Lugoda Street in the semi-industrial area of Gerezani. The paper was a broadsheet (not tabloid-sized as the *Express*), and as the name implied, had business as its core focus. My role was to guide the paper to greater circulation figures by introducing some element of investigative journalism and a broader approach to matters of finance, trade and investment.

Be that as it was, the management also had other bigger ideas. It wanted to add another publication in its stable and asked me to come up with a concept paper for a general English publication specialising in politics, economy, entertainment, health and sports. I worked on the design and layout, borrowing heavily on the style and approach used by Kenya's premier publications, the *Daily Nation* and *The Standard*. The Management gave me complete freedom to fashion the editorial policy of the paper. At the same time I continued to act as chief editor of the *Business Times*. The paper was an authority on matters of business and finance, and attracted a lot of advertising from companies and the government.

The management decided to call the newpaper the *Sunday Times*. On 31 October 1999, the first issue hit the streets of Dar es Salaam with a bang. Every buyer on that day received a *Sunday Times* T-shirt as part of the promotion campaign. I was on the streets myself leading the vendors and getting myself known. At the end of the day the results were good. We had sold three thousand copies of the first edition, thanks to the front-page headline: "The story can now be told of how... An Asian Tycoon Fled with Billions." The tycoon in question was none other than Gulamani, the owner of *The Express* who had fled the country in the heat of a financial scandal involving his companies a month earlier. Gulamani's flight was initially reported by the regional paper, *The EastAfrican*, as a news story on 21 September. The paper had said: "The Tanzania insurance market has been thrown into a panic by the unexplained departure of the Chairman of the country's insurance firm, Tudor Insurance, Mr Riyaz Gulamani, on August 3," and went on to talk of the mysterious withdrawal of a large sum of money from Exim Bank of which Gulamani was Chairman.

Our story on 31 October was investigative and took an inside look at the man. Headlined "Asian Tycoon Fled with Billions," the story talked of the "biggest scandal in Tanzanian history" that had left behind financial ruin and a shattered business empire. It also quoted his domestic workers on the events that preceded his departure. It was a major print coup and awakened the Tanzania media fraternity to a new type of journalism in a country used to bland, non-controversial approach to news coverage. That exposé was part of a three-piece series on Gulamani's financial shenanigans, carried in three consecutive Sundays with front page headlines: "Riyaz Gulamani Arrested in Dubai "(7 November 1999) in which we traced his footprints from his alleged hideout in Canada to his business interests in the Gulf, and "How Gulamani Milked his Firms Dry" (14 November 1999) in which we delved into the alleged plundering of huge sums of money from his own Exim Bank. The series created a lot of interest in the Tanzanian business community and no doubt within government too.

Every week I carried a personal column, *Joe Khamisi On Sunday*, a hard-hitting commentary on the functions of the government, its leaders and the general political landscape. In the maiden issue, under the headline: "The Union: Waffling and Shuffling Won't Do", I warned that the union between Tanganyika and the islands of Pemba and Unguja was "likely to mutate into a political juggernaut," in view of the brewing calls for full autonomy from island leaders and argued that President Nyerere's dream of a united Tanzania was under threat less than two years after his death. I criticised the Tanzanian government for suppressing debate on matters related to the Union. I wrote: "So far, the issue as to whether the Union should remain as it is, modified to allow a third government or whether it should be disbanded altogether has been muted under a political cloak... because no one could dare to raise the issue for fear of upsetting the mercurial Mwalimu Julius Nyerere, the man who crafted, nurtured and protected it. But (with the death of Nyerere) things have changed... and the nation must be prepared to see the Union issue move from the back burner to the front burner. Ordinarily that is where it should have been anyway." Then I went on to add: "Sweeping the matter under the carpet is a sure way of courting disaster. Waffling and shuffling over it only prolong the agony. And just ignoring it is bad politics and goes against the letter and spirit of democracy and risks exposing the government to condemnation by advocates of transparency and good governance."

In the issue of 14 November, my commentary was headlined: "A village Clown? We have One Too!" an attack on opposition leader Reverend Christopher Mtikila of the Democratic Party for his careless celebratory comments following the death of Nyerere. Mtikila, I felt, had shown disrespect by flying his "outdated Tanganyika flag at full mast at his residence in Ilala, by manufacturing hate cassettes and even taunting the police to arrest him... the diminutive man of the cloth behaves like a bully, a spoilt child who wants to draw attention... Through his comical and preposterous action, Mtikila has exposed himself as a man unfit to lead the nation that is Tanzania." In another critical commentary carried in the *Sunday Times* on 21 November, I called for the jailing of corrupt officials in the government who were perennially mentioned in the Auditor General's report. "What the Government must do," I said, "is to move in with alacrity, arrest the culprits and haul them into courts to face the music. If Mkapa cannot do this, then his whole declared intent of ridding the country of corruption will be seen as nothing but political lip service."

Another article which must have infuriated the government and the ruling Chama cha Mapinduzi (CCM) was headlined: "Will CCM Survive a Power Struggle?" In that 7 November commentary, I faulted the nomination process of 1995 in which Benjamin Mkapa was controversially picked as the party's candidate and, therefore, its presidential nominee. I implied that Mkapa did not win the nomination; rather it was stolen from Jakaya Kikwete at the instigation of the CCM old guard. "The weeding out process was by no means popular... But it was the eventual unpopular choice of Mkapa that hurt the party most. Most thought the youthful Kikwete, an economics graduate and an ex-Army Lieutenant Colonel, was the choice of the majority. He never saw the light of day because the process was grossly manipulated at very high level by CCM big wigs."

With that article the patience of the government had run out. Those who had not known my origin found out that I was not even a Tanzanian. How dare, some asked, a foreigner come into the country and criticise our leadership? Some Letters to the Editor supported my position but the old guard did not. Two things went against me almost simultaneously: one, the rage and hidden influence of my former boss, Gulamani; and two, the anger and disgust within the political establishment over my critical commentaries. Interestingly, the management did not say anything about my bombastic style of journalism. The paper was selling well and advertisements were trickling in cautiously. The prospects looked good.

I suspected a third reason for the swift reaction of pro-establishment people. Almost at the very beginning of *Sunday Times*, I brought on board, as a guest columnist, a former detainee and one time political enemy of the administration, Wolfgango Dourado. For those who don't remember Dourado, he was the outspoken Attorney General of Zanzibar during the rule of President Sheikh Abeid Amani Karume. He opposed the Union of Tanganyika and Zanzibar and did not hide his feelings even though he held a senior judicial position. In an interview with the BBC World Service in London in 1984, he called the Union "constitutionally illegal", thus attracting the wrath of President Nyerere who promptly had him arrested and jailed without taking him to court. Amnesty International declared him a "prisoner of conscience" and rallied the world to agitate for his release. Three months later, he was released and reinstated to his job. A Tanzanian-born lawyer of Goan origin, Dourado never forgave the government for that arbitrary detention. So, when I gave him a column to write – he named it: Nothing but the Truth – he finally found a platform to pummel the authorities, further exasperating Dar es Salaam. In his first write-up, he took issue with Mkapa's statement during Nyerere's burial that, as president, he (Mkapa) would deal harshly with those opposing the Union. He asked sarcastically in his column of 21 November 1999: *Who would deal with them?* "There is no one who wishes to break the Union," he wrote. "If there are such persons then President Mkapa should name them and show evidence to support the charge," he added lawyerly. He went on: "There is, however, a big group of persons in Zanzibar and on the Mainland, who wish to have a federal structure with the Government of Tanganyika, the Government of Zanzibar and the Federal Government of Tanzania... If President Mkapa cannot see this he should resign forthwith and not cling to power in the hope that he will, through him, allow Nyerere to rule from the grave." That commentary was vintage Dourado. Nyerereists and Unionists rebuked Dourado. In one rejoinder, Michael Kimaro accused the Zanzibari of concocting "half-truths and distortions" in his arguments over the relations between the two entities, concluding frustratingly that "perhaps it is time for him to be dispatched to his ancestral village (read Goa) where he might be able to speak on behalf of his own people."

The ruling party CCM and the government began to take a serious note of what was being published in the *Sunday Times*. During all that time the management watched on the side lines and not once did it interfere in our editorial preferences. With all those negatives stacked against me, my goose as chief editor of the *Business Times* was cooked. The Tanzania government had finally found a legitimate reason to throw me out. It would have been crude for people to know I had been expelled for abusing press freedom. That would have raised nasty reactions from human rights organisations. Now, they had a legal explanation: being in Tanzania illegally. On 17 December 1999, I was taken to court and fined the equivalent of thirty thousand Kenya shillings, which the company promptly paid. The same day, I was issued with a deportation order to leave Tanzania within seven days.

My expulsion was news. South African papers affiliated to the Independent Group, my former employer, carried a blunt story to the effect that I had been deported for criticising the government. In retrospection, I can now admit I made a tactical mistake by taking an anti-establishment stance against a foreign government. Perhaps I had become too overconfident; perhaps I had carried my hospitality too far or perhaps it was just the journalist in me, applying the old adage popularised by England's Duke of Wellington way back in 1824: publish and be damned! And damned I surely was. I failed to recognise that Tanzania was intolerant to criticism, more so from a foreigner.

I took solace in the fact that I was not the first Kenyan journalist to be shown the border. Way back in the early 1960s, Francis Rafiki Raymond, a reporter for the Nation Group was the first one to be booted out for crossing the threshold of Nyerere's socialist policies. On 29 June 2005, four senior editors – Mutuma Mathiu, Mbogo Murage, Chaacha Mwita and Kizito Namulanda – employed by the Nation Group, but seconded to *The Citizen* in Dar es Salaam, were thrown out for almost the same work permit reasons that got me out. *The Citizen* was owned by Mwananchi Communications Ltd in which the Kenyan company was reported to own majority shareholding.

The following day on 18 December 1999, I boarded a Kenya Airways plane and an hour later I was in Nairobi. I left the *Business Times* to follow up on the issue of my status. Although the deportation order was rescinded six months later I never returned to my job. Nevertheless, I have made many trips to "the port of peace" since then.

Chapter 20

A Lucky Entry into KBC

My wife and I spent Christmas of 1999 at Mtepeni village. We visited my father at Kanamai and took time to celebrate my birthday which, as I mentioned earlier, falls on 31 December. As the New Year began, I was tipped that the position of Managing Director at the KBC was vacant. My informant told me the contract of the previous holder, Simon Anabwani, had expired and the President had declined to renew it. The government was therefore looking for a suitable candidate to replace him.

General elections were only two years away and President Moi was looking for someone he could trust to steer the public broadcaster through what was his most critical polls. After the introduction of multipartyism at the end of 1991, Kenya held elections in 1992 and 1997 and was now gearing itself for the 2002 polls. In the two earlier elections, the opposition had been fragmented and Moi had sailed through easily. This time around, talks were taking place amongst the various opposition leaders to put up a united front against the incumbent. The second President of the Republic of Kenya had a huge challenge ahead of him.

I did not know Moi personally. When I was at the Ministry of Foreign Affairs, he only dealt with the Chief of Protocol. To me, he was a larger-than-life personality who wielded immense powers. I feared him more than I respected him. Moreover, when I was a correspondent for foreign media houses, I had condemned his policies and ridiculed his regime and was on the radar of the Special Branch.

But I personally knew Lee Njiru, his trusted press secretary, who was once my workmate at the Ministry of Information. After he moved to the Presidential Press Service we lost touch. However, he remembered me well. I called him to inquire about the job because I knew he could pull a few strings (in Kenya, influence is everything). Since the vacancy had been open for a few months, there were several other people ahead of me with strong political connections who had expressed interest in the job. Mine was therefore a long shot, but I had nothing to lose, I told myself. I knew professional qualification alone – which I thought I had – would not get me the job. Loyalty and ethnicity, I believed, would top the list, then management and finally experience in radio and television. I may have had problems with Moi's style of governance but I knew I was loyal to my country. As for ethnicity, I was sure my minority background would be a plus. My management and journalism experiences would also come in handy.

Like all public broadcasters in other countries, KBC was considered a strategic organisation and a politically important agency of the government. After I had talked to Njiru and he had consulted, he called me back and told me to go and see Titus Naikuni, the Permanent Secretary in the Ministry of Transport and Communication. I knew at that point that things were not bad at all. Moi may have been swayed by the fact that I was the son of his one-time friend and LegCo colleague, Francis Joseph Khamisi. I was known to be apolitical although I was a registered member of the ruling party, KANU. In other words, I was safe to work with as his broadcasting guru.

Naikuni, formerly Managing Director of Magadi Soda Company Limited, had been hired as part of the so-called Dream Team, a group of half a dozen top technocrats recommended by the World Bank to rid Moi's government of corruption and mismanagement. The team was led by palaeonthropologist-cum-conservationist, Richard Leakey, as Head of the Public Service. Naikuni assessed me and then sent me to Leakey, who asked me a few questions of an integrity nature. I informed him of my immigration troubles in Tanzania, but he shrugged them off and thought they were inconsequential. I wanted to make sure the government was fully away of the matter to avoid any questions in future. Leakey then sent me to the Minister for Communications, Musalia Mudavadi. It was the Minister, I was told, who was the appointing authority and who was to draft a Gazette Notice for the President's signature, but it took two days to see him. I started worrying that somebody somewhere was trying to play tricks. Kenya is a country of intrigues, and in those days, one was not sure of an appointment until an announcement was broadcast on KBC.

I finally got to meet Mudavadi who showed me a draft contract that had the same terms and condition of service as those of the departing Managing Director, which carried a basic salary of seventy thousand

Kenya shillings per month. I did not complain, but when the draft went to Naikuni he amended it and hiked the salary to two hundred thousand shillings per month. He told me to report to Broadcasting House only after I heard the announcement. That evening my family and I sat attentively before the television set, and there it was at the top of the news. "President Daniel arap Moi has appointed Joseph Matano Khamisi as the new Managing Director of the Kenya Broadcasting Corporation." We jumped in excitement. At that time, I remembered the saying: when one door closes another opens, a saying uttered by telephone inventor Alexander Graham Bell.

At 7 o'clock on the morning of 17 February 2000, I reported for work at the Broadcasting House (BH) where I found Naikuni waiting to introduce me to senior staff. My wife, Doretha, drove me to KBC in our old Toyota Corolla. In the evening I returned home in a chauffeur-driven Volvo saloon. I was returning to work at the broadcasting station for the second time having been there thirty-five years earlier as a reporter and news editor when KBC had been nationalised and renamed the Voice of Kenya (VoK). In 1989, it reverted to its old name KBC through an Act of Parliament, and now I was going to be the Chief Executive. I found not much had changed. The tiny newsroom and its bruised desks were still there. The toilets were where they used to be, except this time around the stench was unbearable, sipping through the corridors like a spike. The only new things at BH were a huge, colourful gate and sentry house at the entrance to keep away trespassers and several pre-fabricated houses sandwiched together to provide additional room capacity. Other than cosmetic changes, the public broadcasting facility remained virtually the same outwardly and inwardly. The library containing the largest selection of music was still intact, but the brand new carpets in the studios were faded and the electronic equipment rather outdated. Nevertheless, the popular shows of my days, the Sundowner and Lunch Time music, continued to serenade people with soothing, soft soul and rhythmic beats.

* * *

For about a year my father had been ailing. He had a prostrate condition that was making it difficult for him to control his bladder. At eighty-seven years old doctors did not see the need for an operation and decided instead to keep him comfortable by prescribing medication and installing a catheter to facilitate urination. When I visited him at the end of February 2000, I found him not in the best state of health. A man who had once been robust now looked frail; his eyes darting about the room and his skin wrinkled. I knew then that his days were numbered. I had started work at KBC only two weeks earlier and had gone to Mombasa to give him the good news. I knew he would be proud to know that the kid who used to skip school and cause trouble at home was now the Managing Director of the largest media organisation in Kenya.

Unfortunately, I did not get that chance to make him proud. He was in no condition to hear and comprehend anything around him. I left that room regretting that I had missed the only opportunity in my life to make my father happy in his deathbed. A few days after I saw him, on 1 March 2000, he passed away. The pillar of the Khamisi family had finally gone to rest. I found out later that my daughter, Pili, who had earlier visited her ailing grandfather, had informed him of my promotion. She thought he understood what she was saying. The irony was that a man who had sacrificed so much for his country, who had made so many friends at high places in Kenya and beyond during his active days, was all alone in death. What consoled the family were the many messages of condolence that poured in from many quarters including from the surviving LegCo Members, President Moi and Taaita Towett and Dr Gikonyo Kiano who was my Chairman at KBC.

As practical as my father was to reality, he had bought a white suit to wear on his way to his maker years in advance. He even picked his burial site, next to his dear wife, Mary Tabu, and ordered that there should be no *matanga* (after-burial vigil). We followed his will to the letter and buried him in a befitting Catholic requiem mass at his Kanamai farm. With his death, I assumed the leadership of the family.

* * *

At KBC not everything was going on well. I quickly found out that something was terribly wrong; that the Corporation was losing millions of shillings through corruption and fraud. Much of the loss was taking place in the Marketing Department. I ordered an internal probe which confirmed illegal payments of commissions to sales representatives. I informed the Permanent Secretary and the Board, and we all agreed that everyone in that department had to be vetted to weed out the culprits and save the innocent. I hired three marketing practitioners from the private sector on the recommendation of the Permanent Secretary to carry out the interviews and make recommendations to the Corporation. Suspecting some of them would lose their jobs the marketers ganged up and took me to court alleging a plot to fire them. The case dragged on for weeks but nothing came out of it. Meanwhile, the interviews went on and those found culpable were fired. By restructuring the marketing department I saved the Corporation millions of shillings which had been going into individual pockets.

At the time of my arrival at KBC staff morale was at its lowest. There had been no salary revisions for years, there were too many artists who had worked for a long time on casual terms, there was rampant malingering, the buildings were in a state of disrepair, the equipment was from the 1960s, and some managers were occupying positions they were not qualified to hold. Bottom-line, KBC was not making money. It was accumulating debts. It had huge outstanding bills with foreign lenders, with the power company, with the water authority, with the taxman, with the staff pension, and with medical schemes, among others. On the other side of the balance sheet, government institutions, politically connected people and others owed KBC millions of shillings, which the Corporation could not collect for one reason or the other. With an accumulated deficit of six billion shillings the Corporation was technically insolvent.

Unfortunately for a Corporation as important as KBC, no financial support was forthcoming from the Exchequer despite the fact that the broadcaster was spending a large chunk of its air time promoting government projects, broadcasting government functions, and running civic education programmes. KBC was the only public broadcaster in the world that I knew was operating without public support.

Despite all that, I knew I had to move fast to secure staff confidence. I ordered a review of all salaries including emoluments paid to correspondents and artists, and launched a vigorous exercise of mopping up outstanding debts from individuals and companies. I also launched an incentive award system for marketers to ensure active marketers were rewarded. I made a point of personally visiting offices of Ministers and government institutions to demand and collect outstanding monies.

In the meantime, new privately-owned radio and television stations were entering the market like swarms of locusts and eating into the KBC market share. The previous administration had launched Metro Radio, a sports and entertainment channel. When I came in and saw the precarious financial condition of the station, I mooted the idea of a commercial television station, so Metro Television, an exclusively entertainment channel was born. I went around the country collecting from our various stations surplus but usable transmission equipment and from the salvaged pieces and a little financial injection I launched two FM stations, Coro FM for Central Kenya and Pwani FM for the Coast. The stations were meant to compete with newly installed stations like Kameme FM. I had hoped that by doing all that, the Corporation's financial situation would improve but the problem was so big that the situation did not significantly get better. And since the government was not coming through with support, we got to a point where we had to resort to bank overdrafts to pay salaries.

The Board of Directors, chaired by Dr Julius Gikonyo Kiano, ran out of ideas on how to lead the management. We had written so many letters to the Treasury for funding without any success. We operated literally on a month-to-month basis, ensuring in the process that salaries were paid on time, while we negotiated for time with our debtors.

As head of KBC I was automatically Chairman of Multichoice Kenya in which the public broadcaster had interest. Multichoice was established as a joint venture between KBC and the South African-based Multichoice Africa in February 1995, when the only major competitor was the Kenya Television Network (KTN). It was the time when the country had begun a programme of liberalising broadcasting, and Multichoice was permitted to broadcast through DStv. I chaired the local board of Multichoice and attended company meetings in Nairobi and at its headquarters in South Africa. In 2001, I had an opportunity of attending a Multichoice Board function in Cape Town, one of the most beautiful cities in Africa. The modern buildings, the super highways and the sheer cleanliness of the city stood out as a major achievement of the government. Most of the infrastructure was built by the apartheid regime but the new African-led government had done wonders in maintaining the town's ambiance.

The most memorable moments were when my wife and I took a cable car and went atop the Table Mountain, the most visited attraction in Cape Town. The cable took only five minutes to transport us to over one-thousand metres above ground and gave us a spectacular three-hundred-sixty degree view of the city centre and the Atlantic Ocean. Robben Island, the jail where Nelson Mandela spent most of his twenty-seven years as a political prisoner, was in plain view beyond the waters. After independence, the island was declared a historical monument and can now be reached by boat. We didn't get a chance to go to the island, but I promised myself that one day I will go there as a pilgrimage to Africa's most prominent citizen who died on 5 December 2013.

In the meantime, political interests in government were making it difficult for us at KBC to create a level and just playing ground for all political players. Even as Moi's nemesis, Raila Odinga, was discussing disbandment of his National Development Party (NDP) and a merger with KANU, the government did not want to let go its stranglehold on the station when it came to opposition coverage. We were under constant pressure to headline Moi regardless of whether or not an event was newsworthy, and to follow down the line with coverage of officials according to seniority as had been the practice before I joined. So, the President's story or stories would be followed by the Vice President's, then Ministers', Provincial commissioners', District Commissioners', District Officers' and Chiefs' in that order. Where there were stories involving more than one Minister, the editor was expected to use common sense and ascertain who among the two was closer to Moi. I didn't think it was Moi who gave that directive and suspected it came from officials either at the Office of the President or at State House itself.

I remember a time when James Orengo, an opposition politician, was touring and addressing meetings at the Coast. As usual he castigated Moi on issues of human rights abuses (such criticisms were common in those dark days of rights violations). Ordinarily our reporter would not have bothered to file such a story, but for the changing nature of news gathering we were trying to introduce at KBC. The news editor did not know what to do with the story when he received it so he referred it to me. I read the story and decided that we would air it. That decision triggered a chain of reactions and threats of dismissal from State House.

For a while I thought the news editor was going to be fired. However, I told Lee Njiru, Moi's press secretary, that I was fully responsible and if there was anyone to be sacked it was me. That matter ended there. Such was our determination to bring changes in the way KBC handled political news. Those small steps gradually led to positive reforms so much so that by the time Moi left in 2002, the KBC newsroom was offering much equitable coverage of events. There was no turning back.

As part of a programme to foster closer relations with other public broadcasters, I was invited to visit China by the CCTV (Central China Television) station early in 2001. I chose two other officials from KBC, Joseph Murema from TV and Engineer Otieno from the Technical Department, to accompany me. I also bought an extra ticket for my wife, Doretha. Our first city of landing was Guangzhou, one of the largest Chinese cities on the picturesque Yangtze River. The vastness of the city seen from the air was mind-boggling. I had heard a lot about the masses of people in China, which I confirmed when we got to Guangzhou, to Shanghai, a shipping and trading region on the eastern coast, and to Beijing, the capital. The streets were crowded with people and all manner of vehicular vessels. The cities were noisy, and the air was polluted with fumes mixed with the sweet smoke of fried foods emanating from every corner.

The Chinese are fantastic hosts. They spoilt us. We were booked in top hotels and, at times, it looked as if we were spending more time eating rice, noodles, dumplings, duck and even frog, than doing anything else. We did a lot of sight-seeing in the company of official guides. We toured the Tiananmen Square, venue of the Cultural Revolution of the 1960s and 1970s, the Forbidden City, which was once occupied by former Emperors, and the Great Wall of China, the ultimate attraction north of Beijing built many centuries ago to stop nomadic incursions and military intrusions. However, the purpose of our visit to China was not lost. Our objective was to visit radio and television facilities, including transmission stations and studios, and to hold talks with senior broadcasting and government officials.

Both CCTV and KBC had expressed interest in entering into a bilateral exchange of programmes and the visit was intended to lay the foundation for that agreement. We had very useful discussions, which were followed by a visit to Kenya by a Chinese delegation led by Xu Guangchun, Director of State Administration of Radio, Film and Television. Eventually, an agreement was signed for an exchange of programmes. At the end of the day, the two countries did implement that exchange.

Back at the village, construction work on our house at Mtepeni was nearing completion. The original one room had mutated into three very comfortable bedrooms, a modern kitchen, a huge sitting room with big windows that projected an illusion of openness and warmth. The gardens were immaculate. Eventually generators for power were replaced with electricity, when I "pulled a line" to my house from three kilometres away. That gave households on the power line and those beyond my own house an easy and cheaper way of installing electricity for their own personal or business use.

The house was finally ready in 2003, in time for the wedding of my second daughter Pili to Chiza, a schoolmate from the International School of Kenya in Nairobi. From Nairobi they had travelled separately to America for University education, graduated and were now ready to marry. For the second time, Doretha and I were the proudest of parents. Maria, our eldest daughter, had been earlier married in America to Sydney from Ghana, a fellow medical student. When they visited Kenya we took them through the Catholic rites. Now it was her sister's turn. Chiza's relatives came all the way from Tanzania and my uncle, Leones Matano, came with a large group of distant relatives and dancers from Dar es Salaam. A live band led by Mwaeba, an old musician friend played as the two took the traditional Mijikenda vows of *kuhaswa*. Advice was given to the newly-weds and instead of using *mnazi* – because both did not drink and did not want to smell like booze – the elders who blessed them, sprayed water unto their chests to signify their acceptance in the community. Afterwards, we danced and ate until the wee hours of the morning.

* * *

While at KBC in 2000, I started looking for a project that would be of benefit to the community at Mtepeni. We consulted and the villagers settled on a health facility. Although I took it up as a personal challenge I wanted everyone to be involved by contributing the little they had to a common kitty even though I knew of the extent of poverty in the area. I held three fund-raising meetings and led from the front by making much bigger contributions. We estimated we would need one-point-five million Kenya shillings to complete the first phase of the project which was to comprise a clinic, a toilet and an open well. By the end of the third *harambee* we had collected over three hundred thousand shillings. By that time, the villagers were weary and their contributions became fewer and smaller. I had to reach out for outside help. I sent a proposal to the Ministry of Health for assistance and the response was good. The Permanent Secretary, Dr Julius Meme, agreed to mobilise finances from various departments in his Ministry. At our next fundraiser event, Dr Meme and several senior officials from the Ministry attended and pledged huge amounts. With about seven hundred thousand shillings now in the bank, I wrote to the Chandaria Foundation and Manu Chandaria, always gracious and magnanimous, agreed to take over the project. We sent our monetary share to the Foundation and the Foundation brought in materials and artisans. Within a few weeks the Chandaria Community Health Centre was ready for use.

The dispensary was one of my biggest personal achievements in any community. The bug of development had caught up with me. I wanted to do more though. So I started bee-keeping projects for self-help youth groups. I bought the necessary materials, brought in experts from Honey Care, a private sector social enterprise, to teach the youth how to set and maintain beehives as well as how to harvest honey. Company personnel made regular visits to purchase the produce. That gave members of the groups a big financial boost. Mtepeni self-help project was one of the most active and continues to benefit from the initiative even today. In addition, I acquired, through my friend in Nairobi, Niru Patel, thousands of tissue culture banana plants for distribution to farmers across Bahari Constituency. I built water wells and purchased school uniforms for the less privileged children.

That good work did not go unnoticed and people in the village started urging me to go for an elective position. However, I had been away from Kilifi District for too long and I didn't think anyone would take notice. My motivation for community projects was driven by the state of poverty and hopelessness I was witnessing. Many times I saw sick people being transported on beds to health facilities away from the village. Moments later, the same people would return wailing, their loved ones having died on the way.

After weighing all the options and opportunities, I decided to take the plunge. I booked an appointment with the President to inform him of my desire to resign from KBC to go into politics. He was very supportive and from him I received my first campaign contribution of one hundred forty thousand Kenya shillings. I was immensely thankful. When the head of public service issued a notice advising public servants desiring to enter politics to resign, I was the first one to leave on 15 August 2002.

Chapter 21

A Political Journey Begins

After resigning from KBC I also resigned from the ruling party KANU and joined the Liberal Democratic Party (LDP) as Life Member No. 0017. The day was 14 October 2002, the same day the opposition held a huge rally at Uhuru Park, Nairobi. The rally was the first serious move by the opposition to demonstrate a determined willingness to unite in a drive to oust President Moi. LDP, which was led by Raila Odinga, had agreed to go into an alliance with the Democratic Party of Mwai Kibaki, the Forum for the Restoration of Democracy–Kenya (Ford–Kenya) of Kijana Wamalwa, and the Social Democratic Party (SDP) of Charity Ngilu. The alliance was to be called the National Rainbow Coalition (Narc). It was during that meeting that Narc was unveiled and Kibaki was declared the group's presidential flag bearer.

My entry into politics was a realisation of a life-long dream of following in my father's footsteps. When he was in LegCo my father represented Mombasa, and Shimo la Tewa was part of his constituency. As I planned to go to Parliament, Shimo la Tewa was now part of Bahari, the constituency I hoped to represent. Shimo la Tewa and its adjacent locality, Mtwapa, can be described as both urban and rural, places where wealth conflates with poverty. Among all urban areas in the old Kilifi District, Mtwapa township was the highest revenue generator, thanks to its innumerable bars, nightclubs and eating joints. *Matatus* ply all night long between Mtwapa and Mombasa island, perhaps the only commuter minibuses working on a twenty-four-hour basis. Edwin Nyaseda, a senior police officer who served in the township and who later became the Commissioner of Police had once told me jokingly that if there was anywhere in Kenya that harboured criminals from multiple nations of the world it was Mtwapa. Indeed, its labyrinth set-up of narrow passageways, the perfunctory way in which European tourists mingle with locals and the nebulous lifestyles of many make it enigmatic, yet a saucy entertainment haven.

Like all vibrant urban enclaves, Mtwapa also has its share of baneful activities including prostitution and illegal drugs. The town is unplanned and the houses are packed so tightly that getting in and out of the neighbourhoods is a challenge. Interestingly, it is those negatives that make Mtwapa a much sought-after location by locals and foreigners looking for adventure.

A short distance out of the township the environment changes. Villagers in surrounding areas live in penurious conditions. The huge contrast in the standards of living is laid bare when rich Kenyans and international jetsetters live luxuriously behind high security walls in one part of the constituency, while a few yards away, squatters struggle for the next meal.

I had known Mtwapa and the lower part of the constituency since childhood. When I was growing up, the whole stretch from Mombasa to Malindi was one giant forest inhabited by buffalos and rhinos. When my father bought a farm at Kanamai from a Swahili inhabitant I was in my pre-teens. The road to Malindi was murram. From Kengeleni (the place of the freedom bell) the road veered through Mlaleo and into Bamburi and then shifted right to emerge at the present cement factory and into what is now the Mombasa/Malindi road. I knew this area well because I used to pass through it on the way to our farm about thirty-seven kilometres away. It was my responsibility and Charles's to haul seedlings on bikes all the way from Majengo to Kanamai, sometimes as part of a punishment. I remember being stricken with fear of animal attack as I cycled feverishly along that not too busy road. At the time of our return, the sun would be setting in the horizon, the black crows would be settling on the giant baobab trees and the air would be pregnant with a creepy feeling of vulnerability.

At the time of the Uhuru Park rally in 2002, less than three months remained before the general elections. I had done my homework and found my record on the ground to be favourable. The various development projects I had initiated were well appreciated. I was leading from the front, engaging with the people and working on solutions. I was not giving them fish, but a rod and a bait to go fishing. I was sensitising them on their rights and how to fight for those rights. Because the district had one of the highest illiteracy rates in Kenya – well above sixty per cent

– civic education was paramount. I traversed the constituency holding public meetings and explaining to the people why it was important to get rid of the Moi regime. It had been in power for too long and had done nothing to ease the plight of the ordinary people of Bahari.

Landlessness was a big issue in the area. People had been dispossessed of their plots and were living as squatters. They had also been impoverished, partly because of the closure of the Kilifi cashew nut plant. Farmers no longer had a reliable market for their produce, and middlemen and women had invaded the market and were exploiting them. Considering all those reasons, Kilifi people had no reason to vote for Moi. I went around convincing them to vote for Kibaki. We wanted to open a new chapter, a chapter of hope and veritable freedom.

Elsewhere too Kenyans were generally tired of the status quo: corruption, mismanagement, nepotism, human rights violations and impunity. They were ready for change. I supported the LDP because it stood for constitutional and judicial reforms, equal distribution of resources, good governance and respect for the rule of law.

Kibaki's point man at the Coast then was Emmanuel Karisa Maitha, a popular former Mombasa Councillor known for his belligerent demeanour and aggressive campaign prowess. He was the leading light of the National Alliance of Kenya (NAK) and therefore of the Narc coalition in the region. The Mijikenda loved him and recognised him as their bona fide leader. Since the death of Ngala in 1972 the community had not produced any political leader of equal clout. Of the nine tribes that make up the community, the Giriama is the biggest and most influential, and sets the agenda for the rest of the community.

Karisa Maitha had spent most of his early adult years in Mombasa. With the limited education he had, he could only get small jobs here and there before he became a KANU youth winger and trouble shooter. In 1979, he was nominated a Councillor in the Mombasa Municipal Council and in the 1997 elections he was elected to Parliament on the Democratic Party ticket before he followed Kibaki to NAK and again won the Kisauni seat in 2002. Maitha's popularity at the Coast soared in 2003 in Parliament when he pushed the government to exempt *mnazi* from the list of illegal brews. Until then, it was illegal to drink, transport or trade in the brew.

As far as I know, Maitha was under some pressure from his community to support only Mijikenda candidates in the 2002 general elections. He refused because he knew the Coalition would lose if he did so. He did not want to be seen as a Mijikenda leader only; he wanted to be able to influence the politics of the entire coastal region. He therefore took a middle road and supported all popular candidates. In Bahari he urged the Mijikenda to vote for me, a non-Mijikenda. They listened to him and I won with a decisive majority.

* * *

LDP was undoubtedly the most vibrant party both in and outside Parliament. I was the party's vice president and a member of its key national executive committee. It was this committee that sat and deliberated on all policy matters regarding day to day running of the party and gave directions on matters such as membership mobilisation, scheduling of public meetings and party elections. Although Raila Odinga was the party leader, the administrative secretariat was headed by Larry Gumbe as Chairman and Mumbi Ng'aru as Secretary General. There was also a political wing, with David Musila as Chairman and Joseph Kamotho as Secretary General. As a partner in Narc, LDP played a major role in getting Kibaki elected President of Kenya in 2002. What happened thereafter – the betrayals and the intrigues – leading to the break-up of Narc are now part of Kenya's political history and are elaborately explained in my first book, *The Politics of Betrayal: Diary of a Kenyan Legislator.*

Within the first year of the Narc government, Maitha – who had been appointed Minister for Local Government – became a victim of corruption allegations. It was alleged he had used his influence to get the Nairobi City Council to issue a fifty-four-million-shilling tender to an insurance company under dubious circumstances. Connected to that accusation were allegations that a briefcase containing five million shillings had been found in his office, raising suspicion that the money could have been a bribe from the company. The matter was raised in Parliament and Maitha was put to task to explain why he did not report the find to authorities. Together with others, I called for his resignation and asked the CID to investigate him for possible prosecution.

The allegations were serious, but instead of sacking Maitha, the President transferred him to the Ministry of Tourism and Wildlife. That month, in retaliation for my attacks, Maitha called a public meeting in my constituency, verbally assailed me and, speaking in Kigiriama, questioned my origins. In the same breathe, he asked Mijikenda elders to reconcile us. I immediately called a press conference in which I dismissed the idea of reconciliation and told Maitha to answer questions raised over his integrity. I felt accepting reconciliation by Mijikenda elders would be a waste of time since they would most likely side with him, their kin. In the meantime, Maitha maintained his innocence saying he had done nothing wrong.

My political war with Maitha was headline news for weeks. We could not agree on anything political. I was disappointed that Kibaki did not take action against Maitha despite his repeated declarations of his desire to fight corruption. In his inaugural address and in subsequent speeches, Kibaki had vowed to vigorously tackle corruption which by then had permeated all sectors of Kenyan society. By failing to take action against one of his wayward ministers, Kibaki had failed to walk the talk. It proved that he was no different from Kenyatta and Moi.

Maitha died in 2004 while on an official visit to Germany. His exit precipitated a by-election in Kisauni that same year. This time around, the battle was clearly between the Mijikenda and the rest. Anania Mwaboza, a Mijikenda from the Chonyi sub-tribe who was contesting on the National Labour Party was facing stiff opposition from a Narc candidate, Ali Hassan Joho, a Mdzomba with unknown ethnic origin. Mwaboza had contested against Maitha, a fellow Mijikenda in 2002 and lost. This time around, the large population of Mijikenda in Kisauni came out in support of Mwaboza, a lawyer and an advocate of land rights. Although Joho was a candidate of the coalition Narc, he was a novice and of limited education. I felt that Kisauni, being a densely populated cosmopolitan constituency north of the island, required a more combative, more educated representative. Between Joho and Mwaboza, the latter had better credentials. For the first time, I broke away from my party, Narc, and supported Mwaboza. He won.

* * *

With Maitha out of the picture, the Coast region had become rudderless. The majority Mijikenda no longer had a single leader to inspire them and offer direction in a fast changing Kenya; the Luos had Raila, the Kikuyus had Kibaki, the Kalenjin had Moi, the Maasai had William ole Ntimama, the Abaluhya had Michael Wamalwa, the Merus had Kiraitu Murungi, the Kambas had Kalonzo Musyoka, but the Coast had no one as a flag bearer. The Coast Parliamentary Group (CPG) which was expected to bring legislators together had failed the test due to petty jealousies and ethnic divisions. It had been in existence since the 1980s when Noah Katana Ngala was Chairman, but it had been unable to galvanise the people under one leader.

One reason for the group's failure was that the upper Coast, comprising the Taita and Taveta, had always felt overshadowed by the powerful Mijikenda of the lower Coast. The former felt they were not being given a fair chance on leadership. That perception of isolation manifested itself when I became Chairman of the CPG immediately after the 2002 elections. Whenever I called a group meeting, legislators from the upper Coast almost always did not attend. However, when a Taita MP was elected Chairman, legislators from the lower Coast similarly boycotted his meetings. The organisation soon became moribund.

Seeing that the CPG was not making any headway in exciting coastal people, I came up with the idea of a pressure group, the Coast Leaders' Forum (CLF). The forum was intended to create a fresh awareness about the need for unity among leaders and all coast people. With the support of former Mombasa mayor, Taib Ali Taib, I invited sitting and former MPs to a meeting to discuss our future. At least two dozen leaders attended. I explained the need for a strong lobby to fight for peoples' rights. The CPG, I told the meeting, had failed to make a mark and a stronger, more focused group was required. The leaders endorsed the formation of CLF. We all agreed to meet again to crystallise our ideas on the way forward. However, when I called a follow-up meeting, only Taib and a few others showed up. I felt betrayed, but I was not completely surprised.

It turned out that some Mijikenda leaders had boycotted the meeting because they felt uncomfortable associating with a group headed by non-

Mijikenda. I was a descendant of slaves and the others were *adzomba*, a derogatory reference coined by the locals in reference to Muslims and Arabs. Sitting MPs complained that the lobby was part of a plot to eject them from their seats, a vacuous argument. I was not discouraged and went ahead to organise the CLF launch in Kilifi in which Taib and I took the lead in recruiting members. From the Coast I took the campaign to Nairobi where I convened several meetings of Coast residents living there. Everything was going on well. Little did I know that a silent coup d'état was in the works.

Some Mijikenda members called a secret meeting without my knowledge, and ousted Taib and me from the leadership. I never protested and from thereon I never attended any of the group's meetings. The new leadership changed the name from the Coast Leaders' Forum to the Coast Peoples' Forum (CPF). Although the group started excitedly, soon it faded away. It was dominated by the elite and failed to understand the mundane issues facing the people at the grassroots. My original idea was to unite the leaders. It was only after uniting the leaders that we would be able to trickle down the message to the people. By turning the group so quickly into a people's forum, the organisers had in essence decided to put the cart before the horse. There is no way it could have worked.

For the record, my efforts to unite Coast leaders did not start with my entry into Parliament. Way back in 1997 when I was running Copy Deadline, I started a pressure group in Nairobi called the Coast Development Group. We held several meetings in my office before it was infiltrated by the Special Branch and forced to fold up within a few months. The CLF was therefore a continuation of that initiative.

After the CLF debacle I mooted the idea of starting a full-fledged political party. In July 2006, I went to Ukunda in South Coast and made an announcement at a public meeting to the effect that I would be ready to start or to support any Coast-based political party. The idea was received with aplomb from the crowd. The following day, however, some Coast MPs called me a lone ranger, arguing that I was "frustrating efforts to form a common political bargaining power". That was a complete misreading of my intentions. I felt let down by my Coast colleagues in Parliament. What I was proposing was not intended to frustrate anything. Instead, it was aimed at starting an intelligent conversation about the direction we wanted to take the people. My colleagues in LDP also castigated me for planning to form a rival party and called for disciplinary action.

At the time of writing this book, my views about a Coast-based political party have changed. I no longer believe such a party is tenable. The leadership at the Coast has been unable to speak with one voice. Those parties that emerged since the coming of multiparty politics in 1991 have failed to gain support and most of them are dormant. The following parties come to mind: The Islamic Party of Kenya (IPK), KADU-Asili, the Uzalendo Party, the National Labour Party of Kenya, the Federal Party, the Republican Congress, Mwangaza, and the Shirikisho Party of Kenya (SPK).

For almost four years I had been a committed member of the LDP and had stood by all its decisions. In 2005, I had even volunteered to put my name as the lead plaintiff in a civil suit against the Attorney General in a case in which we at LDP objected to the Report of the Parliamentary Select Committee that endorsed the Kilifi Constitutional Draft. We argued that the report did "not faithfully reflect the views and wishes of the Kenyan people" and that Parliament and its Committee "had failed to promote or achieve a national consensus on contentious issues." In the meantime, Kibaki made several visits to the Coast ahead of the referendum on 21 November 2005, to try to lure Coast leaders to support the government-inspired draft constitution. One meeting was in May and another one in early August. He also held one meeting with Coast MPs in Nairobi in March. These meetings bore fruit when Morris Dzoro, a Cabinet Minister, and Joseph Kingi, an Assistant Minister, agreed to support the constitution along with Ali Chirau Mwakwere.

Despite the strong opposition, the government pushed ahead with a referendum based on the Kilifi draft. The government was soundly defeated. After that the country went back to the drawing board to find a solution to the constitutional stalemate. A few days later, Kibaki, annoyed that Raila and his supporters had campaigned against the draft, promptly sacked all the Cabinet members allied to LDP. The sackings created vacancies in the Executive that Kibaki wished to fill with "friendly" members of the opposition. He aimed at raiding LDP, and two people on his radar were Orwa Ojode, the MP for Ndhiwa, and me, two people considered to be among the most disgruntled members of the party.

A month later, a parastatal boss close to Kibaki called me to his office at the Jomo Kenyatta International Airport in Embakasi, Nairobi, and tried to convince me to defect from LDP to Kibaki's Narc in exchange for one of the cabinet positions vacated by my colleagues. I told him that the move would be politically risky for me given the fact that Kibaki was unpopular in my area after failing to settle squatters. I told him that the only way I could even consider the matter was if the government met certain conditions: I wanted the government to re-open the closed Kilifi cashew nut plant, issue title deeds to squatters, and appoint Coastarians to key government positions. I had complained in Parliament once before that people from my area had been left out of senior government appointments. He responded that since those were political issues he could not answer me immediately, but he agreed to arrange a meeting with Njenga Karume, a Minister and also a confidant of Kibaki.

The meeting among the three of us – the parastatal boss, Karume and me – took place at a hotel in the Upper Hill area of Nairobi. On the issue of re-opening of the Kilifi factory, Karume was confident that the Treasury would not be averse to parting with money from the Exchequer to buy off the plant from its Asian owners. Originally, the plant was run by local farmers and the government, but mismanagement and corruption had led to its closure rendering hundreds of workers jobless and leaving farmers in pecuniary difficulties. As for settlement of squatters, Karume assured me that the President would personally visit my area in the near future to issue title deeds. Knowing the intrigues of politics, I insisted that my conditions had to be fulfilled before I could make any move of shifting camp. We left the matter pending as Karume went to consult further with the government. I also arranged a meeting with my elders to get their opinion.

When we met again at Lord Errol's restaurant in Runda estate, Karume did not have anything new to tell me other than repeating promises he had made earlier. Rumours were already circulating within political cycles that I planned to defect to the government side and take up a Cabinet position. When that rumour reached Raila he issued a stern warning to LDP members thinking of joining Kibaki to brace for expulsion. I viewed that declaration as dictatorial and selfish since he himself had been in government, but was now barring others from joining it. Luckily, the government failed to meet most of my demands, so I stayed put in LDP. However, the disciplinary action against me for supporting the formation of a coast party was still pending.

What had become a strong relationship with Raila ended when I resigned as Vice Chairman of the LDP on 22 August 2006. However, I remained in the party as an ordinary member. At a press conference in Kilifi, I protested against the intended disciplinary action which I thought was unfair. In my statement I said: "In view of the above, I feel I have lost the confidence of the higher echelons of the party and I have consequently decided to resign as Vice Chairman and Member of the National Executive Committee of the Liberal Democratic Party (LDP)." On rumours that I planned to move to Kibaki's party, I stated that such speculation was misplaced. "In Parliament I will vote with my conscience and I will support Government motions and Bills if such motions and Bills are beneficial to the people of Bahari, the Coast and Kenya in general."

Raila's reaction to my resignation was tempestuous. In comments captured on camera, he called me *takataka* (garbage). With all the respect I had for my party leader, I was shocked at that description of me. That comment clearly showed that Raila was not an honourable person. I decided not to respond to his outburst. At the time of writing this book, I have never met nor talked to Raila since then.

* * *

After the cabinet reshuffle, Raila and others moved away from the coalition and announced the formation of the Orange Democratic Movement-Kenya (ODM-K) at a public meeting in Kisumu. Soon, wrangles between Raila and Kalonzo, the two presidential contenders, that had been simmering underground, exploded in the open. Each one of them wanted to become the party's presidential flag-bearer and neither wanted to give way.

Finally, at the end of July 2007, Kalonzo staged an internal coup by resigning and taking to his side the registered party Chairman, Daniel Maanzo, who had custody of the registration documents. Given my tumultuous relations with Raila I decided to follow Kalonzo. Given these developments, Raila founded another party, the Orange Democratic Movement (ODM). The battle was now on between Kalonzo's ODM-Kenya and Raila's ODM.

Chapter 22

Things to Remember in Parliament

I had many enjoyable moments during my tenure in the Ninth Parliament from 2003 to 2007 as the representative for Bahari Constituency. One of the first things I did upon being elected was to call a Leaders Meeting in my constituency to identify the most urgent problems and to chart the way forward. Two hundred delegates attended the meeting at the Kilifi Institute of Agriculture, now Pwani University. After two days of deliberations leaders identified three issues as being top on the priority list: education, water and health. That did not mean other pressing problems such as landlessness, poverty, youth unemployment and early pregnancies were to be ignored. We needed a pathway to achieving the best results by tackling each problem forcefully and systematically. With the financial assistance of Action Aid, a non-governmental organisation, and technical support from Oscar Nyapela of the Kilifi-based Community Development Services Centre, Bahari became the first constituency to draw a five-year development programme. That plan was launched in 2004 by Vice President Moody Awori at Mnarani Club in Kilifi.

The introduction of the Constituency Development Fund (CDF) through an Act of Parliament in 2003 was a big boost to development, and every year during my tenure, Bahari received the highest amount of money over all the other 209 constituencies, giving us the resources to initiate a total of 140 different projects. We constructed five secondary schools – Roka, Mnarani, St Thomas (in Kilifi town), Kibarani School for the Blind, and Ngerenya; sixteen nursery schools; a one-thousand-seater social hall for women; eight dispensaries, science laboratories at Lustangani; Msumarini and Dzisoni Secondary Schools; a fence at Arabuko Sokoke to bar elephants from invading farms, multiple open wells and piped water projects; and many other projects. We also offered bursaries to hundreds of high school and university students both in the constituency and abroad.

In Parliament, I was active in proposing and debating motions and in asking questions, most of them about land issues. My proudest moment was when I tabled, on 5 July 2006, a motion for the enactment of legislation on cashew nut development, which, after recommendations of MPs, became the Kenya Nut Development Authority Bill. As the cashew is one of the key agricultural products at the Coast, I wanted a body that would streamline the industry and provide economic safeguards for farmers in the region. In my contribution, I told the House that farmers had been discouraged from growing the crop because of low prices, exploitation by middle men, and high costs of seeds, and that many of the trees had been cut down and replaced with crops such as maize. I blamed the incumbent government and the previous ones for doing nothing to encourage production of the crop. "The fact that the Government has not found it fit to enact legislation in the past 40 years," I said, "speaks volumes about the goodwill and commitment of this country to agriculture in Coast Province." The motion was seconded by the Lamu West MP, Fahim Twaha, who told MPs that it was the duty of the House to support all initiatives towards economic growth and development. He also said that the motion was long overdue and urged the Members to support it. It passed. When Parliament dissolved on 22 October 2007, the Bill was still at the Law Office awaiting to be re-drafted for further debate. When I lost my seat, the incoming MP did not follow up on the Bill.

There was another issue that occupied my attention in Parliament. It had to do with the fate of the Kilifi Cashew Nut Factory. Since its closure in 1998 due to corruption and mismanagement, the factory had become a matter of heated political debate, especially during elections. Politicians used it as bait for votes, and the government rode on it to elicit support. Established during the Kenyatta Administration jointly with the Kilifi District Cooperative Union in 1973, the factory became an example of how a government can partner with people to achieve development and raise the living standards. At the height of production, the company was employing 3,000 people and supporting thousands others. There was a high demand for housing and goods in Kilifi town and farmers were busy. Three parastatals had a total shareholding of 65 per cent in the company: the Industrial and Commercial Development Corporation (ICDC), the Industrial Development Bank (IDB) and the National Cereals and Produce Board (NCPB). The rest was held by the Kilifi District Cooperative Union (KDCU). When the three parastatals offloaded their shares to KDCU, some unscrupulous individuals in the company failed to register the 65 per cent shares as required by law and instead sold the investment to a group of politically-correct individuals meaning that, although the union acquired the entire equity – 100 per cent shareholding – the transaction was not legally registered. Company directors only filled forms to sell the shares to two companies owned by the individuals mentioned. The plant was eventually closed and equipment transferred to other factories.

On 11 April 2007, I asked Parliament to form a select committee to investigate the circumstances that led to the factory's collapse and punish those who were responsible. If approved that was going to be the second body to investigate the closure. The first one was undertaken in 1991 by the Parliament's Public Investment Committee, but its recommendations were not acted upon. While moving the Motion I told Parliament that as a result of the closure, Kilifi's economy had crumbled causing untold suffering to the residents. I wanted the people responsible prosecuted and the equipment which was taken away from the factory including a complete macadamia cracker unit, two hundred plaster cranes, one electronic weighing scale of 20-kilogramme capacity, shelling machines, calibrators, computers, printers and fax machines – returned, and the farmers compensated for loss of investment. My seconder, the MP for the neighbouring Malindi Constituency, Lucas Maitha, whose constituents were equally affected by the closure, described the Motion as a very serious issue: "The government is not doing anything because it is simply not interested. Could the government wake up and assist our people?" he asked desperately.

The motion attracted a lot of interest in the House. Thirteen MPs contributed to the debate before the Motion was put to a vote. It passed with an amendment proposed by Hon. Justin Muturi to broaden the committee membership to include MPs from the opposition. The following names were approved: Hon. P. K. Sang, Hon. Lucas Maitha, Hon. J. Ojode, Hon. A. A. Bahari, Hon. W. Osundwa, Hon. N. N.

Shaban, Hon. Zaddock Syongo, Hon. N. Balala, Hon. M. Mukiri and Hon. M. K. Waithaka. As the proposer, I was to chair the Committee.

The committee moved to Kilifi and took evidence from former executives at the factory, farmers and government officials who had been involved in the management of the company. At the end, recommendations were made in which the committee called for the prosecution of certain individuals and further investigation of others. On 1 September 2006, while on a visit at the Coast, the Agriculture Minister, Kipruto arap Kirwa, admitted that no action on my Motion was taken because the government was not involved in its drafting. He suggested that I re-table the motion through the government because the latter had "more weight". I sensed a lack of seriousness on the part of the Minister and I never took any further action.

What will remain as the most memorable event in my life in Parliament is the investigation into the disappearance and murder of former Kenya Foreign Affairs Minister, Robert Ouko. I was among the twelve MPs selected to serve in the parliamentary committee chaired by Hon. Eric Gor Sungu. The others were Hon. Dr Oburu Odinga, Hon. Prof. Christine Mango, Hon. Dr Abdulla Ali, Hon. Amina Abdalla, Hon. Paul Muite, Hon. Peter Munya, Hon. Samuel Leshore, Hon. Kiema Kilonzo, Hon. Samuel Moroto and Hon. Raphael Wanjala. The Committee also had the support of the Assistant Deputy Public Prosecutor, Oriri Onyango, and four police officers under Maurice Amatta. While I wouldn't want to go deep into the deliberations that took place in that Committee (they are comprehensively covered in the subsequent reports and presented in my book, *The Politics of Betrayal: Diary of a Kenyan Legislator*) it would be an omission of history if I was to ignore this event completely. This is even more important because the killer or killers who committed that heinous act on the night of 12/13 February 1990 are still at large.

Robert Ouko was a brilliant cabinet official who defended Moi internationally at a time when Kenya was on the spotlight on the basis of human rights abuses. We in the committee found no evidence to implicate Moi directly, but a number of questions remained unanswered about the suspicious conduct of some senior government officials immediately before and after the murder at his village area of Koru in Kisumu, Nyanza. I continue to suspect that there was a high level conspiracy by people who wanted to derail Ouko's popularity within and without the country. That explains why all investigations – including the one conducted by the British Scotland Yard – were never acted upon because of political interference. Recommendations that certain people should be investigated further were also not followed up by the government and the matter was put on the back burner.

When Ouko was appointed Foreign Affairs Minister by President Moi in 1988, I had already left for Namibia. While there, Ouko was killed and his charred body found in a thicket. So, I never got to work with him to know the kind of individual he was. On my return, Ndolo Ayah had been appointed to take over the portfolio.

One of the people to be investigated further, according to our report, was President Moi. We felt he had questions to answer. The inclusion of Moi's name angered some members of the committee and a bitter argument ensued between two members, Hon. Samuel Moroto and Hon. Raphael Wanjala, resulting in an almost physical fight. Consequently, a number of the Committee members refused to sign the report. Nevertheless, Hon. Sunguh did present the report to Parliament and it was adopted. Unfortunately, the recommendations were never implemented. In 2010, a member of the Tenth Parliament, Gitobu Imanyara, re-introduced the report for debate in Parliament, but it was rejected as a collection of unsubstantiated hearsays and falsehoods.

Ouko's killing joined a long list of unresolved political murders starting with Pio Gama Pinto in 1965, Tom Mboya in 1969, Ronald Ngala in 1972 (he died in a mysterious car accident on the Mombasa-Nairobi road) and J. M. Kariuki in 1975. Listening to witnesses during the hearing of the Parliamentary Committee I detected lies and contradictions which made me believe Ouko was indeed murdered and did not commit suicide as the government pathologist, Jason Kaviti, and others had claimed. How did Ouko leave his home on that fateful night? Was he abducted or did he leave voluntarily? Why the contradictions about when Ouko's body was found? Who first discovered the body? Was it the herdsboy Shikuku or a search team? What happened to his briefcase said to contain important documents related to a corruption scandal and which was reportedly collected by security officials? All these questions remain unanswered. The roles of senior government officials, including

President Moi himself, were not also adequately examined. Moi declined to appear before the Committee to shed light on that particular issue.

My lowest moment in Parliament was when on 7 July 2006, the Assistant Minister for Information and Broadcasting, Hon. Koigi wa Wamwere, falsely accused me of practising nepotism while I was the Managing Director of KBC. During a member's question on the retrenchment of 253 KBC employees, Hon. Wamwere alleged that I employed three unqualified persons from my home area to positions in the newsroom. He informed the House that Eric Ponda had been a petrol pump attendant at Broadcasting House and that Alfred Kiti had been my driver. Another employee, Peter Mrima had faced several disciplinary actions for poor attendance. The accusations were far from the truth. All of the three were employed before I joined KBC in 2000, and although Kiti had been a driver he had attended and obtained a diploma in journalism from the Kenya Institute of Mass Communication before he was promoted to a clerical officer and then to a news assistant.

Because of the seriousness of the allegations, I asked the Speaker for time to make a personal statement as per House Standing Orders. I told the House the allegations were false and were "actionable in a court of law" and challenged the Assistant Minister to repeat them outside Parliament and face legal action. I also tabled in the House letters of appointment, academic and professional qualifications and letters of recommendations from supervisors to prove that I had nothing to do with their employment and whatever promotions they earned were properly done.

There are many times when I felt Parliament was nothing but a talking shop. Ministers promised things they knew they could not deliver and MPs were often dismissed with statements such as: "The government will do this and that when funds become available;" "The government is looking into the matter;" and, "It will be included in the next budget." Those were clichés used to disarm backbenchers and sweep matters under the carpet. Many times I was promised the government would confiscate land owned by absentee landlords and that squatters would be settled, but none of the Ministers for Lands during my five years in Parliament – Amos Kimunya and Kivutha Kibwana – did anything substantial to settle the landless. At one time, names of squatters and absentee landlords were collected on orders of the Provincial Administration, but nothing was heard after that. On 30 August 2006, President Kibaki visited Kilifi and issued hundreds of title deeds, but numerous beneficiaries later complained that some of the titles were faulty and could not be used as collateral for bank loans. And since Parliament did not have an implementation committee, many decisions by the House, including action on Motions and Petitions, ended up in government files. Such was the fate of the Kenya Nut Development Bill.

***

In September 2007, during the heat of the election campaign, I was invited to Kathmandu to attend a Round-Table Conference hosted by the Speaker of the Nepalese National Assembly. The conference was held under the aegis of the New York-based Parliamentarians for Global Action (PGA) of which I was a member. PGA is a non-profit, non-partisan network of more than one thousand parliamentarians from more than one hundred countries across the globe. It aims at mobilising legislators to promote peace, democracy, rule of law and human rights. PGA has a Kenya chapter, and at the time of my visit to Nepal, the chairman was David Musila, my former chairman of LDP. I was scheduled to deliver a keynote address before a group of Nepalese legislators on the Accession and Implementation of the Rome Statute of the International Criminal Court (ICC). Two years earlier, the Nepalese Parliament had passed a resolution to join the Rome Statute, but the actual accession had not taken place. I was asked to give Kenya's experience and challenges that preceded the signing of the international statutes in a move to encourage the Nepalese to move faster in accenting to the Statute. I called Maina Kiai, the human rights crusader who had worked on ICC issues to help me with notes for my speech. He was kind enough to send me some raw material which, combined with information I had gathered from other sources, enabled me to come up with a draft speech.

I made all the arrangements to ensure I got to Kathmandu on time for the meeting. My ticket was paid for by PGA, but I purchased an extra ticket for my wife to accompany me in our first visit to that mountainous region. We were to travel aboard Kenya Airways to Mumbai and then board Nepalese Air. The travel officer at Parliament informed me that there was no need of applying for visas in Nairobi because we could easily get them at the airport in Mumbai for transit into another part of the airport where we were to catch the flight to Nepal. On arrival at Mumbai however we discovered that visas were not issued at the airport, meaning we could not make a connection.

The first time I knew something was wrong was when we got to the immigration counter. Instead of being cleared to pass through, we were directed to a waiting area. As we sat there, I noticed an animated discussion in Hindi among the immigration officers whose eyes were now focused on the two passports. The person who took the documents from us turned the passport pages as if shuffling a pile of cards, and then called a colleague who did the same. Within a short period of time, there were at least four officers on our case. A fifth one came, took one of the passports, flipped its pages, jabbed at one of the pages with his index finger, shook his head, and joined what had now become a rather noisy circus. Periodically I could hear the word "deportation" followed by a sudden burst of laughter. I turned to my wife and I saw grim signs of pessimism written all over her face. I tried to remain positive, but my mind was going helter-skelter. I approached the group and tried to convince them it wasn't our fault that we didn't have visas; that I was given wrong information, and that we meant no harm. To use the Kenyan approach, I introduced myself as an MP and even flushed out my speech as a confirmation that I was a keynote speaker at an important meeting in Nepal. They just looked at the speech, pretended to understand it, and gave it back to me.

What we didn't know was that the Kenya Airways plane had been stopped from leaving without us. Once they had finished preparing the deportation documents, we were directed back to the aircraft for the return flight home. Our passports were taken and handed over to the flight purser with instructions to pass them on to the immigration officers on arrival. That harrowing experience got me thinking about the abundant hospitality routinely showered on foreigners at points of entry in Kenya. An incident such as that would not have turned into such a mess in Kenya. Visitors would have been asked to pay, passports would have been stamped with a smile, and they would have been allowed to proceed. Not in India.

We spent the return journey sleeping in the business class of the plane. At the airport in Nairobi, an immigration officer handed back our passports, and with a blithe wave of the hand, said *"Pole mheshimiwa"*, Sorry sir! I thanked him and we headed home. I was worried about my no-show at the meeting and was prepared to book another ticket once we obtained visas from the Indian High Commission in Nairobi, but it was a Saturday and the chancery was closed. In any case, the two-day meeting would be over by the time we made a turn-back. I didn't think somebody either in government or parliament sabotaged the trip. I thought it was purely accidental.

At the time of this incident, it was only a few weeks to the December general elections. Temperatures and expectations were high in the Kibaki and Raila camps, the two leading presidential contenders. Kalonzo was far down at third position. One opinion poll after another tipped Raila as the possible winner, but all indications pointed to a very close contest. When results came Kibaki had apparently won. Despite the fact that the ODM got more parliamentary seats, Raila had for the third time failed to win the presidency. At the Coast, the ODM wave was too strong for Kibaki's PNU. The former won thirteen out of the twenty-three parliamentary seats. As I had supported Kalonzo of ODM-K in a perceived Raila zone I failed to re-capture my seat.

***

For years, my mother had been under the good care of Dr Moses Thuo, a specialist cardiologist at the Mombasa Hospital. She did not only have a serious high blood pressure condition, but her heart also appeared to be failing her. I made arrangements for her to be evaluated every month by the doctor. With regular medication, her condition stabilised and she continued to live a normal life. For some reason she became unusually vulnerable to allergies. She could no longer eat certain types of foods such as beef, which she had consumed without any problem all her life. One day, her tongue swelled. We rushed her to hospital and she recovered within a few days. But one evening a week later, her heart began to pound rather unusually and she started to talk things nobody could understand. She was restless and could not eat. Some of her children and grandchildren gathered to monitor her that night. I was in Bahari and was informed of her deteriorating condition. I rushed to Rabai and found her in a rather worrying condition. I sought the assistance of a nurse from a government clinic nearby who came and managed to stabilise her. I left Rabai and returned home convinced the emergency was over. The following day as I sat in a campaign meeting, I received a call that she had died that morning. I cancelled all my activities and rushed to Rabai to take charge of the situation.

I had no time to properly mourn my mother during the whole period of burial preparations. I was in charge of the arrangements and there were so many things that needed my attention. It was on the day of the burial, as I was giving my speech, that I felt something stifling my ability to talk. At the time I was trying to explain to the mourners what my mother meant to me. Before I could finish the sentence, I choked, and big round balls of tears dripped down my cheeks.

Mine was not just the pain of losing a mother, but a realisation that the last remaining person who mattered most in my life was now gone. I was now an orphan. Ten years earlier I had lost my father. Now, the last of the siblings of Nyanya Pauline and Mzee Stephens had also gone to join her maker. Even the step-mother who I had loved to hate had also departed. It felt weird and lonesome. Relatives from Tanzania came to commiserate with the family. With her rosary beads around her neck – as always – we buried her next to her parents in the family cemetery at the Kinyakani farm.

***

The situation that followed the announcement of results was total chaos. The tallying centre at the Kenyatta International Conference Centre (KICC) was turned into an arena of shouting, shoving and exchange of insults before security officers moved in. At one point, the lights went off and the situation became even more convoluted. It was the chaos that forced the Chairman of the Electoral Commission of Kenya (ECK), Samuel Kivuitu, to withdraw to the confines of a private room at the Centre and announce the results. Within an hour, as the sun set, Kibaki was sworn in for a second term in office at a hurriedly convened ceremony at State House.

In the meantime, the announcement ignited instant reaction in some parts of the country. Youths allied to ODM in sections of Nairobi and in the lake town of Kisumu swarmed the streets, uprooted railway lines, smashed shop windows and looted property. Raila was seen on television calling people to mass action to protest the results. Elsewhere, clashes erupted between ODM and PNU supporters, a church was burnt and many people were killed. Before calm was restored following the intervention of the international community, more than one thousand people had lost their lives and tens of thousands of others had been left homeless. Other than a few skirmishes in Mombasa, the rest of the Coast remained relatively calm. People went about their businesses normally and only followed the unfolding events on radio and television. What followed until the formation of the Grand Coalition government between Kibaki and Raila has been documented adequately in my book, *The Politics of Betrayal*.

Chapter 23

The Pain of Losing

I was now no longer an MP. I didn't have to deal with constituents visiting my home at all times of day and night with bagful of problems for me to solve. My cook did not have to prepare kettle after kettle of hot tea and serve loaf after loaf of bread. I did not have an office to go to. I did not have meetings to attend. I had plenty of time on my hands.

Losing an election can be a traumatic experience. It's not like losing a loved one where anger and hurt connive to create a psychologically enduring depressive state of mind. Political loss is different. The hurt is dull and segmented. It is stubborn and piercing. One minute you are alive and cheerful, the other you are thoughtful and dispirited, the mind tracing over and over again every campaign details to find out what went wrong. Like all political losers, I went through what Sigmund Freud, the celebrated Austrian clinical neurologist of the nineteenth century, called a "denial of reality", the refusal to believe that one had actually lost. The thought of forfeiture of privileges, the perceived loss of respect and recognition, the shame, and more importantly the financial uncertainty, all combine to make life miserable for a political loser. What happens immediately is that the henchmen disappear and the usual crowds that sang, danced and praised you vanish into thin air. From the day the results were announced, even those who routinely showed up at my house for a free cup of tea stayed away.

I remember that morning vividly. I was gripped with a visceral wave of panic and confusion. The more I thought of the millions of shillings I spent in the campaign the more galled I became. I could see myself dishing out money to people who pretended to support me, people I didn't even know. I visualised all the weddings I paid for, all the funerals I attended, all the school *harambees* I supported, all the school uniforms I bought, all the medical expenses I paid for, all the women groups and youth groups and church groups, and Muslim institutions I contributed to, and I realised how rotten Kenyan politics was. I thought of my father when he lost his elections.

Once one loses, many things change almost immediately. I almost couldn't recognise my own surroundings. The birds may have been there – like they always did – but somehow I didn't hear them sing that morning. The chickens and the ducks and the goats – which would normally be scratching the ground and chewing away my flower plants – had all taken into the bush perhaps as a sign of mourning. I didn't even hear women chatter and laugh as they drew water from the open well in my compound. They had withdrawn to another watering hole. My wife was away and the only person in the house with me was the cook. Normally a babbler, he too had surprisingly become dumb. The house was eerie and the compound had become frighteningly ghostly. I checked my phone. On a normal morning I would have had a dozen messages in the inbox waiting for my attention. On that day, there was only one – from Kenya Airways confirming my flight out.

If my loss in 2007 was a slap to me, the loss in the 2013 elections of Prime Minister Raila Odinga and Vice President Kalonzo Musyoka must have been a stinger. If my fall dug a small hole, theirs must have opened a crater. Shortly after the results were announced they became ordinary citizens. Their elaborate armed security was withdrawn. They no longer had cushy offices to go to and no flags fluttering on the bonnet of their cars. The trauma must have been particularly painful for the duo. They were a breath away from the presidency. With the loss, their future was as uncertain as mine had been five years earlier.

I had purchased an air ticket several months before the 2007 elections for travel out of the country, win or lose. I needed time off to rest and to recover from the torturous campaign schedule that I had put myself through for more than a year. After confirming the results, my immediate thought was to be as far away from home as possible. That evening my driver took me to the airport for a flight to Nairobi and on to New York.

As I settled in the cabin for the trans-Atlantic journey, and as I took a glimpse of the Nairobi skyline with its glittering night lights, my mind turned to a post-mortem of what could have led to my defeat. I knew I had done everything well. My record in Parliament was satisfactory. I had raised all the issues that were pertinent to my constituents. I had fought for the landless and for the unemployed, and I had prepared and tabled a motion for the establishment of an authority to manage the cashew nut and the coconut industries – a move no other coastal MP had made in history. My use of the Constituency Development Fund was the best among all the 210 constituencies during my term. I had done extremely well in the use of my CDF so much that Ngumbao Kithi, a Coast-based writer with *The Standard* took notice of that in an article on 29 March 2007, less than a year to the polls when he wrote: "Bahari legislator, Joe Khamisi is perhaps the only MP in the country who will fight for a second term on the strength of what he has done with the Constituency Development Fund (CDF). He can stand on top of a mountain and tell opponents that he has put Bahari on the national map as the constituency with the best run CDF projects."

In addition, I had opened three offices across the constituency and I was available once a week, every week, at each of those offices. I frequently toured the constituency to meet people in their own surroundings and to hear and find solutions to their problems. I had bought hundreds of school uniforms, paid medical expenses for the poor, dished out tens of thousands of shillings for funeral expenses and paid school fees for those not covered by the bursary – all for the good of my constituents. I felt I had done everything that a Kenyan MP was required to do except one thing: I refused to bribe voters. Experience shows majority of voters do not care about performance, they only care about money. It has to be upfront and good, otherwise they dash to those who can satisfy their hunger for cash. To me, direct hand-outs belonged to the past.

* * *

One of my hobbies, picked from years of working in the media, was collecting newspaper cuttings. I cut, paste and file anything I consider useful for future use. I had piles of files in my office at home, covering various subjects such as politics, corruption, energy and land. I also kept notes of events and people I met in the hope that one day I would get a chance to use the material. That chance came in 2008 after my defeat.

When I left for the United States I took with me files, notes and diaries I had kept over some years. I had plenty of time in my hands to do whatever I wanted. So, I decided to write a book. At the beginning I didn't know what kind of a book I actually wanted to write, never mind how I wanted to write it. At the end I settled on a political memoir.

I decided to document events that took place over a ten year period; starting with the alliance between Moi and Raila in 2001, and ending with the formation of the Grand Coalition government of Kibaki and Raila in 2008. The problem was that I was an active player in some of the events during that period. The question then was: should I be a spectator in the story or should I be a participant narrating the story from the inside. After some thought, I decided to mix the two. Hence, *The Politics of Betrayal: Diary of a Kenyan Legislator,* was born.[16]

It took me two years to complete the book. For purposes of inspiration, I read several memoirs and autobiographies of leaders including those of American Presidents Barack Obama, Bill Clinton, Ronald Reagan, and British Prime Minister Tony Blair. From the local scene, I chose Tom Mboya's *Freedom and After,* Njenga Karume's *Beyond Expectations: From Charcoal to Gold,* Simeon Nyachae's *Walking Through the Corridors of Service,* and Oginga Odinga's *Not Yet Uhuru.* I perused through Andrew Morton's *The Making of An African Statesman,* a biography of Daniel arap Moi, and Babafemi A. Badejo's *Raila Odinga: An Enigma in Kenyan Politics.*[17]

Once the manuscript was ready I hired an American firm to edit it (a big mistake) and tasked a Kenyan designer to do the cover (a good idea). Because of its politically-sensitive content and to avoid any possible leakages, I decided to publish the book in the US rather than in Kenya. I chose Trafford Publishing of Bloomington, Indiana, a self-publishing company for the work.

By February 2011, the book was ready for the stores. In preparing for the launch, I considered a number of prominent people as guest speaker. I didn't want the political type. I wanted someone with a good record of genuinely caring for the people. I narrowed the list to two people: Father Dolan, the fiery priest who had been at the centre of land wars for years, and Davinder Lamba, also known as Bwana Filimbi, the respected

---

16 Joe Khamisi, *The Politics of Betrayal: Diary of a Kenyan Legislator* (Bloomington, IN: Trafford Publishing, 2011).

17 Tom Mboya, *Freedom and After* (London: Andre Deutsche, 1963); Njenga Karume, *Beyond Expectations: From Charcoal to Gold* (Nairobi: Kenway Publications, 2009); Simeon Nyachae, *Walking Through the Corridors of Service: An Autobiography* (Nairobi: Mvule Africa Publishers, 2010); Oginga Odinga, *Not Yet Uhuru: An Autobiography* (Nairobi: East African Educational Publishers, 1967); Andrew Morton, *Moi: The Making of An African Statesman* (London: Michael Omara, 1999); Babafemi A. Badejo, *Raila Odinga: An Enigma in Kenyan Politics* (Nairobi: Yintab Books, 2006).

advocate of human and environmental rights. Dolan was in Mombasa and was unavailable. Fortunately, Lamba was in Nairobi and he gracefully agreed to be the guest of honour. At the event held at a Westgate Shopping Mall bookshop in Westlands I sold my first thirty copies.

The publicity was instant. The serialisation in the *Daily Nation* newspaper was a big boost. Radio and television stations picked up the story, zeroing in on corruption in Parliament and the intrigues and back-stabbing in political parties and government. Alex Chamwada of the Citizen TV carried a series of articles in the evening news bulletins, and Caroline Mutoko made the book a subject of discussion at Kiss FM. I must also commend Oscar Obonyo of *The Standard* for his contributions. That kicked off a sales boom and a reading frenzy never seen before since the release of Michela Wrong's *It's Our Turn to Eat*.[18]

After some months, things somehow settled down to normal routine. The question I had asked myself early in 2008 when I lost the Bahari parliamentary seat still begged for an answer at the beginning of the 2012 election year. I could not make up my mind whether or not to go back to active politics or retire and write more books. The family was certainly not enthusiastic about my going back to politics. They felt I had done my share and should exit. I was caught in the middle. My head was telling me to leave, but my heart was still in politics. Someone once said, "Once a politician always a politician." But was I really a politician or an itinerant adventure seeker? Yes, I was passionate about politics. I liked the unpredictability, the risks and the excitement of crowds and even the *mheshimiwa* (honourable) tag. Seriously, I asked myself: Was I really a politician? And if I wasn't, what was I?

My journey from journalism into politics was defined by two things: one, I wanted to make a statement: "My father did it. I too want to do it." Two, I wanted to give back to my people. Had it not been for community support, I would not have been able to reach the level of comfort I was blessed with. There were so many people who helped me along the way to success. In most cases I didn't even know who they were – relatives, neighbours and even strangers. I have never considered myself rich, but I have been blessed with abundant opportunities that have given me

---

18 Michela Wrong, *It's Our Turn to Eat: The Story of a Kenyan Whistle-Blower* (New York: Harper Perennial, 2009).

profound gratification. While I know of many people who went to bed hungry, I have never experienced hunger, nor have I been homeless. My general state of health has been good and trouble-free. So, giving a little back to the community always gave me a lot of pleasure.

On 19 October 2010, while planning for the 2013 elections, I was appointed Chairman of the planned Ronald Ngala Utalii Academy at Vipingo in Bahari Constituency. The appointment was duly recorded in the *Kenya Gazette*. The project was finally coming to fruition after all, so we thought, after years of legal and bureaucratic hurdles. Way back in the 1980s, Rea Vipingo – the largest sisal producer at the Coast – donated forty acres of its prime land for the construction of a tourism hospitality wing of the Kenya Utalii College. Nothing was done until Najib Balala became Minister for Tourism in the NARC government. With the growth of tourism the Kenya Utalii College, which was built in 1975 with assistance from the Swiss government, had been overwhelmed by demands for trained workers. Since the Coast handled sixty per cent of all the tourists visiting Kenya, it was considered prudent to have a training facility at the point of use. The new college was named in the memory of the famous Coast politician.

With the help of a Board of Directors, I was expected to work with professionals to construct a model college from scratch to include administrative offices, staff housing, hostels and a training hotel for practical lessons. The plot of the Academy was located just behind Vipingo shopping centre facing the open Indian Ocean. Funding was expected from levies administered by the Catering and Tourism Development Levy (CTDL) Trustees, a branch of the Ministry of Tourism in charge of collecting training levies from hotel and restaurant establishments. Additional funds were expected to come from the government. However, after a few Board meetings and benchmark visits to leading tourism institutions in the world including Le Roche in Switzerland and Cornell University in the United States, the project came to a standstill due to internal squabbles in the Ministry over tendering issues. It appeared there was a tussle between certain individuals over how to allocate the design and construction works. The Board was kept in the dark so Board meetings were stopped and the project collapsed. Seeing that confusion I tendered my resignation in February 2012 to go back to politics.

I had resigned from Kalonzo Musyoka's ODM-K in 2010 to have time to strategise, away from the influences of party politics. For about two years I was party-less. When I finally made a decision to re-enter politics, I registered with Raila Odinga's ODM on 1 May 2012, as Life Member No. 001240. But my membership was short-lived due to frustrations meted at me by party leaders both at the headquarters and at my branch in Kilifi. Three months after my registration, my name was still not recorded in the database of the Registrar of Political Parties, which was a mandatory requirement. After complaining on the phone to the Secretary General, Prof. Anyang Nyong'o, I sent an e-mail to the Executive Director, Jane Ong'era, on 13 August, complaining that I was encountering "hostility and resistance" from both Nairobi's Orange House and the Kilifi branch officials. An official who was also contesting the same parliamentary seat directed that I should not be allowed to use the party offices. "I find these matters to be critical...and I am worried that some people may be planning to uneven the ground and possibly deny me a fair chance of the nomination." That letter was never responded to. On 1 October 2012, I resigned from ODM and headed to the United Republican Party (URP) led by William Ruto.

The following month, Eliud Owalo, Raila's chief campaign manager, called me to try to entice me back into ODM. Since I was on my way out of the country, we agreed to meet at the Nairobi airport, but after a lengthy talk in which I expressed my anger at the mistreatment I got from the party, I told Owalo my resignation from ODM was final. I knew ODM was still popular in my constituency and by moving away I was risking my chances, but my principles did not allow me to remain in a party that had no desire for my membership.

Because of the long political association between the Rift Valley people and Coastals dating back to the KADU days in mid-1960s, the region had no problem accepting Ruto as the party's presidential candidate. In fact, during Ruto's several visits to Mombasa and the surrounding areas, many leaders pledged support for his presidential bid. However, when URP eventually entered into a coalition arrangement with The National Alliance (TNA), and Uhuru Kenyatta was chosen to be the flag-bearer, the mood of the Coast URP leaders changed. The Kenyatta name did not resonate well with the people because of its association with land grabbing as explained earlier.

There was also something else that did not excite Coastals about the Uhuru candidature. He was a Kikuyu. In 2002, Karisa Maitha had made a statement that shocked Kenyans. He said after Kibaki, Kenya would never again be ruled by a Kikuyu. That statement was still ringing in the ears of the people in 2013. Already two of Kenya's three Presidents had been Kikuyus – Jomo Kenyatta and Mwai Kibaki. There was a feeling of Kikuyu-fatigue. Although Ruto was a Kalenjin like Moi, Coast people had a softer spot for Kalenjins than they had for Kikuyus. Hence, after Ruto had joined Uhuru and had accepted the number two position, our challenge as URP leaders at the Coast was two-fold: one, to convince the people that Uhuru was not Jomo and that he had done nothing wrong to the people of the region, and two, that, despite his ethnicity, he was the most suitable candidate for the presidency. He was young and educated and – from his own proclamations – dedicated to change. What I knew was that Uhuru was clean and not linked to any scandal and that his record in the public service, especially as Finance Minister, was good.

As Uhuru began his forays into the region, peoples' perception of him began to change, but because Raila had long won their confidence and enjoyed the goodwill of wealthy personalities in the sea-side town, Uhuru's task of wooing Coastals became an uphill task.

The 2013 elections in Kenya were said to be the most complex in Kenya's history. After the election dispute of 2007 in which many people died, there was a push for an electronic system of voting and tallying of votes. The government spent a lot of money in acquiring the biometric voter registration (BVR) kits that were supposed to register voters and then produce what was called a certified voter registry. Things went awfully wrong because the kits failed to work and the process of voting had to be conducted manually, fuelling fears of widespread rigging. At some places within the Coast, including my own constituency of Kilifi North, matters were exacerbated by violent attacks on police and polling stations that disoriented personnel leading to many polling stations remaining shut and others opening late and closing early. The secessionist group, MRC, was blamed for the violence but no evidence was adduced to support that assertion. MRC, itself denied it was involved. However, the people at Chumani, Zowerani, Mkombe and Jezazhomu polling stations did not vote at all. Thousands others at Tezo, Fumbini, Mtondia and centres in Matsangoni ward, the Children of the Rising Sun, Gede Youth Polytechnic, Gede Primary, Mijomboni, Mabuani, Mbaraka Chembe, Kizingo Baptist Church, Bethel Nursery School, Jacaranda Primary School and SDA Primary School opened late and closed early. Also, regulations barred ballot boxes from being moved from stations. In Kilifi North, the boxes were transferred to Kilifi at night and my agents were not allowed to accompany them. Moreover, many computers malfunctioned and the whole voting process was doubtful.

From my discussions with local people in affected areas, I am convinced the violence was politically instigated to scare people and rig the polls. Twenty-three people lost their lives in that violence, among them senior police officers. I am still convinced today that the elections conducted in Kilifi North did not meet the threshold of free and fair elections. As Raila said, and I agreed with him, the management of the 2013 elections by the Independent Electoral and Boundaries Commission (IEBC) was far worse than the ones conducted by the disgraced Electoral Commission of Kenya (ECK) in 2007. Even with the shortcomings in Kilifi North, electoral officials went ahead and announced the winner despite having sent a letter of complaints to the IEBC on 8 March 2013.

Apparently, the current electoral laws are unfair to losers who must carry the burden of an election petition process. The costs of filing a petition are very high, and the penalties for those who lose in court very exorbitant. From the 2013 elections petition losers have been slapped with penalties that have ranged from three million to five million shillings. Personally, I did not have the will and resources to go to court and I let the matter rest.

A major surprise to me was the obvious reluctance by the local media to report objectively and truthfully about events that took place in Kilifi North before and during the elections. The media gave a blind eye to all the corruption, all the stealing of votes and all the conspiracies that surrounded the polls in constituencies and instead spent inordinate amount of space and ink on the presidential dispute. One journalist admitted to me that editors refused to publish election protests because they feared inciting people and triggering the kind of violence like the one that happened after the 2007 elections. I disagree with that position. It should not be the responsibility of the media to stifle information for some imaginary reasons. The media is not there to police the state. The Fourth Estate is there to inform the public about "everything" in an objective, accurate and timely manner as long as that work is undertaken in a responsible manner without malice or bias. There are laws to protect the media.

Since the days of the Moi administration, self-censorship has been the hallmark of the Kenyan media, afraid to antagonise the ruling authorities. Because Moi was hard on the media, the latter invariably lived in a state of fear. Under Moi, presses were ransacked and critical editors jailed or driven into exile. In addition, laws were enacted providing stiff penalties for critics of the government. As a result, the media abandoned their long-held journalistic ethos and chose to publish only what was safe with the State. For a while after Moi's departure, the media appeared to regain their freedom, but the raid on *The Standard* newspapers in 2006 by goons said to have been sent by some government officials shattered all that. After the raid, the media went into a cocoon once again and played safe. As I write, relations between the media and the Uhuru regime are shaky. The controversy that followed the Media Bill towards the end of 2013 was an indication that there was bound to be a bumpy road ahead between the Media and the Government.

Indeed during a function to mark the World Press Freedom day in Nairobi on 2 May 2014, President Uhuru Kenyatta told journalists that there was no absolute media freedom and asked them to be responsible by checking facts before publishing. Uhuru's harsh speech elicited sharp reactions in newspaper editorials and social media outlets that accused him of stifling media freedom.

Chapter 24

Money, Money, Money

I never realised when I joined active politics in early 2002 that being a Member of Parliament required more than just the ability to represent, make laws and conduct oversight. My perception of an MP was of a person whose primary duty was to fight for the rights of his people, advocate good governance and agitate against societal ills. Little did I know that MPs were also expected to "bankroll" the needs and requirements of their people. It was only after I was elected in 2003 that I realised the whole concept of representation in Kenya revolved around one thing: money. Qualities of good leadership – humility, tolerance, honesty, integrity, competence, fairness and even a sense of humour, do not matter in Kenyan politics. If you are a tightwad, such qualities may, to quote an American Vice President, John Nance Garner, "not (be) worth a bucket of warm spit".

To a Kenyan voter money means everything. It determines whether or not they will attend your meeting and whether or not they will vote for you. That makes representation a very expensive affair for those aspiring for elective office. Before independence, the obsession for handouts did not exist. Kenyans were patriotic, volunteering and fully aware why they were fighting for independence. They sacrificed their time, energies and resources without expecting anything back from their leaders. When nationalists Achieng Oneko and Mbiyu Koinange were ordered by Kenyans to go to London in 1951 to present a case for land rights, it was the Kenyans who contributed pounds and cents to buy their tickets and ensure their stay in England. They contributed voluntarily and generously. The same happened when Jomo Kenyatta went on trial at Kapenguria on charges of belonging to Mau Mau, a proscribed organisation. It was Kenyans again who rose up and paid for his legal fees. That was the Kenyan spirit then.

Unfortunately, after independence that spirit vanished. Patriotism and volunteerism no longer mattered, and people had a reason for it. In the first two decades, *wananchi* watched helplessly as their money meant for community causes in the spirit of *harambee* (pulling together) was gulped down by gullible leaders. They saw their leaders getting richer while they wallowed in poverty. Instead of looking out for common interests leaders looked out for their stomachs. They became detached from those they represented. Corruption and nepotism brought fortunes to a few and left the masses in desperation. Those who sacrificed their lives in the forest during the liberation war were forgotten. Instead, rewards sometimes went to those who fought on the side of the colonial regime. Consequently, people cracked and the spirit of volunteerism died. They stopped subscribing to the common good and looked for a way to survive. More disastrously, they sat back and waited for largesse. They demanded handouts from politicians, sold their votes to the highest bidder, and decided that all their personal problems belonged to leaders.

Today, politicians have become hostages of their constituents. They are expected to pay school fees, medical expenses, bus fares, weddings, funeral costs, food and everything else. What this means is that greed is no longer the preserve of politicians. Kenya has become an avaricious society, the kind of man-eat-man society that President Julius Nyerere once described of Kenya years ago. People who go to political meetings expect to be paid. Leaders who refuse to pay are heckled and chased away. Rent-a-crowd has become big business complete with brokers and cheerleaders. The more people demand, the further politicians go in devising new ways of getting more money.

I saw it all during my ten years in politics: people rushing to my office panting and sweating and asking for money for their wives to be admitted to maternity. It never occurred to them that women conceive and nine months later they deliver. Struggling parents with half a dozen children in tow coming to ask for school uniforms as if they didn't know, from the very beginning, the consequences of procreation. People also come up with lies of family tragedies that never occurred and diseases that did not exist. It was not surprising therefore that in their first order of business, MPs in the Ninth Parliament doubled their salaries and allowances.

The Bill to hike MPs' salaries was passed in a record time of less than two hours despite widespread opposition from *wananchi*. Only three MPs, myself included, opposed the Bill on the floor of the House. The passing of the Bill opened a flood gate for future legislatures to follow suit. In 2007 the Tenth Parliament fought and got perks that were well above what had been negotiated by their predecessors. However, it was the Eleventh Parliament that took greed to a new level.

Although changes in the 2010 Constitution no longer permitted MPs to increase their own salaries, the drama that ensured immediately after the inauguration of the Eleventh Parliament showed that greed had taken root in our legislature beyond all expectations. Parliamentarians threw all manner of tantrums to intimidate the Salaries and Remuneration Commission (SRC), the body mandated by the constitution to determine all public salaries. Despite protests by Kenyans at the gates of Parliament, MPs blackmailed the Commission to submission and got their way, earning much more than any Parliament in the country's history. What is clear therefore is that leaders and *wananchi* have become gluttonous and foolishly unreasonable.

When Moi was in power MPs routinely trooped to State House every Friday to receive handouts for weekend expenses in their constituencies. Their salaries were modest, but they had a constant flow of money to contribute to *harambees* and at funerals and enough left over to pay school fees and wedding expenses for their constituents. In addition, they enjoyed preference on government tenders and benefited from free land. As Moi continued to amass wealth so did political leaders in KANU, the only political party then. In essence, Moi encouraged the dependency syndrome, made leaders lazy and encouraged corruption. *Wananchi* knew about Moi's generosity and every weekend waylaid their MPs along the streets, in their houses and in public meetings for a piece of the largesse.

Enter Kibaki, and the whole game changed. Kibaki shut himself in State House and closed the door for freebies seekers. Visitors to State House murmured about the small glasses of juices and the absence of snacks in State House, and complained when he advised those who wanted financial favours to go to the bank for loans. But *wananchi* continued to demand money from their leaders. With the introduction of the devolved government many expect the level of greed to go even higher because of the large number of elected representatives at the county level.

The solution to *wananchi's* unquenchable demands for money cannot come from increased salaries for elected leaders, but from heightened national civic education initiatives about the role of leaders vis-à-vis that of the people they lead. Majority do not know why they elect leaders; what they want in leadership and how they want to be governed. That may explain the reason why there is a high turnover of MPs at each election, and why people always complain about the leaders they had voluntarily elected. Furthermore, many people have not read the constitution and have no clue about common laws that govern them. This ignorance is largely responsible for perennial frictions between the governors and the governed, making it difficult for the two to work together for the good of the nation.

After what I believed was stolen 2013 elections, my thirst for politics waned. I no longer had the urge to continue in a game which, by all intents and purposes, was flawed. So I made a decision to retire from active politics. I saw my change of direction as a continuation of a journey I had begun many years before. This change was not any different from when I left the media to go into the diplomatic service or when I left the diplomatic service to go back to the media. *The Politics of Betrayal*, which I launched in 2011, was certainly a turning point in my life. It was after the success of the book that I started thinking about writing books on a full time basis. It is a branch of literature I find challenging and pleasurable. In their book, *Literature: The Human Experience*, Abcarian, Klotz and Cohen, contend that literature can help us get closer to life, (and) to understand it in a new way when we get back from our literary journey.[19] That could be said of politics. But unlike politics, writing is a lonesome travail. There are no chanting crowds when I sit in front of my laptop. No praises, no insults, no demands. Just me, and my silent thoughts. Those thoughts automatically drag me to my own life experiences, which I then harness and translate into letters and manuscript for others to share. Through writing I am able to broaden my understanding of life, and through that understanding I subconsciously transform myself into a magnanimous, tolerant and loving person. So, for me, writing books is the best alternative after politics. I know that rewards from writing are few and cannot be compared to those obtained from politics, but the joy of seeing my work displayed in bookshops far outweigh any monetary gain.

---

19 Richard Abcarian, Marin Klotz, Samuel Cohen, *Literature: The Human Experience, Reading and Writing* (Boston and New York: Bedford/St Martin's, 2013): 3.

I would be much happier if more Kenyans were writing and reading for pleasure. Perhaps this poem by Emily Dickinson,[20] written around 1873, may offer some inspiration:-

> There is no Frigate like a Book
> To take us Lands Away
> Nor any Coursers like a Page
> Of prancing poetry –
> This Traverse may the poorest take
> Without oppress of Toll –
> How frugal is the Chariot
> That bears the Human Soul.

Many years ago I tried my hand in poetry, and even sent a sample to Double Day Publishers in London who liked my work but thought they were too few for publication. Doubleday encouraged me to write more. I could have done that, but I lost interest in poetry. Now that I have the time perhaps I would go back to writing verses once again.

I want to say something about the *The Politics of Betrayal*.[21] The book was not about any one individual or any one event, but a catalogue drawn from personal diaries and other records accumulated over the period 2001 to 2008. In commenting on the book, some critics thought I had been too harsh on my one-time party leader, Kalonzo Musyoka; that I had betrayed him by divulging information on how Kibaki settled on him as Vice President. The late Mutula Kilonzo, the ODM-K Secretary General, even went public to deny that a meeting I wrote about with Kibaki at State House, Mombasa, ever took place. Let me reiterate what happened.

In mid-October 2007, politician Johnstone Muthama and I went to State House Mombasa for a secret meeting with President Kibaki on how ODM-K could support Kibaki's PNU in exchange for the Vice Presidency. Also present were presidential advisor Stanley Murage and our adviser, Justice Kasanga Mulwa. Our intention at ODM-K was to salvage Musyoka's dwindling political career. We knew chances of him beating Kibaki and Raila in 2007 were nil, so a few of us in the party agreed

---

20　Mathew Curtis, Two Poems of Emily Dickinson – Balanced Voices, 16 October, 2013, M3 Downloads.
21　Joe Khamisi, *The Politics of Betrayal: Diary of a Kenyan Legislator* (Bloomington, IN: Trafford Publishing, 2011).

that, for Musyoka to be politically relevant in the coming five years, we had to support either Kibaki or Raila. Opinion polls were showing either Raila was on the lead or the two were close. Kibaki was worried and sent feelers wanting to cooperate with ODM-K. We used his anxiety as a bargaining chip but we refused suggestions for a formal merger. We chose to back him. However, we insisted on getting something in return which was the Vice Presidency. That is how we ended up at State House, Mombasa, on that dark, rainy night. The mission was restricted to a small group of party officials and as it happened, the negotiations were successful and Kibaki – most likely influenced by our negotiations – agreed to appoint Musyoka as his principal assistant.

I believe such events in our political history need to be recorded for posterity. The future generations must be in a position to read about the past, analyse it, and make their own judgement.

Chapter 25

Bombay Africans

At the beginning of this book, I painted a picture of my ancestry and talked about how my great grandparents found their way from the hinterland of Tanzania and Nyasaland to the villages of Rabai. I also indicated that my great grandparents, from my father's side and Nyanya Emilia, came from Nyasaland and my father Francis was born in Kenya. Pauline, my grandmother on my mother's side and her husband, Stephen, were both from Tanzania, while my mother, Maria, was born in Kenya. Although that makes me a full-blooded Kenyan, it also makes me a third generation Kenyan Mnyasa. That is important to me because it clears the air about my ancestry and answers many questions people have been asking about my origin. Through this book I am able to explain, in a more holistic way, how the Khamisis and the Stephens involuntarily came to Kenya. The slaves who were rescued from the sea and the descendants that were born in Kenya have, without doubt, made significant contributions to the evolution of the Kenyan nation.

The slave settlements in Freretown and Rabai were established in the nineteenth century by the Church Missionary Society (CMS). Freretown was named so after Bartle Frere, the one person credited for stopping the Zanzibar slave trade. Rabai was the site of the first CMS church in Kenya and it provided refuge to thousands of rescued and recaptured slaves.

The tales of slave victims in Kenya was more or less the same told by slaves on the Atlantic route. Human beings were captured, chained and marched to processing points. They were packed in dhows and the lucky ones were rescued by British Navy vessels in the high seas. The ill-fated ones were tossed into the sea. This is the description of a slave scene in the trans-Atlantic slave corridor as portrayed by Christine Hatt:

> "Bound in iron neck rings and linked together with chains, the prisoners staggered towards an unknown destination. On reaching the coast, they were imprisoned in the Europeans' forts and castles. As the trade grew, holding pens called barracoons were built, where Africans awaited the arrival of the slaving ships. European traders did not buy all the people who were brought from the interior. They preferred healthy men and

women up to the age of 25, and they rejected the injured, the old, the weak and the sick."[22]

The treatment of all slaves was the same. It was a story of chains, brutality and human degradation. In East Africa slaves were sent to Freretown in Mombasa and Rabai in Kilifi, but others were shipped to orphanages in Bombay. Those came to be known as Bombay Africans – slaves who had been liberated by the British on the high seas or those who had been rescued from slave merchants in the interior of Eastern Africa and sent to India. There they were placed in Christian homes and taught English, Hindi and technical skills.[23] Records also exist of a settlement in Leopoldville (present-day Kinshasa) in what is today the Democratic Republic of Congo.

According to the Royal Geographical Society, which ran an exhibition in London in conjunction with historian Cliff Pereira and some non-governmental organisations,[24] some of the Bombay Africans were recruited by British explorers to work on caravans across the continent. The most famous of such recruits were Abdullah Susi and Chuma who travelled with David Livingstone, a Scottish explorer and missionary, who died in Central Africa (Zambia) in 1873. Susi and Chuma carried his body to Bagamoyo from where it was transported to England.

The life of slaves in Rabai and Freretown was not without challenges. Firstly, freed slaves always lived in fear of being recaptured by marauding gangs. The *kengele* at the Kongowea junction, opposite the slave-built St Emmanuel Anglican Church represents that grim period of history. The bell was rung to alert people to go into hiding whenever such gangs approached. The slave trade along the East African coast went hand in hand with trade in ivory. Captured slaves were made to carry the ivory poached from animals in the interior to ports for export, and both the slaves and ivory were auctioned in markets to the highest bidder. Just like slaves that were shipped to America, African slaves were forced to work

---

22 Christine Hatt, *Slavery: From Africa to the Americas* (New York, NY: Peter Bedrick Books, 1997): 14.

23 Royal Geographical Society, "Bombay Africans 1850–1910 (Part 2)", available at https://www.rgs.org/NR/rdonlyres/831B3822-2330-4773-8B53-A2E3328D2FBD/0/BombayAfricansPartTwo.pdf, accessed on 22 April 2014.

24 The NGOs include Tanzania Women's Association (London), Friends of Maasai People (Harrow), Congolese Community in the UK, Lancaster Youth Group (Ladbroke Grove, London), Ghanaian Elders' Group (Black Cultural Archives, London), O-Bay Community Trust (Edmonton, London).

in agricultural plantations and many were taken to British-held territories such as Madagascar where they laboured for long hours. The death toll was astronomical due to diseases and poor working conditions.

The treatment of slaves in general was abominable. In a letter sent to the *Times* of London in 1885, Fred E. Wingrow, the CMS Secretary, reported that a British ship arriving in Mombasa from Zanzibar found a group of two hundred and forty slaves who "had been left to die on the beach by slave dealers, unable to ship them (overseas)."[25] But records show that there are those who refused to "be treated as little children," according to the Royal Geographical Society.

It is also proper for the record to say that before and even after the abolition of slavery, freed slaves in Rabai particularly faced discrimination from local communities. They were often viewed as undesirable intruders who brought with them strange cultures and habits. In Rabai, the Arahai resented the Bombay Africans. They viewed their way of dressing in English jackets and frocks and their straightening of hair anathema to the local cultures. In contrast, Arahai women wore *hando*, a heavily pleated skirt with little at the bosom, while men wore *shuka*, a wrap-around piece of cloth. For both male and female, hair was kept naturally intact, garnished only with a thin layer of palm oil.

In an attempt to draw the curtain between the slave community and them, the Arahai and Mijikenda in general conjured up different derogatory names to identify different groups of slaves. They called the Bombay Africans *adzungu airu* or black Europeans because of their skin texture and dress code.[26] While in captivity few married Indians and bore children whose skin colour was close to white. They only spoke English and Kiswahili. By 1880, according to some estimates, there were three thousand Bombay Africans in East Africa, the majority of them in Freretown and Rabai.[27]

Then there were the *mateka,* those who had been captured by marauding gangs, but re-captured by good Samaritans and returned to

---

25 *The Gleaner Newsletter*, Church Missionary Society, 30 March 1885.
26 Thomas J. Herletty and Rodger F. Morton, *A Coastal Ex-Slave Country in the Regional and Colonial Economy of Kenya: The Wamisheni of Rabai*, 1880-1963.
27 Royal Geographical Society, "Bombay Africans, 1850–1910 (Part 3)" available at, http://www.rgs.org/NR/rdonlyres/F0AD08FF-4FC6-4569-B0F4-19F51B3063A8/0/BombayAfricansPartThree.pdf, accessed on 22 April 2014.

the settlement camps. There was also a name for Muslims and Arabs from Mombasa and other Islamic areas who felt threatened by slave hunters and ran away from their homes to avoid capture. The Arahai called them the *adzomba* or uncles. The name is still commonly used to describe anyone outside the Mijikenda community. Then there were the Wamisheni, former slaves who resided within the mission area and professed the Christian religion. That word *wamisheni* is still being used especially in Rabai which has seen little physical change since the days of Dr Ludwig Krapf. My mother told me, before she passed on in 2011, that there was a significant amount of conflict between the Arahai and the slave descendants during the early days. The Wamisheni were not allowed to participate in the festivities of the Arahai such as dances and rituals, and vice versa. Sometimes, physical confrontations occurred, further deepening the schisms between the two groups.

But even more annoying to the indigenous Arahai was the fact that the former slaves were more educated than they and could speak English and Kiswahili in addition to possessing artisanal skills that were in demand. Slave descendants were very involved in education at both Rabai and Freretown. A number of schools were established across present-day Kenya, Uganda and Northern Tanzania, and were run by descendants of the Bombay Africans."[28] In fact, the former had the first known technical institute, training Arahai youth in the fields of agriculture and mechanics. The school at Freretown graduated students who served beyond the borders of Kenya. Consequently, it was easy for slaves and their descendants to get jobs as clerks, bookkeepers, railway workers and handy-men in government and private companies than it was for indigenous people. I feel the contributions of slave descendants to the development of Kenya have largely been ignored by historians, and Kenyans have been left in the dark about who these people really were. Being few in number compared to many communities Kenya, the freed slaves' contribution to the colonial economy was minimal. The same was the case after independence with a few exceptions.

One book that is widely quoted in discussions about former slaves in Kenya is Joseph Harris and James Mbotela's *Recollections of James*

---

28 Royal Geographical Society, "Bombay Africans, 1850–1910, (Part 3)", available at: http://www.rgs.org/NR/rdonlyres/F0AD08FF-4FC6-4569-B0F4-19F51B3063A8/0/BombayAfricansPartThree.pdf, accessed on 22 April 2014.

Juma Mbotela .[29] Other than that, there are minimal known narratives by slaves to shed light on exactly what their varied experiences were. The only narrative I came across was contained in a book by Margaret Strobel called *Three Swahili Women*.[30] It gives the experiences of a Mombasa woman called Mishi wa Abdalla who was captured in Central Africa and sold as a slave. She says her parents were settled in Freretown in the 1870s, but she wasn't quite sure how they got there.[31]

In North America, over six thousand narratives are recorded – personal accounts of lives in captivity and freedom. Some of those narratives have been published as books providing a historical background between "the (time of the) importation of the first documented shipload of Africans to Virginia in 1619 to the death of the last former slave in the 1970s..."[32] In the absence of such personal records, East Africans have been left largely clueless about the slave trade and its implications; personal narratives were not documented and died with their possessors. Not very much is therefore known about that part of history. What has been written by foreigners has failed to capture the inner feelings of the slaves.

Many people do not even know – even admit – that Rev. William Jones, a Bombay African, was perhaps the first Kenyan human rights crusader. Together with Abi Sidi, another freed slave, he aggressively and successfully fought for the release of hundreds of African slaves detained by Zanzibar authorities. His oratory and mobilisation skills endeared him to many people at Freretown and Rabai. Every Sunday his church at Rabai was filled to capacity, making him perhaps the first high-flying evangelical preacher in the country. Rev. Jones had been rescued in the high seas and sent to Bombay in 1854. Ten years later he was transferred to Kenya and worked at Freretown and Rabai. His son, James Jones, owned the first commercial printing plant in Kenya, which published the *Coast Express* and *Mwalimu*, both edited by slave descendants, the latter by my father.[33] When the Kenya/Uganda Railway

---

29 Joseph E. Harris and James J. Mbotela, *Recollections of James Juma Mbotela* (Nairobi: East African Publishing House, 1977).
30 Sarah Mirza and Margaret Strobel (Eds), *Three Swahili Women: Life Histories from Mombasa, Kenya* (Bloomington, IN: Indiana University Press, 1989).
31 Ibid: 70.
32 Yuval Taylor (Ed), *I Was Born a Slave: An Anthology of Classic Slave Narrative*, 1772–1849, Vol. II (Chicago, IL: Lawrence Hill Books, 1999),: xv.
33 Royal Geographical Society, "Bombay Africans, 1850-1900: (Part 2)", available at https://www.rgs.org/NR/rdonlyres/831B3822-2330-4773-8B53-A2E3328D2FBD/0/BombayAfricansPartTwo.pdf, accessed on 22 April 2014.

was completed, the colonial government turned to Edward Brenn, a *mateka*, to train indigenous Arahai youth on the craft of telegraphy.[34] Those who qualified were posted to railway stations all over East Africa.

Slave descendants from Freretown and Rabai were also among the first African teachers, two good examples being those of James Mbotela and Lance Jones Bengo, a grandson of Rev. William Jones. Others like Tom Mbotela, and my father, Francis Khamisi, were active participants in the political evolution of Kenya. At one time in the LegCo when the President of the European Electors Union, F. W. Cavendish-Bentinck, said that Europeans intended to make the European power the predominating factor in the whole of East Africa, Khamisi hit back by saying Kenya was a "black man's country" and that the Africans "must see to it that it remains so forever."[35] Mbotela, who is described by one writer as of "a mixed tribal parentage", served briefly as vice president of KAU.[36] He was assassinated in Nairobi on the night of 26 September 1952 because of his moderate political views, which differed with those of the Kikuyu-dominated Central Committee. Like my father, he wanted peaceful change while others called for armed struggle. Both Mbotela and my father were described by one writer as the "most committed of KAU officials", but the writer did not fail to note that, although they were the "best educated, both were descended from former slaves of Central African origin. Without a local ethnicity, they would in some assessments be the only true 'Kenyans' KAU possessed."[37]

Although the original Freretown has been diluted by an invasion of outsiders, descendants of former Bombay African slaves like Grant Ralph, Hosep Douglas, Ishmael Semler, James Deimler, Tom Smith, George David, Mathew Wellington, Jacob Wainright, Charles Isenberg, John Mgomba, Thomas Mazera, the Farrahs, and many more (note their English names) can still be found even today, working in different fields.

---

[34] The End of Slavery in Africa, edited by Suzanne Miers and Richard Roberts; Chapter 8, Thomas J. Herlehy and Rodger F. Morton, "A Coastal Ex-Slave Community in the Regional and Colonial Economy of Kenya: The Wamisheni of Rabai 1880–1963," University of Wisconsin Press, 1988: 254-273.

[35] Assa Okoth, *A History of Africa 1915–1995* (Nairobi: East African Educational Publishers, 2006): 74.

[36] A. Marshall Macphee, *Kenya* (New York, NY: Frederick A. Praeger, 1968): 32.

[37] John Lonsdale, "KAU's Cultures: Imaginations of Community and Constructions of Leadership in Kenya After the Second World War", *Journal of African Cultural Studies*, Vol. 13, No. 1 (June 2000): 107-124.

Other slave descendants are the Mbotelas, the famous one being Mambo Mbotela, the celebrated broadcaster who is the son of James.

It is apparent then that descendants of slaves were not just bystanders, but major players in the evolution of Kenya. Justin Willis and George Gona say that, although Khamisi was a descendant of freed slaves, and (even though) "... he was an articulate exponent of African rights against Arabs, he could be seen as an outsider."[38] That "outsider" tag overshadowed his political career and damaged my own in later years.

It should also be noted that it was the Bombay Africans at Freretown – together with local Goans – who introduced dance music in Kenya in the early twentieth century, which, according *The Origins of Beni*, "killed native dances". In an interview in 1968 with George Mkangi, James Mbotela, son of James Juma Mbotela, talked of the popularity of the pioneering dance music and said the only music instrument used at the time was the accordion.[39] Today, Freretown and Rabai are known for producing some of the most prolific musicians who have gone to become famous beyond their own areas of birth, such as Joseph Ngala, Geoffrey Ngao, Nahashon Gandani and the once popular Pressmen Band of the *Msenangu* fame. Before them, there were Juma Tututu, Donald Jacca, Donald Tunje and many others.

All this discussion debunks some negative perspectives that have followed slaves in all parts of the world since the early days. For example, Thomas Jefferson was once quoted as saying that (slaves) are equal to whites (only) in memory, but "in reason much inferior ... and that in imagination they are dull, tasteless and anomalous." The reference was directed at African American slaves in the West, but could as well have referred to all Africans. African Americans (and Africans on the continent) came to believe that they were indeed inferior to Caucasians. That was seen in the way slave descendants in Rabai and Freretown carried themselves in the early days; assuming English names, straightening hair and pretending to speak the Queen's English. They despised local customs and considered themselves only below whites.

---

38 Justin Willis and George Gona, "Pwani C. Kenya? Memory Documents and Secessionist Politics in Coastal Kenya", *African Affairs*, Volume 112, Issue 446 (2012): 48–71.
39 Terance O. Ranger, *Dance and Society in Eastern Africa, 1890–1970: The Beni Ngoma*, University of California Press, 1975: 15.

It could be surmised that there was indeed a class society within the mission population at Rabai and Freretown with whites at the top of the ladder, followed by slave descendants and the Arahai at the bottom. That explains the apathy that existed through several generations between the Arahai and slave descendants. By failing to recognise them as a "tribe" in the country, the Kenya governments destined them to debasement. It left Freretown to be "run over" by new arrivals and for decades refused to issue title deeds to slave descendants settled in the Rabai mission area. Even St Emmanuel Church at Freretown, which was a religious sanctuary of rescued slaves, has not been spared. Wrangles pitying the descendants and new arrivals have been raging for years as the latter struggle to wrestle its leadership from the indigenous owners. As all this is going on the older generation of slavery is dying, taking with it to the grave valuable information that could enlighten the world about the pain and joy of slaves. The younger generation, given their exposure to modern living, continue to abandon their ancestral settlements for better lives elsewhere, a factor that is further eroding the history and culture of these former slaves.

Looking at it now, Rabai has not changed much from what it was when I was small. The market is no longer there, but the same shops are still trading although under different ownership. The missionary-built Anglican church needs patching up and the Isaac Nyondo school continues to perform badly in national examinations. There are no decent roads, and even though a major electricity plant has been built there many people in the vicinity of the plant still have no electricity. However, a positive addition to the Rabai mission is a museum established by the National Museums of Kenya to preserve documents, books and maps related to slave activities. It was opened in 1998 "to give formal and a perpetual reminder to monumental events during the advent of early missionaries."[40]

---

40 The National Museums of Kenya booklet, Rabai Museum, undated.

Chapter 26

The Last Word

In 1962, as British colonialists prepared to grant Kenyans independence, a cargo ship sliced its way through the choppy waters of the Kilindini channel at the port of Mombasa. On board were sixty thousand bags of yellow maize, a gift from the United States Agency for International Development (USAID) to a nation gripped by severe drought and famine. That was the year I ate yellow maize for the first time. Many Kenyans detested it and spread rumours that it interfered with child rearing. They had no alternative, but to learn to like it.

In the interior of the country, particularly in the scorched north and north-eastern regions, men, women and children were dying of hunger. Dead camels, their long necks miffed and their bodies bloated, and the stinking remains of sheep and goats, their skeletons sparkling in the hot sun, littered the cracked ground. Stench engulfed the air, huge green flies feasted and crows dived in and out of the carcasses like kites. For weeks, representatives in the LegCo had debated the state of famine – one of the worst in Kenya. The colonial authorities in Nairobi finally came to the conclusion that immediate importation of maize was necessary to slow down the human catastrophe. That initial disaster was contained, but only temporarily.

Three years after independence, the country was again gripped by hunger, this time from a serious shortage of maize. It was now the responsibility of the independent nation, under Jomo Kenyatta, to deal with the situation. The strategic reserves were empty and an illegal trade was thriving. Frustrated by what was happening, Kenyatta appointed the first ever commission of inquiry to investigate the cause of the shortage and why there was so much contraband in the midst of scarcity. That is when the commission, under Justice Chanan Singh, discovered a connection of the scam to the Minister for Marketing and Cooperatives, Paul Ngei. The Minister had permitted his wife, Emma, to buy maize from firms against the law; no one was allowed to buy maize directly from farmers, but from the Maize and Produce Board and only with a permit.

In 1987, and thousands of miles away from Kenya, a Hollywood film "Wall Street" was released to an expectant global audience. Based loosely on a real life of Ivon Boesky, an American stock broker who got entangled in a web of insider trading scandal in the United States in the mid-1980s, the film was a blockbuster and won its star, Michael Douglas, an Oscar award. It portrayed the life of a corporate raider who specialised in acquiring troubled companies on the cheap, re-engineering them and selling them at a great profit.

The story of the Ngeis and that of Boesky have one underlining commonality: greed. In the film, Douglas who was acting under the name Gordon Gekko, makes a rather startling and arguable statement to company shareholders to justify his underhand actions. "Greed," he said, "is good. Greed is right. Greed works." He then goes on to make an even more inflammatory statement: "Greed...has marked the upward surge of mankind." The social and political implication of that statement may not matter when made within the context of affluence in a developed country, but made in Africa to a population living in abject poverty the remarks would be considered insulting. Nowhere in Africa has greed been linked to goodness. Instead, it has been one of the major causes of misery, pain and suffering. In the Kenyan scandal, Ngei argued that he was clean, but the commission did not agree. The commission censored him for compromising his ministerial position. In 1966, Kenyatta suspended his one-time detention mate from the government.

As Kenya passed the fiftieth-year independence mark on 12 December 2013, I wondered whether the country had learnt any lessons from the maize scandal – the first in independent Kenya. Given the proliferation of avaricious activities in the three previous Administrations – and what was going on under Uhuru Kenyatta's – the learning process has not even started. From the thefts associated with *harambee* projects and grabbing of lands under Kenyatta to the Goldenberg and Anglo Leasing type scandals under President Moi and institutionalised corruption under Kibaki, greed is the common denominator in all administrations.

PLO Lumumba, the former Anti-Corruption Commission Director, once said Kenyans were living by the "creed of greed". However, nothing can match the shocking revelations contained in the report of the Truth Justice and Reconciliation Commission (TJRC) released in

May 2013. The Commission was set up in 2008 as part of the National Accord to end post-election violence and pave the way for the formation of the Grand Coalition administration between President Mwai Kibaki and Raila Odinga. It showed that 17 per cent of all land owned by whites at independence went to Kenyatta and Moi: "One sixth of the settler lands were found to have been sold intact to the emerging African elites comprising Kenyatta, his wife, children and close associates." Former politicians Mbiyu Koinange, Gikonyo Kiano, J. M. Kariuki, Masinde Muliro, Paul Ngei and Ronald Ngala got large tracts of land on the cheap, so were the Provincial Administrators who worked under Kenyatta like Eliud Mahihu and Isaiah Mathenge.

If Kenyatta was unbothered about what went on around him and Moi had no inclination to stop his cronies from stealing, the entry of Kibaki in 2002 rekindled renewed hope that under his watch the country would drastically reduce or completely eliminate corruption. That hope was reinforced by Kibaki's own personal commitment to fighting graft and a promise that there would be no "sacred cows" and that his government would end impunity and prosecute anyone caught looting the State. Little did he know that corruption was what a section of the media has called "a monster dragon that refuses to die". Despite all his promises, corruption thrived throughout Kibaki's two-term regime. Now, all eyes are on Uhuru Kenyatta. Will he slay the dragon and achieve what his predecessors failed to achieve? Or, will he allow Kenya to remain at the top layer of international corruption indices?

In Kenya, there is no shame in acquiring illegal wealth whether from the public or from other illicit activities. In 2010, during the second term of Kibaki, the US government released a list of five prominent persons it said were kingpins of the drug trade in Kenya. It named them as a recently elected MP, an Assistant Minister, a Coast Province MP, a Central Province MP and a Mombasa-based businessman with interests in other parts of the country. In 2011, the New York-based International Peace Institute claimed in a report entitled *Termites at Work* that between ten and fifteen internal drug trafficking networks were operating in Kenya.[41] It was thought that with this lead the Kenya government would

---

41 Peter Gastrow, *Termites at Work: A Report on Transnational Organized Crime and State Erosion in Kenya—Comprehensive Research Findings* (New York: International Peace Institute, 2011): 8.

undertake investigations and nab the culprits but nothing happened. Later, it admitted it had not found any truth in the allegations.

Even the media, which was voted the most trusted non-state actor in a study by the Nairobi University Institute of Development Studies in March 2012, has not been spared the vice. The worst culprits are correspondents working in rural areas who must hustle to survive due to poor remunerations. They are paid per line and enjoy no benefits from the firms they work for. Thus, they are easily manipulated by the highest bidders; this explains why throughout my last campaign in Kilifi I never received any publicity because I refused to bribe. That does not mean corruption does not exist in newspaper offices in the capital Nairobi. In a comprehensive report published on 19 October 2010, in the *Expression*, which covers media news, Nairobi media houses were cited as being highly corrupt. The report was written by Otsieno Namwaya while on a fellowship from AfriCog, an NGO dedicated to issues of corruption and bad governance in Kenya. Journalists were reportedly on the pay of politicians and corporate executives, stories were either published or killed on payment of cash, and senior editors were rewarded for following or not following story tips.

Greed is pervasive everywhere in the Kenya society. From the school teacher who pockets examination money and the police officer who stashes away millions acquired through bribery, to the civil servant who demands money to process a document and the MP who is paid to move a Motion in Parliament, greed is the driving force. Women sell their children, relatives murder each other over inheritances, religious people con the faithful, and members of the Judiciary dare take home a whopping 80,000 Kenya shillings (almost one thousand USD) in sitting allowances all in the name of greed.

Corruption and greed are fuelled by impunity and there is plenty of that in Kenya. During the past fifty years, very few senior government officials have been successfully prosecuted and jailed. Most of those who were taken to court were either let go for lack of evidence or their cases took years to conclude. As I finalise this book, the Goldenberg trial is still in courts more than two decades since it began. Three of four senior government officials who were taken to court for defrauding the public of 5.8 billion Kenya shilling in a gold exports fraud have died – Eliphaz

Riungu, Deputy Governor at the Central Bank, James Kanyotu, former spy chief, and Dr Wilfred Koinange, former Finance Permanent Secretary. Only Elijah arap Bii, a former Central Bank General Manager, and the person said to have been the chief architect of the scheme, businessman Kamlesh Pattni, remain.

In 2003, Kenya was among the first African countries to ratify the United Nations Convention Against Corruption, enacted the Public Officer Ethics Act and introduced a system of wealth declarations that required all public officials and their spouses to declare their worth. Myself and all the other legislators in the Ninth Parliament from 2003 to 2007 were compelled to fill in special forms which were then deposited in the Office of Speaker of the National Assembly. The forms were supposed to be updated regularly, but for lack of government commitment that system was abandoned as quickly as it was begun. I never got to hear anything more about the forms.

That brings me to the question: Is the Kenya Government really committed to ending corruption? My answer to that question is no. It is not because we don't have the laws, we do. We have also had qualified Kenyans heading the various anti-corruption organisations since 1997 when John Mwau was made the head of the anti-corruption advisory board. Although some progress has been made in the fight against draft, the twin problems of corruption and impunity remain Kenya's biggest social enemies.

My own view is that corruption will end only when we begin to respect laws and end impunity; when we elect ethical and honest leaders; when we get rid of all the brokers and wheeler-dealers who influence decisions in government, and when we are in a position to reward fairly public officials in areas prone to bribery such as the police, the immigration and the judiciary. We must also implement to the letter constitutional provisions relating to integrity issues.

Glossary of Non-English Words

Adzomba – A Giriama terminology literally meaning "uncle" or "nephew", but used to refer to the Waswahili and Arabs

Askari – A native African police officer or soldier, but also used to refer to a security guard

Askari – A soldier or police officer in East Africa

Bango – A music style that is popular at the East African coast, which fuses traditional Portuguese, Arabic and local coastal Bantu music genres

Bhang – A preparation from the leaves and flowers (buds) of the female cannabis plant consumed for its hallucinogenic effect

Busaa – An alcoholic drink made from fermenting sorghum, maize or millet flour

Bwana – A master, boss or lord, and also used as a word of respect

Chang'aa – A popular alcoholic drink in Kenya mostly distilled from grains like millet, maize and sorghum

Dodo – A type of mangoes found on the East African coast

Dudus – (derived from *mdudu*) Usually refers to harmful or irritating insects collectively

Fito – Straight poles used for the construction of houses or huts among most traditional African societies

Gwaride – Street parade with brass band

Habesha qemis – An ankle length traditional attire of Ethiopian women usually worn at formal events

Hando – A popular traditional skirt worn by women

Harambee – A term that literally means, "all pull together" denoting the Kenyan tradition of self-help initiatives

Injera – A national dish in Ethiopia and Eritrea comprising sour dough-risen flatbread, with a unique, slightly spongy texture

Isyo – Traditional Kamba food made of dry maize and beans

Jaza kitabu – To fill the book (a form of punishment)

Jembe – A hoe; commonly used as a household implement

Jiko – Traditional three-stone open wood stove

Kanzu – A tunic; a white or cream coloured robe mostly worn by Muslim men in Kenya

Kaya – The forest regions in the Mijikenda country often regarded as shrines or sacred

Kebelles – Urban dwellers' associations in Ethiopia, known as *kebelles*

Kengele – Swahili word for bell

Kikapu – Basket used as a container

Kikoto – A whip made of braided grass or twigs

Kinu – A traditional form of pestle curved from wood or stone for pounding grain or other items, usually for food

Kipande – An identity document used in the colonial Kenya and featured basic personal details, fingerprints and an employment history; all African males above the age of 15 were required to wear it around their necks at all times

Kuhaswa – A special blessing given to prospective marriage partners as part of the traditional Mijikenda wedding

Kumbe kumbe – Flying termites, which emerge from their underground homes, and are caught and eaten as snack

Kunazi – Small edible berries, known as jujube berries from the jujube tree, *Ziziphus jujube*

Kupiga magoti – To kneel; a form of punishment involving kneeling down

Leso – Also known as *Kanga*, it is a piece of clothing largely worn by women around the waist and torso and screen printed with beautiful sayings in Swahili (or English)

Madrassa – A Muslim educational institution

Mahamri – Mandazi made with coconut milk

Majengo – Areas of makeshift structures found in many major urban centres in Kenya where there is Islamic influence

Majimbo – A movement advocating a federal type of government

Mandazi – A form of fried bread with origins in the Swahili coastal areas of Kenya and Tanzania

Marekani – American khaki

Matanga – A time of mourning where the community gathers to support the bereaved family

Matatu – Privately owned minibuses that are run in many Kenyan cities to provide passenger services

Mateka – captives

Matingasi – a brew made from fermented grains

Mboko – A slim gourd

Mchicha – *Amaranthus dubius,* a common small-leafed vegetable that grows in the wild

Memsahib – A term of Indian origin used for respectful address to an upper-class woman (especially whites during colonial days)

Miyaa – Leaves of the Dwarf palm (*Phoenix roebelenii*), used for making mats, sails and *kikoto*

Mnazi – Coconut palm wine, the common alcoholic beverage along the East African coast

Moran – (sometimes *Il–murran*) A young warrior among the Maasai community

Mpunga – Asian rice (*Oryza sativa*), a cereal that grows on wet ground and becomes white when polished

Mtsunga – *Launaea cornuta,* a bitter lettuce mainly used as a vegetable in East Africa; it is an important vegetable for the coastal tribes who also use it for medicinal purposes

Mtura – (commonly known as *mutura*) A popular meaty snack made of goat intestine wrappers stuffed mostly with inner meat parts and/or blood; it is also referred to as Kenyan or African sausage

Muazin – (also *muezzin*) The Muslim official of a mosque who summons the faithful to prayer

Mvuna – An indigenous vegetable

Mwambao – A movement associated with the protracted struggle among the Arabs and Waswahili along the Kenyan Coast to pull out and join the Sultanate of Zanzibar or form a self-governing territory

Namaste – Customary greeting among people of Asia (especially Indians) spoken with a slight bow and hands pressed together

Ngoe – A type of mangoes found on the East African coast

Nguru – King fish

Nyama choma – Roast meat, especially goat-meat and beef

Nyama – Meat or food that is comprised predominantly of meat

Nyoka – A snake

Paan – A stimulating and psychoactive preparation of betel (*Piper betel*) leaf combined with areca (*Areca catechu* nut) and/or cured tobacco mostly used by Indians

Panda – A form of catapult popular with boy

Pandizo – Steps cut to help wine tappers climb the coconut tree

Panga – A machete; commonly used as a household implement

Papa – Shark

Pilau – A dish common at the Coast, consisting of rice flavoured with spices to which meat, poultry, or fish may be added

Puree – Food made of dry maize and beans

Pyuwa – Coconut palm wine distilled into spirit

Sarakasi – Street theatre

Shifta – A term used in the Horn of Africa to refer to a rebel, outlaw or bandit

Shikio la punda – A type of mangoes found on the East African coast

Shuka – Men's loin cloth

Siturungi – Black tea (tea without milk); probably a corruption of "strong tea"

Sokota – Dry clay marbles

Sufuria – A common utensil among East African households featuring a flat based, deep sided, lipped and handle-less cooking pot or container

Sukuma wiki – A form of kale, *Brassica oleracea acephala*, used as a vegetable and popularly taken with *ugali*

Takataka – Rubbish, waste or dirt

Ugali – A staple food in Kenya generally made from maize flour (or ground maize) and water

Ukuti – A straw, but usually a branch of a coconut tree

Unga – Grain flour, usually maize flour, used in the preparation of *ugali*

Wamisheni – People who lived in the Christian missions (e.g. freed slaves who lived in the Rabai Mission)

Wananchi – Term used to describe the ordinary people or the public

Washihiri – Arabs, especially with origins in Oman

Wot – (also known as *wat*) A thick Ethiopian and Eritrean stew or curry prepared with chicken, beef, lamb, a variety of vegetables or spice mixtures, usually served atop *injera*

Index

A
Abdalla, Hon. Amina 219
Abegunga, Jana 14
Afwerki, Isaias 177
Ahtisaari, Marti 158
Ali, Hon. Dr Abdulla 219
Ali, Shekue 46
Amatta, Maurice 219
Anabwani, Simon 195
Andom, Lt Gen. Aman Michael 110-112
Antonio J. Mendez 161
Armstrong, Jean 76
Armstrong, Louis "Satchmo" 69
Arthur 8, 59
Aslam, Mohamed 172
Awori, Horace 178
Awori, Moody 178, 216
Ayah, Ndolo 220

B
Bahari, A. A. 218
Balala, N. 219
Banda, Dr Hastings Kamuzu 50-51
Baring, Governor Evelyn 62
Barngetuny, Hezekiel 171
Barre, Siad 176-177
Beauttah, James 30
Bell, Alexander Graham 197
Bell, Eric 72
Bengo, Jones 248
Bii, Elijah arap 255
Binns, Edward 29, 52
Biwott, Nicholas 171
Blair, Tony 230
Boesky, Ivon 252
Bolton, Kenneth 72
Boniface, Father 35-36, 39
Botha, Pik 180
Buxton, John 48-49, 65, 69

C
Carmichael, Stokely 97
Carter, President Jimmy 146
Chambati, Omari 75, 78
Chamwada, Alex 231
Chand, Gen Prem Dewan 158

Chandaria, Manu 204
Chang'awa, Arthur 77
Chavanga, Javan 72
Chemponda, Alex 143
Chirwa 38
Chissano, Joaquim 167
Chiume, Christopher Kanyama 50-51
Chokwe, Mwinga 64
Chotara, Kariuki 173
Clinton, Bill 230
Criticos, George 118
Cuellar, Javier Perez de 167

D
Dada, Idi Amin 110, 114, 132
Daudi 36, 46
David, George 248
Dolan, Father 230
Douglas 32
Douglas, Hosep 248
Douglas, Michael 252
Dourado, Wolfgango 192
Dumoga, John 113, 119
Dzoro, Morris 213

E
Egal, Muhammad Haji Ibrahim 89
Eliphaz Riungu 255
Emilia, Nyanya 7-13, 17-20, 23. 27, 30, 57-59, 85, 243

F
Faida, Maria 1, 4, 7, 14, 38, 139, 243
Fanjo, Hary 48
Farrahs 49
Fatuma 70
Florence 8
Ford, President Gerald 94
Fred 59
Freud, Sigmund 227

G
Gachathi, Peter 87, 89
Gandani, Donald 35
Gandani, Nahashon 249
Gandhi, Mahatma 30, 78, 82

Garner, John Nance 237
Gatei, Daniel 77
Gaulle, Charles de 128
Geingob, Hage 156, 160
Gessesse, Tilahun 122
Gichuru, James 29, 63
Gichuru, Mary 104
Gikonyo, Muchohi 29
Githii, George 77
Gona, George 249
Gouba 81
Grant, Bob 89-90
Griffiths, George Thomas N. *See* Ras Makonnen
Gulamani, Riyaz 186-187, 189-191
Gumbe, Larry 209
Gurirab, Theo Ben 160, 168

H
Habyarimana, Juvenal 177
Hamisi, Badi 69
Hardy, Brig. A. J. 74
Hatt, Christine 243-244
Hayes, Charles 75

I
Imanyara, Gitobu 220
Isenberg, Charles 248

J
Ithau, John 77
Jacca, Donald 249
Jahazi, Mohamed 46
Jeffa, Hamisi 182
Jeremiah, Jimmy 29, 52
Jimmy 9, 55
Johnson, President Lyndon B. 94
Joho, Ali Hassan 210
Jones, James 247
Josiah 14
Josiah, Samuel 29
Joyce, Bai 15
Juma, Charles 1, 7, 11-12, 14, 19, 23-24, 30, 32, 36, 38, 40, 43, 48, 53, 59-60, 68, 85, 101, 149-150, 207
Juma, Salim 77

K
Kaberere, Rocki 13
Kabila, Laurent-Desire 177
Kabugua, Michael 78
Kabwere 50
Kadzo, Lydia 8
Kalasinga, Omar 183
Kalekwa 4, 7
Kamotho, Joseph 209
Kangwana, James 87, 89
Kanyotu, James 255
Kariithi, Geoffrey K. 87, 106
Karim, H. E. Prince 75
Kariuki, J. M. 92, 122-123, 220, 253
Kariuki, Kinyanjui 102
Karume, Njenga 214, 230
Karume, Sheikh Abeid Amani 51, 192
Kasina, Francis 152
Kathurima, Harry Mutuma 174
Katjimune, First Lady Kovambo 168
Katjiuongua, Moses 161
Kaunda, President Kenneth 89
Kaura, Katuutire 161
Kaviti, Jason 220
Kazikazi, Margaret Nadzua 8
Kazungu 35
Kazungu, Lawrence 40
Keen, John 49
Kennedy, Jacqueline 90
Kennedy, President John F. 90, 94
Kenyatta, Christine 92
Kenyatta, Jane 92
Kenyatta, Mama Ngina 118
Kenyatta, Margaret 104
Kenyatta, President Mzee Jomo 29-30, 52, 73-74, 82, 86-93, 95, 104, 106, 110-111, 113-124, 126-128, 132, 162-163, 171, 173, 179, 182, 210, 217, 233-234, 237, 251-253
Kenyatta, Uhuru 92, 233-234, 236, 252-253
Khamisi, Badi 69
Khamisi, Francis 149-150
Khamisi, Francis Joseph 3, 8, 13, 30, 63, 196, 198, 243, 248-249
Kiai, Maina 222
Kiano, Dr Julius Gikonyo 51-52, 198, 200, 253

Kibaki, Mwai 106, 135, 181, 206, 208-211, 213-215, 222, 224-226, 230, 234, 239, 241-242, 252-253
Kibibi 67
Kibinge, Leonard 97
Kibunja, Victor 93
Kibwana, Kivutha 221
Kikumu, Stephen 77
Kikwete, Jakaya 191
Kilonzo, Hon. Kiema 219
Kilonzo, Mutula 241
Kimani, Stephen 13
Kimaro, Michael 192
Kimathi, Dedan 46
Kimunya, Amos 221
Kimura, Catherine 128
King George VI 39
King, Martin Luther 97, 144
Kingi, Joseph 213
Kinuthia, Julius 72
Kinyanjui, Peter 122
Kiplagat, Bethwel 151, 168, 174
Kiplagat, Hoseah 172
Kirwa, Kipruto arap 219
Kiti, Alfred 221
Kitonga, C. J. 32
Kitonga, Nzamba 32
Kivuitu, Samuel 225
Kivure, Walter Elijah 7, 59
Kiwanuka, Jenkins 78
Klerk, President F. W. de 167, 178-180
Koinange, Dr Wilfred 255
Koinange, Mbiyu 63, 128, 237, 253
Kombo, Msanifu 46
Komen, Francis 71
KomoraYuda 124
Koskei, Inspector Jonathan 163
Krapf, Rev. Johann Ludwig 3, 28, 246
Kuri, Reverend Samuel 28

L
Lamba, Davinder 230
Leakey, Richard 148, 196
Legwaila, Legwaila Joseph 158
Leshore, Hon. Samuel 219
Lincoln, President Abraham 99
Livingstone 7
Livingstone, David 244
Loogman, Rev. Father Alfons 13

Lucy 107
Lumumba, PLO 252
Lydia 59

M
Maanzo, Daniel 215
Maathai, Wangari 95
Macharia, G. N. 126
Machel, President Samora 156
MacLeod, Ian 63
Mahihu, Eliud 253
Mahugu, Njuguna 106-107, 167, 169-170, 174
Maijo, Athanas 143
Maitha, Emmanuel Karisa 208-211, 234
Maitha, Lucas 218
Makange, Robert 186
Makasembo, Dick 55
Makau, Johnstone 180
Makeba, Miriam 97
Makonnen, Ras 127-128
Makwida, Sammy 56
Maliti, John 133
Malu, William Mbolu 46
Manasseh, Edgar 49
Mandela, Nelson 167, 178-179, 201
Mango, Christine 219
Maria 103-105, 119, 130, 140, 143, 162, 169, 203
Mariam, Mengistu Haile 111
Marsden, Eric 72-73
Marshall, Anthony D. 144, 116
Mary 8
Masengo, Edouard 68
Massey, Chancellor T. Benjamin 147
Matano, Anthony 61, 131
Matano, Athanas 7
Matano, Leones 3, 7, 67, 203
Mate, Bernard 52
Mathenge, Isaiah 253
Matheson, Alistair 76
Mathiu, Mutuma 193
Mathu, Eliud W. 29
Mazera, Onyango 36-37
Mazoa, Hassan 77
Mazrui, Professor Ali 95
Mbaria, Josephat 13
Mbela, Darius 119
Mbogori, Mzee 60

Mbotela, Christine 150
Mbotela, James 248-249
Mbotela, Leonard Mambo 71, 249
Mbotela, Tom 248
Mbotela, Walter 150
Mboya, Pamela 90
Mboya, Tom 52, 62-63, 72, 902-91, 220, 230
Mbuguss, George 75
McCaw, Mel 97
McNamara, Robert 104
Mehta 81
Meme, Dr Julius 204
Mengi, Reginald 187
Menya 47
Mgomba, John 248
Michael 36
Miller, Elliot 117
Milliard, Dr. Peter 127
Miumi, James 52
Mkangi, George 249
Mkapa, President Benjamin 50, 191-192
Mlamba, Dawson 88
Moi, President Daniel T. arap 49, 52, 62-63, 106, 123, 126, 142, 146, 160, 165-176, 178, 180-182, 195- 198, 201-202, 206, 208, 210-211, 219-221, 230, 234, 236, 239, 252-253
Moroto, Hon. Samuel 219, 220
Morris, Uncle 57
Mortimer, C. E. 29
Mountbatten, Prince Philip 73
Mpanda, Augustine Louis 8
Mrima, Peter 221
Mtikila, Reverend Christopher 191
Mudavadi, Musalia 196
Muema, Chrispas 152
Muema, Elizabeth 133
Mugalo, Boaz 75-76, 133
Muganda, Emmanuel 143
Mugo, Beth 106, 115, 118-19, 121-122
Mugo, Nicholas 106, 115, 118-119, 121-122
Muhsin, Sheikh Ali 51
Muimi, James 62
Muiruri, Peter 128
Muite, Hon. Paul 219
Mukeka, W. 46
Mukiri, M. 219

Muliro, Masinde 49
Mulwa, Justice Kasanga 241
Mumo, David 52
Mungai, Dr Njoroge 116
Munya, Hon. Peter 219
Muoria, Henry 30
Murage, Mbogo 193
Mureithi 78
Murema, Joseph 202
Mushala, Y. B. B 144
Musila, David 209, 222
Mussolini, Benito 163
Musyoka, Kalonzo 211, 228, 233, 241-242
Muthama, Johnstone 241
Mutisya, Mulu 173
Mutoko, Caroline 231
Muturi, Justin 218
Muya, Titus 128
Muyongo, Mishake 161
Mwaboza, Anania 210
Mwaeba 203
Mwakwere, Ali Chirau 213
Mwang'ombe, Frederick Elijah 8
Mwanyumba, Dawson 52
Mwashumbe, Claudis 52
Mwau, John 255
Mwidau, Abdulla 46
Mwita, Chaacha 193
Mzungu, Tom 102

N

Nadzua, Margaret 8
Naikuni, Titus 196-197
Namulanda, Kizito 193
Nasibu, Sylvanus 49, 75, 150
Nassir, Sharif 173
Ndegwa, Duncan 87
Ndesandjo, Stephen 77
Ndolo, Brig. Joseph 74
Nehru, Jawaharlal 78, 82, 85
Ng'ang'a, Frederick 29
Ng'aru, Mumbi 209
Ngala, Joseph 68-69, 249
Ngala, Noah Katana 211
Ngala, Ronald Gideon 49-50, 52, 62-65, 100, 208, 220, 232, 253
Ngao, Geoffrey 249
Ngei, Paul 251
Ngilu, Charity 206

Ngugi, Joseph 13
Nguru, Swalee 33
Ng'weno, Hillary 75, 140
Njenga, Nahashon 91
Njeru 78
Njihia, Francis 107
Njiru, Lee 195-196, 202
Njonjo, Charles 124
Njoroge, James 29
Njoroge, Paul 13
Njuguna, Mohamed 89
Nkrumah, President Kwame 87, 113, 127
Nora 30-31
Nora, Bai 30-31
Ntaryamira, Cyprien 177
Ntimama, William ole 211
Nugi, Joe 72
Nujoma, President Sam 158, 160-163, 165-168
Nyagah, Jeremiah J. 52
Nyapela, Oscar 216
Nyaseda, Edwin 206
Nyaulawa, Richard 188
Nyerere, Mwalimu Julius Kambarage 50-51, 114, 177, 190-193, 238
Nyondo, Isaac 14, 147, 250
Nyong'o, Peter 233

O
Obama Sr., Barack 95
Obama, President Barack 95, 230
Obondo, Alex 56
Obonyo 58
Obonyo, Oscar 231
Obote, Milton 110-111
Obunga, Alois 13
Odede, John Likoko 165-168
Odinga, Dr Oburu 219
Odinga, Jaramogi Oginga 30, 52, 54-55, 62-63, 73, 86-91, 93, 95, 115, 230
Odinga, Raila Amollo 46, 201, 206, 209, 211, 213-215, 228, 230, 233-235, 241-242, 253
Oguda, Lawrence 52
Ogutu, Mathews 124-125, 129
Ojode, Orwa 213, 218
Okoth, Mzee 46
Okungu, Sammy 128

Olindo, Peres 125
Omori, Boaz 75-77
Oneko, Ramogi Achieng 76, 78, 237,
Ong'era, Jane 233
Onyango, Oriri 219
Opande, Lt. Gen. Daniel 156-159, 164
Opiyo, Christopher 104
Osore, Sammy 77
Osundwa, W. 218
Otiende, J. D. 29
Otieno, Engineer 202
Ottaway, David 113-116, 118-119
Otunga, Maurice 40
Owino, Albert 29

P
Padmore, George 127
Patel, Niru 204
Patels 80
Pauline, Nyanya 3-7, 12, 139, 225, 243
Pienaar, Louis 158
Pili, Josephine 17, 130, 140, 143, 162, 169, 198, 203
Pinto, Pio Gama 90, 220
Pohamba, Hifikepunye 160
Ponda, Eric 221
Price Uledi 49

Q
Queen Elizabeth II 39, 73

R
Ralph, Grant 248
Reagan, President Ronald 146, 230
Rebmann, Johannes 3, 28
Regina 7, 61
Rodrigues, Joe 75
Ruto, William 233-234

S
Sadala, Juma 7-9, 31, 58
Sadala, Khamisi 4
Salama, Emilia 7, 9, 31, 60, 150
Sambo, Harry 75
Sang, P. K. 218
Saul, John 117-118
Savage, Doretha 96
Savage, Ephy 98-99

Savage, Mattie 98-99
Savage, Mrs 99
Seale, Bobby 97
Selassie, Emperor Haile 106-108, 110-112, 115, 127
Selina 31
Sepetu, Babu 7
Sepetu, Stephen 3, 6, 139
Sese Seko, Mobutu 177
Shaban, N. N. 219
Shakombo, Suleiman 183
Shastri, Lal Bahadur 85
Shermarke, President Abdurashid 176-177
Shikuku, Martin 49, 52, 253
Shultz, George 146
Sidi, Abi 247
Sidi, Willliam Jones 247
Sikobe, Shadrack 77
Silas 32
Silas, Joseph 67
Silverstein, David 172
Singh, Chanan 251
Skane, James 115
Smith, Captain Edwin 122
Smith, Tom 248
Stephen, Babu 4-6, 12, 243
Stephen, Mzee 13, 225
Strobel, Margaret 247
Susi, Abdullah 244
Syongo, Zaddock 219

T
Tabu, Mary 38, 55, 149, 165, 198
Taib, Taib Ali 211-212

Thiong'o, Ngugi wa 75
Thuo, Dr Moses 224
Tipis, Justus ole 49, 52
Toivo, General Toivo ya 160-161
Too, Mark 171
Toure, Kwame 97
Towett, Taaita 52, 198
Tsola, Joel 75
Tunje, Donald 249
Tututu, Juma 249
Twaha, Fahim 217

W
Wafula, Sammy 131
Waithaka, M. K. 219
Wamalwa, Michael Kijana 211, 206
Wambugu, Mureithi 30
Wamwere, Koigi wa 221
Wandera, J. D. 128
Wanjala, Hon. Raphael 219, 220
Wanjiru, Bishop Margaret 247
Wanjiru, Terry 92
Warrakah, Mbwana 182
Waruhiu, Senior Chief 45
Washe 16
Washington, George 92, 95, 96, 146
Waudi, Joseph Okoth 46
Weinberger, Caspar 146
Willis, Justin 249
Wingrow, Fred E. 165

www.ingramcontent.com/pod-product-compliance
Lightning Source LLC
Chambersburg PA
CBHW072109010526
44111CB00038B/2470